SYMPHONY OF LOVE

By

George Jenki

ISBN: 978-0-9734655-9-4

© George Jenkins 2015 ©

All rights reserved. No part of this publication may be reproduced, distributed, stored in a retrieval system or transmitted in any form or by any means, including photocopying, recording, or other electronic or mechanical methods, without the prior written permission of the author, except in the case of brief quotations embodied in critical reviews and certain noncommercial uses permitted by copyright law. For permission requests, write to the author: "Attention: Permissions Coordinator," at the address on page 266.

All Scripture references ate taken from the King James Version unless indicated.

Table of Contents

Introduction – Page 3

A Simple Song of Love – Page 9

Orchestrated Surrender – Page 24

Fanfare of Man – Page 38

Surrendered Sea Music – Page 49

Ballad of Galilee – Page 62

Symphony in "A" Minor – Page 75

Lyrics of Power – Page 88

Harmony of a Romance – Page 99

Oratorio of Ruth – Page 119

Anthem of a Throne – Page 136

Canticle of Mary – Page 148

Opus of Love – Page 163

Quartet in Surrender – Page 174

Temple Worship – Page 195

The Trumpet Shall Sound – Page 218

Hallelujah Chorus – Page 248

An Invitation – Page 272

About the Author – Page 274

Introduction

Love! We have all thought about. Perhaps we have questioned as to what it really is. Maybe we have struggled with it. Knew the joys and tears that some forms of love brought our way. I'm sure we have known something that wasn't really love at all. We have longed for it, dreamed of it and even prayed for it. In this, we are no different from many people whose stories are portrayed in the Bible. Love, is so complex that it's simple!

In this book, we will journey with many who have struggled with, searched for, and finally embraced loving submission in their lives. They wanted the freedom to love. They wanted the freedom to choose. Still many fought, not for it, but against it.

To understand the stories we are about to read, to have a better understanding of love itself, we have to go and speak with the Creator of all love. In so doing we will discover that love is not something, but rather someone!

Is there such a thing as a forever love? Together we will look full in the face of real love. There the questions we have asked for years will be answered.

The stories of relationships, you are about to enjoy, oozes with devotion, betrayal, immorality and restoration. They carry for us, real life lessons directing us back into the heart of perfection that we once knew. We will encounter successes and failures through every chapter. Plots that unfold with every page turned!

The saga of Adam and Eve is played out again and again as man journeys back towards the perfection of Eden. Their symphony of love will carry us across time and space until we come to the greatest marriage feast that will ever take place! Testimonies that edify and build up that help us make the right choices are ours for the reading! Options that will lead us beyond Eden. Past the Cherubim with a flaming sword who guards the way to the Tree of Life! (Genesis 3:24)

If ever a marriage was made in heaven, Adam and Eve had it all. It was perfectly organized and perfectly complete by a perfect God. The very first couple were molded by the Masters loving hand.

Adam doubtless had a wonderful build and sported rugged handsome features. She Eve, was the most beautiful woman to ever live. They were made in God's own image. They were made in the image of Love. All reasons for a marriage breakdown, all excuse for failure was absent. They had godlike personalities, perfect intellect, emotions, and will. They possessed brilliant minds!

Adam gave names to every single animal on the earth. The choices of those names were his to make. (Genesis 2:19) They had faultless emotions, including a capacity to know tender and totally unselfish love, the love of God Himself. Their wills were in perfect harmony with the purposes of their Creator. No half rhymes existed, in their beginnings with love. For some time they flowed in oneness in a symphony of splendid love. Physically, emotionally, and spiritually they were impeccable! We all know, their Shangri-La of love soon faded, crumbling into brokenness.

What were the consequential effects upon relationships ever since? How do these effects, dictate to our relationships today? Can we in our homes or churches ever know forever love again?

When it comes to expressions of real love, there are few things more poignant than sacrifice. It's inherently wonderful to tell someone, "I want you to be happy and I don't care what it costs." Of course, the greater the sacrifice, the greater the expression of passion and love. In this book, your will encounter firsthand many declarations of such love not just in word, but in, deed.

Together we will explore how life takes amazing twists and turns. We plan, we grow moving steadily towards our dreams. We think that life goes on forever! Then, disaster strikes with uncaring cruelty. We will confront truths that drip with the reality of the days in which we live.

In her story, Opus of Love, our precious Shulamite heroine offers us insights into how to keep our connection's pure. When a relationship begins in song and dance many pronounce, it will not last! When a country girl marries a city boy, some question the cultural exchange. So it was for the Shulamite in Solomon's Song of Songs. A young dark, farm girl was destined for the throne!

Have you ever considered divorce? A list of names appears in your local newspaper almost daily. Just below the names of those just born and those who passed away, there are other names of couples filing for divorce. Maybe our name has been on that list. Certainly we have had a family member or friend who has gone through the pain of a broken marriage.

It's pretty shocking to open the pages of Scripture and find one of the Bible's heroes contemplating divorce. When Joseph makes his first appearance in the biblical story, that's exactly what he is doing.

Taking our journey from the Garden of Eden we will discover a word alien too many hearts. A word, so expensive, so demanding, and its price we could never naturally pay. Still along that road we must journey if we are ever to return to paradise. That road is called abandoned! It is the only highway back to paradise along which Peter had to travel!

"Abandoned," is a word seen everywhere in nature and in things around us. By the command of God, the sun, the moon, the stars, the flowers, the trees, and even the grass came into existence. (Genesis 1) These and much more submitted to His word, hold in their courses as they travel through the voyage of life. Isaiah said:

"Who hath measured the waters in the hollow of his hand, and meted out heaven with the span, and comprehended the dust of the earth in a measure, and weighed the mountains in scales, and the hills in a balance?" (Isaiah 40:12)

God created; and are they not all absolutely surrendered to Him? Do they not allow God to work in them and do everything He pleases? They can't do anything other than to live in complete surrender to His desires and will. When God clothes the lilies of the fields with their beauty, is the earth not yielded up, surrendered, given over, to God as He works His beauty? Everything in the cosmos exists in abandonment to the divine. By His choice, He can change the rules of the game. That's what makes Him God.

There are times in the Bible when He contravened the very laws of nature. Joshua spoke this into existence and time stood still. It is there that we can see how surrendered they are to Him.

"Sun, stand thou still upon Gibeon; and thou, Moon, in the valley of Ajalon." (Joshua 10:12) The results came swiftly. The sun stood still and the moon stayed where it was in the sky. This condition remained for an entire day. (Verse 13) Since the earth revolves around the sun what happened was the earth stopped in its course.

Have we ever cried out; "Stop the world and just let me of?" Still life went on and tears cascaded down our faces. Perhaps we felt abandoned by everyone around us, forsaken in a swirl of drowning emotions. How many times have we walked that lonely mile? How can we find our way back onto that other path where joy bursts from our innermost being? Are we just pawns in some hideous game of life? Condemned to be tossed to and fro at the will of unseen forces. Is there a way out? Can we ever know happiness again?

This book will carry us through the mysteries of life. Past pain and despair to a joy unspeakable and full of glory we will sail. We will walk through the garden of the prophetic. The place where truth past, present and future blooms. Strolling with the great prophets of old we will share with them all that the LORD has planned from the very beginning. Through song after song that fills that garden air, we will come to the truth of our day. We will see how in these last days Satan has launched his end time's manifesto against the church. At length we will come to a day when we will laugh and play again. Then...

In the end we will journey to heaven. The sights! The Sounds! The Bridegroom! The Wedding Feast of the Lamb. All are ours to discover with fresh new light and understanding. Climb the mountain of grace. Soar to the ramparts of glory. Stroll down the avenue of faith. Walk with the giants of the faith. There we will touch the heart of the bride who has waited so very long for her Bridegroom to come.

He will come as promised and transport us to that great banquet hall. We will soar to the heights of glory on an ever-increasing crescendo of revelation as together we explore the music of heaven. We will understand the symbolism of the precious stones, the streets of gold and the colors that explode from all around. We will even, come face-to-face with God Himself and stand in amazement at whom or what we see. Is it any wonder that we will shout, sing and dance to the strains of the Hallelujah Chorus? Have you ever wondered what God looks like? He is ours to discover through the pages of His, "Symphony of Love!"

A Simple Song of Love

There is nothing more powerful than the story of a man's life. It's simply life's experiences, devoid of theology and therefore cannot be argued with. Still many try. The stories about the life of Jesus; they have made movies about Him! Enthroned His story, in the halls of big business to suit Hollywood! Tried to destroy its simplicity and pollute it with foul accusations of defilement with Mary Magdalene. Others wish that He would just simply go away. He will not! Love will never go away! His story has survived the test of centuries! It's a forever love that grows with every passing day. A love so deep that even in eternity, His symphony will echo glorious melodies of truth.

The love stories of those in the Bible, they too, have come down through the centuries. Couples and individuals who forever sing love's simple song. Many are prophetic of all that is coming in our day. They pave our way out of some pointless existence and deliver us safely to another shore. Making our way down that road, we will see the pain in their eyes as they share with us their tears. If we can find joy in their eyes, then, they will share with us their smiles, their love unblemished, love divine!

The Greek language (*the language of the New Testament*) uses three different words to describe and define love. The most commonly used Greek word translated "love" in the New Testament is "agape." This love, is represented by God's love for us. It is a non-partial, sacrificial love probably best exemplified by God's provision for our rebellion:

"For God so loved (*agape*) the world that He gave His only begotten Son, that whoever believes in Him should not perish, but have eternal life." (John 3:16)

The gift of God's Son as the only provision for sin is given to all humans, regardless of who we are. God's love is unconditional!

In contrast, our love is usually conditional and based on how other people behave toward us. This kind of love is based upon familiarity and direct interaction. The Greek word "phileo" defines this kind of love, often translated "brotherly love. "Phileo is a soulish (*connected through our emotions*) kind of love - something that can be experienced by both believers and non-believers. This is in contrast to agape, which is love extended through the Spirit. Agape love requires a relationship with God through Jesus Christ, since the non-regenerated soul is unable to love unconditionally. Agape love gives and sacrifices expecting nothing in return.

Then, there is "Eros," the love of a friend. We have all had friends, some good, some not so good. Even others were not really friends at all. All they wanted was their own way in everything and sought their own ends. They schemed and manipulated to have us do everything their way, what they wanted, how they wanted and when they wanted. Sounds like a few people around today in our churches!

With all that behind us, let's leap forward into the kind of love we need to have in our life.

Love is patient! (1 Corinthians 13) At no time has Jesus ever forced Himself upon us. Unlike pushy people around us, He has waited patiently. Even when we were not interested in Him, He watched over us. His love letters to us are written in every blue sky. He whispered His love for us on the winds. He causes a thousand birds to sing of His love for us. Perhaps we were just too busy to notice. Still, He never pushed Himself upon us. When we were sick the doctors gave us medicine, but He was the one who healed us. He was right there by our side, ever so quiet so as not to disturb us. When you wept, He collected your tears in His bottle. He was with us, through it all. Perhaps we had no idea He was even there! Other believers perhaps ignored us. They were too busy with their own lives. Off to church they went, for some manifestation appearing and had no time, for real grace to be manifested in our life. It was then...

He held our hand! Sometimes we got so angry and frustrated at events happening in our life and we were unable to access any loving place. Instead, our eyes darted from side to side as our fists clenched and our minds filled with angry thoughts. Maybe we even spewed those thoughts out into the world with our words and actions.

At that moment, He wanted to sweep down from the ramparts of glory and jump into our circumstances. He didn't though! He would not touch our life without our permission. He wants us to make all our own decisions. Good or bad they are ours to make. It was then that tears streamed down His face. He knows everything, He knew that a day would come when we would turn to Him. Only then will He come to us! Still and for all of this, He Jesus, Love, remained ever patient, singing His simple song of love. A serenade from His heart to you!

  Love is kind! Maybe we have known a whole lot of deluded kindness in our life. It seems to be all around us these days. Kindness is not about self-interested politeness, calculated generosity, or superficial etiquette. People being nice to others because they believe that this will manipulate us into giving them, what they want in life, or as a means of controlling us. This, isn't kindness! Nor is kindness about pretending to care for someone all the while repressing anger or contempt; hiding rage or frustration behind false pleasantries. Sadly this is the story of many false apostles, prophets and teachers. (2 Corinthians 11:13-15) Some are very angry people. They are more interested in the numbers of people in their churches or full offering plates. The Lord told us they would be with us through the end times. Their name is Balaam!

Peter warned us against "the way of Balaam, Jude against the error of Balaam and John against the doctrine of Balaam. (2 Peter 2:15, Jude 11, Revelation 2:14) God evidently considers these warnings necessary and appropriate for Christians even today.

"The way of Balaam" was a readiness of a false teacher to prostitute his higher spiritual gifts and privileges for the wages of unrighteousness." (2 Peter 2:14) Being willing to preach something contrary to God's Word for personal gain or recognition. Something that was contrary to our final authority, the Word of God.

The error of Balaam, was evidently his willingness to compromise his own standards of morality and truth in order to greedily accommodate those who were his pagan listeners. (Jude 11)

Finally, the doctrine of Balaam! Even in John's day it was already infiltrating the church. He used his teaching authority to persuade God's people that it was all right for them to compromise the standards, of the final authority. To, have them accept less than the full manifestation of the Lord. These use spiritual tyranny to achieve their goals. Spiritual adultery with their idol-worshipping enemies. (Revelation 2:14)

No wonder Micah (*the faithful prophet*) urged God's people to "remember" Balaam and his tragic end. (Micah 6:5, Numbers 31:8)

If Balaam lived among today's evangelicals, he would be considered a great man. His public proclamations would be widely known, and his "ministry" would have great impact. (Numbers 22:6) Why should we settle for less than the pure agape love of God? Love always puts you first in everything.

I'm sure we have encountered the people pleasers, they don't know anything about kindness. Real love is kind in every way. Another word for kind is compassionate. True compassion is not like sympathy. Human sympathy stinks! Real compassion sees the situation and does something to change our circumstances even if we don't respond in kind. There is a story in the Bible.

One day Jesus was called to by ten lepers. They could not come near to the crowd because of their condition. They were lonely and isolated. When Jesus saw them He had compassion on them and healed them. Later only one came back to say thank you. (Luke 12:17-19) When He saw this, He didn't get upset or call judgment down on the ungrateful. Rather, He loved them just the way they were, all that they were and never demanded change.

The unscrupulous of our day only concern themselves with us giving testimony to increase their standing in the eyes of men! See me, they shout! They care little about us. Still, we must love them just the way they are and in silent love, believe for their change.

Have there been times in our life when we felt isolated or alone? Maybe we lying on some bed of sickness and it seemed like no one cared. We felt so terrible! Did we whisper, "God help me?" Soon we were well again and forgot all about our prayer, which Jesus answered.

Do we remember thinking, 'stay away from me,' when someone wanted to tell us about the love of Jesus? Perhaps we laughed or made comments behind the back of that one who invited us to church. Maybe we made jokes about a relative who loves Jesus and told us they were praying for us. Still and for all of this, the Lord did not call judgment from heaven upon us. Rather, He loves us unconditionally. In fact, He got us a new job, apartment and prospered us. His love is kind, motivated by compassion and it is all for you! Another verse in His simple song of love tells us...

Love, does not envy! Envious means wanting what another person has. It's different from jealousy in that it often reflects a kind of free floating self-loathing, which expresses itself in wanting something that belongs to another. I'm sure we have experienced this when we got that new job, new home or were prospered by the kind heart of the Lord. At first others envied us. Then, when we no longer had that job that income or worse they no longer cared about our position in life, the envious person lost all interest. They were gone!

This is rampant in the church in our day. A young minister studies, worships, prays and for a very short time he/she is the flavor of the month. The moment they challenge leadership through the power of being themselves. The second the congregation delights in their message, leaders toss a bucket of cold discouragement on them. Their support is then all gone! The senior pastor could not have them recognized any more than themselves. (1 Samuel 18: 5-9) They were only interested in what you (*the praise of the people*) had and not in whom you are.

On the other hand, Love, Jesus, His sole motivation is too bless us. His heart's desire is to see us walk in happiness, health, joy, gladness, freedom, contentment and that eternally. Everything in heaven and earth was created with us in mind. He wants us to become all we can be!

Love, does not boast! Many people or church leaders, speak with exaggeration and excessive pride, especially about themselves. They want to be the center of attention. Everything is about them. They think to impress others by their self-inflated egos. We don't matter! They are the end all and be all. I am sure we have been friends with someone like that. Their heads are swelled with pride. Maybe their favorite topic was their accomplishments, ministries or talents.

Sometimes these even boast with their threats. This one or that one did this to me, but I took care of them. Soon we discovered that we were better off without that one in our life. Jesus, has never boasted of His accomplishments even though everything He achieved for us, cost Him everything. He has never threatened or hinted at replacing us. When He was put on trial for us and suffered in our place.

"And they stripped him, and put on him a scarlet robe. And when they had platted a crown of thorns, they put it upon his head, and a reed in his right hand: and they bowed the knee before him, and mocked him, saying,

Hail, King of the Jews! And, they spit upon him, and took the reed, and smote him on the head." (Matthew 27:28-30)

They stripped Him! This was the ultimate dehumanizing ordeal and is an experience faced by all prisoners everywhere. The cowards wanted to strip Jesus of more than His clothes. Obviously that gang of thugs understood much about the psychological effect of stripping a prisoner. It's psychologically designed to remove all sense of control from the victim and provide the ultimate of control to the soldiers of the dungeons of darkness. This act sent a clear message to the world as to the contempt they held for Jesus. Those that boast want to do the very same thing to us! We have seen it time and again where pastors became controllers.

They pleated the crown and placed it upon His dear head. It wasn't a crown studded with rubies; rather it was His, own precious blood. Can you see the grin on their faces as they forced that crown into His head? Every drop of blood was forced from His brow by those cruel thorns. Falling were His teardrops of love for you. Every droplet was a declaration that no matter what, He loves you. If we see this kind of giving in the life of our pastors, love him, honor, keep him and don't let him go.

The fiendish worship that they offered Jesus was their filthy spittle, which ran down His cheeks. In mockery they bowed their knees before Him. They saluted him with the cry.

"Hail, King of the Jews!" (John 19:3)

It was done in contempt. In His silence He reigned supreme. His quiet demeanor did not concede defeat rather it echoed grace through faith. Even when contempt reached its pinnacle the King of Kings loved

His abusers and granted them silent grace. Do we in like manner offer the same grace to our abusers? His response to their spit was to carry it all the way to the cross. Still and for all His accomplishments for us He does not boast.

Love, is not proud! The proud are so consumed with themselves that their thoughts are so far away from us. In all their reflection, there is absolutely no room for us. It's an inward emotion that carries people far from humility. The proud thinks we should accept them because they deserve our acceptance. Relationships with such people will end in disaster. Their haughty spirit will end them in a fall. (Proverbs 16:18) The proud, are so blinded by their self-love that they think they have no need of anyone else.

Real love, and pride are a million miles apart. Just listen to these words for they are the very essence of love. "The Son can do nothing of Himself." (John 5: 19) "I can of my own self do nothing; my judgment is just because I seek not mine own will." (John 5: 30) "I receive not glory from men." (John 5: 41) "I am come not to do Mine own will." (John 6: 38) "My teaching is not mine." (John 7:16) "I am not come of myself." (John 7:28) "I do nothing of myself." (John 8:28) "I have not come of myself, but He sent me." (John 8:42) "I seek not Mine own glory." (John 8:50) "The words that I say, I speak not from myself." (John 14:10) "The word which ye hear is not mine." (John 14:24) He was saying that The Father is everything. Does our church leaders say that next to Jesus, you are everything? Jesus says that about us!

Love, is not rude! Rude is an unfinished state! Is it rude to be wakened when we are snoozing at the wheel? It sure feels rude! But it is actually proper and necessary for our safe keeping. There is more than one application to this word. Rude is the lack of polish and gentleness that also applies to either thought or behavior. A good example is slamming a door in one's face. Have we ever done that? Perhaps we said they deserved it! Did Love deserve it? How many times have we slammed the door shut to love? Jesus many times came knocking on our heart's door with loving correction only to get it slammed shut in His face as we tried to justify our behavior with Scripture taken out of context.

Unlike us, Jesus is patient and loving, even when He has to say difficult things. When he told the rich young ruler to sell his possessions and give them to the poor, He spoke compassionately, like a loving father pleading with his son to make better life choices. (Mark 10:17-22) Some have said that Jesus was rude. They are incorrect!

Jesus did sound rude on occasion. However, He was trying to wake the people up in the face of danger. He spoke in ways designed to alert people that they were headed towards hurt. He didn't immediately publicly rebuke, but bore patiently with them.

When a man is drowning, they thrash around in the water. Sometimes they fight the rescuer. The one who answers the call to help sometimes has to punch them in the mouth to be able to stop them fighting so as to save their life. That's a rude awakening! It's positive and beneficial! Has a rude awakening ever come to us to waken us up to the truth? In the process of time we will be glad we were awakened.

Love, is not self-seeking! Many seek their own advantage, comfort, ease, honor, pleasure, and profit. Many in relationships, especially in churches, have known such people. They were one way before we took membership, but as soon as we said, "Yes," things changed. Churches are to provide for family integrity, stability, security, and contentment. A place of safety to grow in the Lord.

Real love, Jesus, wants us safe and secure from all alarms. His desire for us be stable in every area of our life. To this end He gives us power, love and a sound mind. (2Timothy 1:7) By sound mind I mean; one that knows peace and stillness even in the worst storm. His desire for His church is to provide for our every need, physical, emotion and spiritual. They are all provided for the moment we enter into a relationship with Him. (Ephesians 1:3)

Love is not easily angered! We should not be touchy, easily provoked, fretful, resentful, suspicious, or oversensitive with our feelings. Instead, we are to be very slow to get angry, and we're not to let little things cause us to "fly off the handle." That has not always been the case, has it? Not even in church.

Reality says that from time to time we have faced the brunt of other people's anger. In fact, they too, have faced the weight of ours. Then, we justify ourselves by saying that everybody has their times. We let the pressure of finances, what others say to us or about us, employment or even life's circumstances get to us. Real love demonstrated by Jesus is far different.

When they accused Him, spit on Him, beat Him, He remained silent. When they called Him a heretic and said that He did miracles by the power of Satan, He loved them and blessed them. (Matthew 12:24) He lived every day what He said in Matthew 5:44.

"Love your enemies, bless them that curse you, do good to them that hate you, and pray for them which despitefully use you, and persecute you."

Never did He show malicious anger to anyone. He did however, say through Paul in Ephesians 4:26, "be angry, but sin not." Once more there are two aspects of anger we need to look at. There is malicious anger that causes nothing, but trouble. On the other hand, there is righteousness indignation or righteousness anger. An example of that would be when we have gone to church and discovered they were more interested in manifestations than the one who manifests grace.

When I see people take out flashlights to check hands for so-called gold dust. When others speak of angel feathers, orbs of light or oil dripping from the hands. When even more tell the congregation that their healing will come through sessions (*Sozo*) instead of instantaneously. We should become righteously angry. All are contrary to the pattern of Scripture.

Love does not delight in evil, but rejoices in the truth! We are to stand up and speak up when we discover anything that is not found in the Bible. To many this will come as a rude awakening. Just like Jesus we are to challenge others to better, biblical based, life choices.

Naturally there is a price to pay for contending for the faith delivered to us once and for all time. (Jude 3) They will say we are the ones who are wrong. Our names may be thrust out as being of the devil. Let them be warned!

In Isaiah 5:20, the writer warns us about the end times in which we live: "Woe to those who call good evil and evil good!" Our culture calls "good" truth, evil.

Love always protects! I wonder have we always felt safe and protected in our church family? Real love wraps

His arms of comfort around us! There in His arms we feel so safe and warm inside. Why we are alive again! When real Love, Jesus, is part of our life, we can go to Him and feel secure once more. He offers us His all-powerful protection. Love is our place of safety, our fortress. There we can trust securely. Love hides us from all danger. Like a bird spreading its wings over its babies so He shelters us. All around us is His shield that nothing can penetrate. Very quickly we learn that there is nothing to fear anymore. In His arms He tenderly whispers to us in strains so sweet and low. He tells you how beautiful you really are. That's something many have not heard in such a long time. What you have to say is important to Him and He hangs on your every word.

Love always trusts! Have we ever felt we were not trusted? What about others, can we trust them? Miserable is the church where trust has failed. It wasn't like that in the beginning, but then something went wrong. Often we have wondered if we will ever see the passion of our first love again. In real love there is no room for mistrust. It is like a cancer that eats away and eventually destroys. All through the Bible, in melodies of truth, Jesus shows us how to trust again.

When things went against David he sang a song. "I hear them whispering about me. They have turned against me and plan to kill me. LORD, I trust in you. You are my God." (Psalm 31:13-14 ERV) Coming to trust again may be difficult at first. Yet, Love leads the way!

Jesus said: "Father, into your hands I commit my spirit." (Luke 23:46) It was a moment of intimacy. These two verses belong together: trust nurtured by intimacy; intimacy nurtured by trust. The confident words of Jesus, carried Him far away from His circumstances and into the very heart of The Father's love. Can we hear love calling to us right now? Calling us away from the dark days of yesterday. Calling us to the brightness of a brand new day. "Do not let your hearts be troubled. You believe in God; believe also in me." (John 14:1)

Love always hopes! Perhaps, because of our situation all our hopes, our dreams our worth is all gone. All that we hoped for in that church now lies in shambles at our feet. Getting up every day is nothing, but a chore.

When we have real love in our life things are completely transformed. Hope is born again. Hope that is sure and certain. Belief based upon the promises of God that things for us will change, forever rises. Ascends on the wings of a crescendo of love. This kind of hope will never disappoint you. We know this because God has poured out His love to fill our heart through the Holy Spirit. (Romans 5:5 ERV) In Him, Proverbs, tells us that hope will never be lost again. (Proverbs 24:14) I say this because He knows the plans that He has for you. Listen as He speaks to our heart.

"I have good plans for you. I don't plan to hurt you. I plan to give you hope and a good future." (Jeremiah 29:11) "

Hope springs eternal in the human breast; Man never is, but always to be blessed." – Alexander Pope. What he meant was that hope seems to spring up from nowhere and never dies when you are in Jesus.

This has been just a small sampling of what the Lord has for you. Love never fails! No matter what comes, Jesus will never let you down. His love is ever constant and not affected by or diminished through the choices we make. There is a faith that causes us to soar on the wings of love! It's a hope that looks to a brighter tomorrow! Its love ablaze in our heart that draws us closer and closer to Him with every passing day! All these are mandatory for our journey through the end times until we come to the rapture. Without total surrender, abandonment of all, there is no surrender at all. Here is the pattern, our life must follow!

'Where there is no faith, there cannot be hope. Where there is no hope there cannot be love. To be without one element, is to be incomplete. To be incomplete is selfish. To be selfish is to know not God. Therefore, let faith, hope and love abide. These three, but the greatest of these is love. He is the very Breath of Life!' (*Poem by George Jenkins based on 1 Corinthians 13*)

Orchestrated Surrender!

"Abandoned," "surrendered," are words seen everywhere in nature and in everything around us. By the command of God, the sun, the moon, the stars, the flowers, the trees, and even the grass came into existence. (Genesis 1) These and much more, submitted to His word, hold in their courses as they travel through the journey of life. Isaiah said:

"Who hath measured the waters in the hollow of his hand, and meted out heaven with the span, and comprehended the dust of the earth in a measure, and weighed the mountains in scales, and the hills in a balance?" (Isaiah 40:12)

God created them; and are they not all absolutely surrendered to Him? Do they not allow God to work in them and do everything He pleases? They can't do anything other than live in complete surrender to His desires and will. When God clothes the lilies of the fields with their beauty, is the earth not yielded up, surrendered, given over, to God as He works His splendor?

Every piece in an orchestra, are they not given over to the dictates of the conductor? Every player understands their instrument and the sounds they create. There are specific music principles that produces the beauty of every vibration emitted. Without adherence to the composition, without the surrender of every musician to the director, bedlam ensues. Certainly the musician by his own will, can produce whatever sound they want. However, if they are not abandoned to the written score or the desire of the director, all results is utter confusion. Put a group of talented musicians, into unity with the composer, every other instrument and the director, together they paint a picture that fills the air.

Everything in the cosmos exists in abandonment to the divine. By His choice, He can change the rules of the game. That's what makes Him God. There are times in the Bible when He contravened the very laws of nature. Joshua spoke this into existence. It's there we can see how surrendered everything is to Him.

"Sun, stand thou still upon Gibeon; and thou, Moon, in the valley of Ajalon." (Joshua 10:12) The result was swift. The sun stood still and the moon stayed where it was in the sky. This condition remained for an entire day. (Verse 13) Since the earth revolves around the sun what happened was the earth stopped in its course. This requires a greater miracle than what comes to mind.

Universitytoday.com says, "At that moment everything would immediately be launched in a ballistic trajectory sideways. Imagine the oceans sloshing sideways at 1600 km/hour. Devastation all around the globe would have ensured. God however, used His power to prevent all of this and it all came about at the spoken word of a man." A man who was totally surrendered to Him.

Talk about the keeping power of God! In this case, the very universe, time and space, the planets everything abandoned themselves to God through the word of a man. Endless possibilities exist for the church today, but we have turned the love of God into a humanized theology. Some teach that man can speak things into existence! There is nothing wrong with that statement, but they (*Prophetic Prayer Ministry*) take it out of biblical perspective. They declare that man can speak judgment on the earth.

This is a perfect example of where the Word is taken way out of context. Yes, Moses did command judgment to fall, it did so, however, at the command of God and in the timing of God. (Exodus 7) In this it was initiated by God and not man.

These teachings came about when people preached about calling things into existence. For this premise they used, Romans 4:17. The latter part of that verse says: "God, who quickeneth the dead, and calleth those things which be not as though they were." Beyond a doubt the Lord can use us in this way. However, some think that we can, just like the Lord, create and speak things into existence. What they miss is the aspect of God's will and His timing. Without both of those we can speak all day long and nothing will happen. It was here, the enemy ran this off the rails.

In their defense they are quoted as saying: "Well, we would expect you to be against it since you haven't had the experience." That is Gnosticism! (*Esoteric knowledge*) It's believing that they are elevated to a higher level of comprehension which the uninitiated have no understanding. All false apostles, prophets and teachers resort to this argument. The very moment they use it, the true nature of their hearts they expose! There is certainly no abandonment, no surrender to God's calendar, found in their belief structure.

In daily life we can also see total abandonment, total surrender even in the things we use. Everything has to be given up to its special definite purpose and service. This computer and software I'm using to communicate with you; they are both absolutely surrendered to my hands for my chosen purpose of writing. There are of course, certain rules that govern my use of the software and computer within which I must remain, unless God chooses to alter those laws. Still if it is not perfectly abandoned to my will, to the commands of my keyboard, the results will be worthless. If it's broken, then I can't write effectively, nor can the desired result be available for you to read.

My clothes are absolutely given up to cover my body. My apartment is given completely to serve the Lord. My time, my books, my finances, my family and friends all have been given over to the Master. Just like my computer if I only half submit them, as with my commands on the keyboard, what use is it? By the same token how can the Lord work His work if there is only half or part of us that is surrendered? He can't do it. God is life, love, blessing, power, and infinite beauty, and God delights to communicate Himself to everyone who is prepared to receive Him; but ah! This lack of absolute surrender is just the thing that hinders God. It keeps us from fulfilling our mission in God. The only aspect of the universe not surrendered to the LORD is man except by his choice.

We all want to be used of the Lord. We have prayed for it, wept over the possibilities, longed for it and waited one endless night after another. Our day didn't come! Why?

Are we willing to give to Him everything as did the heroes and heroines of the Bible? The Master is here right now. He comes to reclaim us and restore His church. The Lord cannot work His works of love and beauty every day and every hour unless we are entirely given up to Him.

The Temple of Solomon was absolutely surrendered to God the hour it was dedicated. (2 Chronicles 7) That day the glory of the Lord filled the house as revival fires roared. We are temples of the most High God. The Lord requires no less from us. He claims it, He is worthy of it and without it He cannot work among us in absolute power.

The word, "abandoned," in speaking of godly matters means to be left without any need for self-preservation. It means wholly and completely surrendered to the Lord. It has been a doctrine of the church long forsaken by believers. If we are to see transformation as we desire to experience the power of God, it must be resurrected to its rightful place!

Right from the outset some may be thinking that what I am speaking about is too much for many to give.

'You just don't know what I have been through in my life,' they claim. 'There has been so much brokenness, hurt and pain in my life. How is it possible for me to permit myself to be that vulnerable again?'

Hold up a minute. The message of the New Testament is good news. I have a truth for you that should settle your heart forever. The Lord has never asked anything of us that He has not empowered us to give. Any thought that speaks less than His perfect loving provision are cruel thoughts towards Him. Whoever said that He has asked us for a perfect surrender, accomplished by our own strength or by our willpower? Our will, other than to accept His will is all that is required! The Lord has always been willing to do it within us.

"It is God that worketh in us, both to will and to do of his good pleasure." (Philippians 2:13)

This is what we should be looking for. The days of one session after another in counselling through Sozo ministry where people are asked to do much, must come to an end. Total abandonment must come back to its rightful place in our life!

Now there is a word, "Sozo." It's been bandied about in our day with little or no understanding of its real meaning. Teachers of what has come to be known as, "Sozo Ministry," say:

"SOZO," is the Greek word translated "saved, healed, and delivered. Sozo ministry is a unique inner healing and deliverance ministry aimed to get to the root of things hindering your personal connection with The Father, Son and Holy Spirit. With a healed connection, you can walk in the destiny to which you have been called.

A Sozo session is a time for the Sozo team to sit down with you and with the help of the Holy Spirit walk you through the process of freedom and wholeness. Sozo is not a counseling session, but a time of interacting with Father, Son and Holy Spirit for wholeness and pursuing of your destiny." – Bethel Sozo.

When Jesus spoke to the woman with the issue of blood He said: "Woman thy faith hath made thee Sozo." Healed, free, delivered and whole at that very second. According to Strong's the word, "Sozo also," speaks of salvation, of wholeness, of healing and of freedom. This is what that woman received the moment she by faith touched the hem of His garment. At no time has Jesus ever said that salvation was a process. The word, "Sozo," is used 106 times in the New Testament. Let's look at a few of those verses in their context!

Salvation

"She shall bring forth a son, and thou shalt call his name JESUS: for he shall save (Sozo) his people from their sins." (Matthew 1:21)

"For after that in the wisdom of God the world by wisdom knew not God, it pleased God by the foolishness of preaching to save (Sozo) them that believe." (1Corinthians 1:21)

"Wherefore he is able also to save (*Sozo*) them to the uttermost that come unto God by him, seeing he ever liveth to make intercession for them." (Hebrews 7:25)

Forgiven, Healed, and Delivered

Sozo was translated another fifty-three times as "saved" (past tense) in reference to forgiveness of sins. However, there were also times where this same Greek word was translated as "healed."

(*Jairus*) besought (*Jesus*) greatly, saying, my little daughter lieth at the point of death: I pray thee, come and lay thy hands on her, that she may be healed (*Sozo*); and she shall live. (Mark 5:23)

This word, "healed" is referring to physical healing. As the story unfolds, Jairus' daughter actually died, and Jesus raised her from the dead. (Mark 5:35–43) So in this instance Sozo "healed," refers to physical healing, even physical resurrection from the dead. This girl was dead! Jesus didn't say that her resurrection was a lengthy procedure, come back for another session next week!

This same word that's used for both forgiveness of sins and physical healing also applies to deliverance from demons.

"They also which saw it told them by what means he that was possessed of the devils was healed." (*Sozo*) (Luke 8:36) Commonly known as the demoniac of Gadarene, nobody could hold this man. In fact, he often broke the very chains which bound him. Jesus cast the demons out of him. Nowhere does it say that this was a process. He didn't use, "Theophostic Therapy,"

"Theophostic Prayer," or "Sozo Ministry." He didn't say that his freedom would come down the road. It was instantaneous. Jesus spoke a word. The moment He spoke they left! Another example is found in these words.

"The same heard Paul speak: who steadfastly beholding him, and perceiving that he had faith to be healed." (*Sozo*) (Acts 14:9)

Paul beheld this crippled man, (*Lame from birth*) and perceived that he had faith to be healed (*Sozo*), and he was in that instant he abandoned himself to God.

If we take a moment to consider the emotional aspects of these very few people we discover even more truth. The man who was blind, spent years begging on the streets. His condition isolated him and he was condemned to beg on the streets. In those days such was their social welfare program. Ask someone who is on Social Assistance if their experience does not bring to them emotional upset. Sure his emotions were broken, yet his healing was instant. His surrender was total and complete. He laid down his condition and everything that tracked with it. Jesus did not say come back next month and we will go deeper.

The woman with the issue of blood, had spent all she had on doctors and was none better. For twelve long years she searched. I bet at times she felt like giving up. When Jesus healed her that healing was instant, spiritual, emotional and physical she was made whole, "Sozo," the very moment she believed. Jesus never said to her, you are healed, but more is to come down the road. You and I, with the help of the Holy Ghost will work through the issues.

When the Apostle Paul was used in the, "Sozo" of the impotent man, he was faced with much more than, a physical condition. He had been handicapped from the day he was born. Tell me that such does not bring with it many emotional issues. Just ask the person sitting in a wheelchair outside some building hoping someone will come along and open the door for them. From personal experience I can tell you it does.

For seven long years I was confined to a wheelchair, the result of a stroke. His connection, my link with, "Sozo," healing, not the ministry was also instant. (Acts 3-4)

Those who teach, "Sozo," like Bethel attempt to fit God into the experience of man and not fit man into the realities of God. In this, they psychologically manipulate people into something that is far from Scriptural. There is much that has been taught in our church that is not according to Scripture. Things that have kept people in bondage when they could be free.

Personal revival because of the very nature of that word brings the reliving of truths abandoned by the church. The instantaneous truth of Jesus must be reclaimed.

"It is not only desirable, it is essential; we must either be revived by the Lord himself, or the churches will descend until error and ungodliness swallow them up. This calamity shall not happen, but only divine grace can avert it." – Charles Haddon Spurgeon

The courageous Luther, much to the disapproval of the Catholic Church encouraged people to return to the doctrine of justification by faith.

John Bevere, boldly contends: "The church has fallen hard for a teaching that puts lives at eternal risk." He is speaking about hyper-grace, a cheap grace idea that floods the churches in our day. In his book, "Rescued," he presents five marks of the cheap-grace doctrine.

God is taking His church back to the seat of truth. Many who have been deluded by error will challenge ever written word, every step of the way. We are going back to, "Expensive-Grace," to total surrender.

Abraham was absolutely abandoned to The Father. It was no accident that God chose him over all other men in the world. It was no coincidence that he became the father of the faithful. He without God enabling him, could never have come to a place where he was set apart for God. Nothing he ever did was accomplished in his own strength or a result of his will. How without God was he able to obey the King to the sacrificing of his son, or father a baby when he and Sarah were well beyond the physical ability? (Hebrews 11:11)

By which act of his will, did Moses open The Red Sea? (Exodus 14:21) What example can be given of the will of man being used when the Jordan opened up? (Joshua 3) Was it the strength of Joshua that brought down the walls of Jericho? (Hebrews 11:30) Naaman was healed not through his ideas, but in abandonment to the desires of the Lord to wash in the Jordan River. (2Kings 5:1-19) Who among us by taking thought can add so much as one cubit to our height? (Matthew 6:27)

All had to come to that place of total surrender. A surrender orchestrated and empowered by heaven. Abandonment has nothing to do with personal gain. Many today are self-centered and may want to surrender with some idea of personal advancement. Real abandonment is about giving up all control without personal benefit. Often we go to God wanting something from Him. True surrender is captured in the words of an old song. From Rock of Ages by, Augustus M Toplady.

Nothing in my hand I bring,
Simply to Thy cross I cling;
Naked, come to Thee for dress;
Helpless, look to Thee for grace;
Foul, I to the fountain fly;
Wash me, Savior, or I die.

Oswald Chambers in his book: "My Utmost for His Highest," says: "True surrender will always go beyond natural devotion. If we will only give up, God will surrender Himself to embrace all those around us and will meet their needs, which were created by our surrender. Beware of stopping anywhere short of total surrender to God. Most of us have only a vision of what this really means, but have never truly experienced it."

God comes and offers to work this absolute surrender in us. Perhaps for years we have felt that something has been missing in our walk. We have hungered for something more. What that something was we had no idea. The cry of our day has been, "more Lord." Preachers have answered that call with the superficial, the external and steered us away from the internal. The Lord is drawing us like some gigantic magnet into the depth of the river, Jesus Christ. A river of transformation and not warm fuzzy feelings. Jesus lived a life of absolute surrender. He desires to help us take hold of Him entirely and walk with Him in complete abandonment. How will we respond?

If someone were to stick a gun in our ribs the very first thing we do is to raise our hands. It means, I surrender! We do the same in our meetings, but the surrender aspect of our raised hands is not even thought about.

This surrender, the Master not only claims it, He deserves it, He works it and The Father accepts it when we bring it to Him.

Often the un-surrendered pain and wounds in our life prevents us from such abandonment. We always want to hold back from anything that is so absolute, anything that makes us vulnerable. Then, we hesitate and chose the pain rather than the freedom. Such a surrender requires us to abandon everything. The wounds, the pain, all the broken promises and every betrayal. The very moment we surrender, in that instant our healing to complete and we walk away from everything that was. We see this truth played out on every page of the Bible. Let these words call you forward.

"If thou canst believe, all things are possible to him that believeth." (Mark 9:23)

The heart of the young man's father in this story was afraid, just like ours and he cried out:

"Lord, I believe, help thou mine unbelief." (Mark 9:24)

His faith unleashed even though fear and uncertainly lurked on every hand. He was saying: "Lord, I yield myself in absolute surrender to you. I'm trembling and I don't feel your power, I don't feel any assurance." It's the same feeling that comes when someone sticks that gun in your ribs. A terrible feeling of helplessness may set in. Nonetheless, He works for us if we come.

Don't be afraid! Come, just as you are, and even in the midst of our trembling the power of the Holy Spirit will work. Jesus showed us how to take this step. He did it in Gethsemane.

He "through the eternal Spirit," (Hebrews 9:14) offered Himself a sacrifice unto God. The Holy Ghost enabled Him to do it. Even in the face of agony, when terrible sorrow came over Him. Before going to prayer, He told His disciples!

"My soul is exceeding sorrowful, even unto death: tarry ye here, and watch with me." (Matt 26:38; Mark 14:34)

You can be certain this battle arose not through any fear of death. Nor did it come through any fear of physical pain or for the humiliation and shame that He would soon endure. You can also be sure if Sozo ministry was around in those days they would have prescribed sessions to rid him of that sorrow or as they call it, emotional pain.

The battle was set in array, the agony in Gethsemane raged and the great burden that was already upon Him as the people's substitute exploded in all its urgency. It was this great sorrow that pressed Him down even into the dust of death. He was to carry the full weight of sorrow upon the cross, but His passion began in Gethsemane. There, He carried our sin and the terrible weight of that sin began to crush Him. He came to that olive press (*Gethsemane*) and the attending pressure was beyond words. It was a pressure that grew in intensity with every passing moment. Then, soon, nailed to that rugged old cross, there would be forced from Him the agonizing cry.

"My God, my God, why hast thou forsaken me?" (Psalm 22:1; Matthew 27:46; Mark 15:34)

Through it all He, trusted, relied upon the Holy Ghost as He surrendered it all for us.

Externally, we may see no sign of the mighty power of the Spirit, but the Spirit of God is there as we come to surrender. Even so, while we are feeble, fighting and trembling, in faith in the hidden work of God's Spirit do not fear, but yield ourselves.

When a baby is born there comes tremendous pressure as they descend along the birth canal. It is the same when we come under the mighty hand of God. This is why many in historic revival have cried out to get out from under that hand. Choosing to remain brings a life beyond compare! A life filled with all the beauty of the Lord as we His new creatures come into the brightness of a brand new day! A day when we emerge through the birth canal of total and absolute surrender. It was through this gateway of life that the heroes of the Bible came to the strains of that song of old.

"All to Jesus I surrender. All to Him I freely give; I will ever love and trust Him: In his presence daily live." – Ruben Studdard

Regrettably, this fanfare of man does not always echo His melodies of truth in love!

Fanfare of Man

If ever a marriage was made in heaven, Adam and Eve had it all. It was perfectly orchestrated and perfectly complete by a perfect God. To build His fanfare of man, first He created Adam. (Gen. 2:7) Molded by the Master's loving hand! Adam doubtless had a wonderful build and sported rugged handsome features. He was made in God's own image. (Gen. 1:27) He was made in the image of perfect Love. All reasons for a marriage breakdown, all excuse for failure was absent. That means he had a godlike personality, perfect intellect, emotions, and will. He possessed a brilliant mind. Adam gave names to every single animal on the earth. The choices of those names were his to make. (Genesis 2:19) He had faultless emotions, including a capacity to know tender and totally unselfish love, the love of God himself. His will was in perfect harmony with the purposes of his Creator.

Eve! Her preparation for love that too was absolute. "So the Lord God caused a deep sleep to fall upon the man, and he slept; then He took one of his ribs, and closed up the flesh at that place. And, the Lord God fashioned into a woman the rib which He had taken from the man, and brought her to the man." (Gen. 2:21, 22)

Standing there that day Adam gazed at Eve with awe and appreciation. God's creative genius at its best, unblemished grace and beauty, pure loveliness of face and form appeared before him. Eve, was the most gorgeous creature whoever walked the face of the earth. Like Adam, she was made in God's image. Her mind, emotions, intellect swept across the dance floor of creation.

Adam immediately recognized her similarity to himself. He said, "This is now bone of my bones, and flesh of my flesh; she shall be called woman because she was taken out of man. (Genesis 2:23)

Revelation from God had burst in to view at the dawn of creation. Adam knew that Eve was made from him; she was part of him; she was his equal; she was his complement and counterpart. Such revelation only comes from the heart of God to the essence of a surrendered man.

He called her woman, "female man." She was the mother of all living. He drew her to himself in tender love. His arms were warm and inviting. His embrace ever assuring.

She had ended his long days of loneliness and filled his life with happiness. She was just exactly what he needed. His embrace brought her no greater satisfaction than the assurance that her husband needed her so very much.

What intense and indescribable pleasure they found in each other's arms! How they loved each other! No half rhymes existed, in their beginnings with love. For some time they flowed in oneness in a symphony of splendid oneness. Physically, emotionally, and spiritually they were impeccable!

Their home was located in Eden, the perfect place. (Genesis 2:8) The word Eden means "delight," and delightful it was. Their real estate agent none other than God himself. What a listing! What a purchase! He offered them gold tried in the fire! (Revelation 3:18) Eden was well watered and the fountainhead of four rivers. It was a luscious green paradise, blanketed with every beautiful and edible growing thing. (Gen. 2:9, 10) Even the "Tree of Life," Jesus, was right there with them in their garden of splendor. (Genesis 2:9, Revelation 2:7) They cultivated a ground that knew no thistles or weeds. Their work was totally effortless and enjoyable. Side by side they lived, loved and worked in perfect harmony, sharing a sense of mutual interdependence, enjoying a freedom of communion. All exchanges possessing a deep-flowing affection that bound their spirits to each other. Nothing could separate them at least not at that moment.

A closer look at Scripture shows that there was order of authority in their relationship. Adam was formed first, then Eve. (1 Timothy 2:13) Eve was made for Adam! Nothing was lacking! The Father, Son and Holy Ghost were there! The Father spoke, the Word, Jesus created and the Holy Ghost brought everything together. (Genesis 1:26, John 1:3, Genesis 1:2) To top it off, God gave him, His wonderful Eve. Not to dictate to her, manipulate or control her. She was his helper. (Genesis 2:18)

For Eve, to be an effective helper she had to share all of life with him. He could not hold anything back from her. She was with him when God issued the command to subdue the earth and have dominion over it. Consequently, she shared that awesome responsibility equally with her husband. (Genesis 1:28) She did everything an equal would be expected to do. She assisted him, encouraged him, advised him, and inspired him, and she did it with a spirit of sweet submissiveness.

It was a submission not demanded or commanded. It was a submission earned by Adam. Her advice to him was always welcomed. After all that's why God gave her to him. Neither did she resent his leadership. Paul in

Ephesians 5:25, describes Adam. "Husbands love your wives even as Christ so loved the church and gave Himself for it." Who could ever, resent such love? His attitude was never tainted with superiority or exploitation. How could it be? His love was perfect. He was far more than the man of the year! She was someone special to him and he treated her with every respect. He could not give of himself enough to express his gratitude to her. He never had a thought about what he was receiving in return. She could not possibly, resent a leadership like that.

Moses in Genesis says, "And the man and his wife were both naked and were not ashamed." (Genesis 2:25) It was a relationship of perfect purity and innocence. Not one stinking, evil thought was present. Can you imagine the little walks they took together as he named the animals? Picture the moonbeams dancing along the riverbank. Taste the wonders of the fruit of the trees as the stars frolicked in the night sky! One can imagine their laughter, and exclamations of awe as new tastes were discovered, new sights were seen and new things were found. God must have been delighted as His children saw daily, the many wonders of His creation.

Envision a sunny, cloudless day, no breeze, birds twittering and the sweet sound of a woman's voice singing happily and melodiously. It's the stuff of dreams and fairy tales! There was no sin in them. Strife was nonexistent! They were at peace with God, at peace with themselves, and at peace with each other. They were one with God and one with each other.

Well did Jesus pray! "That they be one as you and I are one." (John 17:21)

This was truly the perfect marriage. It was paradise, a utopia soon to be lost. How we wish it had lasted that we could experience the same degree of marital bliss they enjoyed in those glorious days. But, something happened! Their Shangri-La of love faded, crumbling into brokenness. What were the consequential effects upon marriages ever since? How do these effects dictate to your relationships today? Can we ever know a forever love again?

The biblical account brings us to the entrance of sin! The subtle tempter approached Eve. Deception was his instrument! His first approach was to question the Word of God. "Indeed, has God said, 'You shall not eat of every tree of the garden?" (Genesis 3:1) After he questioned God's Word, he flatly denied it: "You shall not surely die!" (Genesis 3:4) Finally, he ridiculed God and brazenly distorted His Word: "For God knows that in the day you eat from it your eyes will be opened, and you will be like God, knowing good and evil." (Genesis 3:5) In reality the very opposite would be true.

His tactics have not changed over the years. This is why hyper-grace, Sozo and a thousand other things pollute our churches today. Easy believism, all that tickles our ears, the external seems to take precedence over the internal. (2 Timothy 4:3)

Adam and Eve, would indeed know evil, but would they be as God? In no way! The likeness to God they enjoyed would be scarred and spoiled. Satan's bait-switch tactics have not changed throughout the centuries. The doubts, the distortions, the denials all have taken their toll, even in our homes. Still we continue to fall victim to them. Can we identify with Eve in her moment of weakness?

Satan used the tree of the knowledge of good and evil to do his sinister work. God had placed that tree in the garden to be the symbol of Adam and Eve's submission to Him. (Genesis 2:17) Satan always uses good things to lure us from God's will and into ill-fated doctrines. "When the woman saw that the tree was good for food, and that it was a delight to the eyes, and that the tree was desirable to make one wise, she took from its fruit and ate; and she gave also to her husband with her, and he ate." (Genesis 3:6)

These three things he used against them. (*1*) The lust of the flesh - "good for food." (*2*) The lust of the eyes - "a delight to the flesh." (*3*) The pride of life - "to make one wise." (1 John 2:16) Ever since that fateful day Satan has continued to use these in attempts to destroy every good thing. The desire to gratify our physical senses, the desire to have material things, and the desire to impress people with our importance is destructive to every body of believers.

Instead of running in the opposite direction, Eve flirted with it. (1 Corinthians 10:14) She had everything a person could want in life, but she stood there and allowed her mind to meditate on the one thing she didn't have until it became an obsession with her. It brought her happy honeymoon to an unhappy conclusion.

Don't get me wrong she was not the only one to blame in their destruction. It always takes two! That same vicious greed that has ended many a honeymoon ever since clawed at Adam.

Husbands sometimes squander grocery money on recreational equipment, hobbies, cars, or clothes. Wives sometimes drive their husbands to make more money so they can have bigger, better, and more expensive things.

These material possessions of this world drive a wedge between couples. When we allow our minds to covet material things, God calls it idolatry. (Colossians 3:5)

Eve did not escape to the safety of God's presence. "She took from its fruit and ate." (Genesis 3:6) Next enters the second culprit to the end of their oneness. Eve, "gave also to her husband with her." He watched in silence as she did it. Why he didn't stop her is simple, he was equally guilty and trapped by the lust of the eyes, the lust of the flesh and the pride of life. He failed her miserably. He neglected to provide the spiritual leadership God wanted him to provide, and instead he chose to follow her. What a powerful influence couples have over each other! We can use it to challenge each other to new heights of spiritual accomplishment, or we can use it to drag those around us into depths of shame. God gave them to each other to be one, but their covetous hearts destroyed them.

Together they waited for the new delights of wisdom that Satan had promised to them. Instead, a horrid sense of guilt and shame crept over them. God had told them that in the day they took off the tree of knowledge of good and evil they would surely die. Listen to His actual words: "Thou shalt not eat of it: for in the day that thou eatest thereof thou shalt surely die." (Genesis 2:17)

That, tells us that God knew a day would come when they would do this. His love for them, kept Him silent as He empowered them giving the will to choose. We know on that day they didn't die physically. The reference to death then had to have a more in-depth meaning. They died spiritually and their physical bodies began the slow process of decay that would mar God's beautiful handiwork and end ultimately in physical death.

The Apostle Paul spoke of physical death when he said, "Therefore, just as through one man sin entered into the world, and death through sin, and so death spread to all men because all sinned." (Romans 5:12)

That's the way it is with sin. It promises so much and delivers so little. It promises freedom, wisdom, and pleasure, but it delivers bondage, guilt, shame, and death. The latter was their choice!

Suddenly their nakedness became symbolic of their sin. (Genesis 3:7) It exposed them openly to the penetrating eyes of a Holy God. They tried to cover their bodies with fig leaves, but it wasn't acceptable. God would later reveal that the only adequate covering for sin would involve the shedding of blood (Genesis 3:21, Leviticus 17:11, Hebrews 9:22)

The painful aftermath was terrible. Sin is always accompanied by disastrous consequences whether or not we are willing to accept the blame for it. Adam blamed his part of the tragedy on Eve and God: "The woman whom Thou gavest to be with me, she gave me from the tree, and I ate" (Gen. 3:12). Eve said the devil made her do it. (Genesis 3:13)

In much the same way, we try to blame our marital problems on someone else. 'If he/she would only stop nagging me.' 'If he/she would be more considerate I could.' God held them both equally responsible, just in the same way, He holds each of us responsible for our part of the blame. In every church relationship failure, blame can be ascribed on both sides. God wants us to face up to it squarely and not skirt around it. We are the ones who permitted error through the doors of the church.

The consequences were almost more than Adam and Eve could bear. For Eve, the pain of childbirth would be a recurring reminder of her choices. In addition to that, she would experience an insatiable yearning for her husband, a piercing desire for his time, his attention, his affection, and his assurance. Have you ever seen this as people make demands on their church leaders?

Eve's need, would be so great and her sinful husband would seldom be willing to meet it. The consequences of the fall to relationships are all around us today are horrific.

The authority Adam possessed over Eve from creation was strengthened by the word rule. "And he shall rule over you." (Genesis 3:16) In the hands of a sinful men that rule degenerates into harsh and heartless domination over a partner. There is then nothing, but disregard for feelings and disdain for opinions. Eve no doubt hurt under the sting of her sin as Adam drifted farther and farther away from her. He paid less attention to her, and became preoccupied with other things. Bitterness, resentment, and rebellion began to settle in her soul.

For Adam, cultivating the ground became an endless, tedious chore. The consequences of his sin brought the birth of a new day. A day of great toil and struggle. Anxiety over his ability to provide for his family added to his agitation and irritability, which made him less sympathetic to his wife's needs. Conflict in their home was the result. Sin always brings tension, strife, and conflict. Never was that more painfully obvious to Adam and Eve than when they stood beside the first grave in human history. Their second son, Abel, had lost his life in an ugly family squabble. The honeymoon was over and paradise gone!

Ever since the fall, man was no longer created in the image of God. We were created in the image of Adam. (Genesis 5:3) Adam was a broken man. He knew heartache and despair. Unhappiness, misery, ill health and poverty governed his life far from their garden heaven. Ever since, every relationship in or out of the church has followed in their footsteps.

This would be the saddest story ever told was it not for a glorious light of hope by which God illuminated the darkness. Speaking to Satan He said, "And I will put enmity between you and the woman, and between your seed and her seed; He shall bruise you on the head, and you shall bruise Him on the heel." (Genesis 3:15)

God promised that the seed of the woman, a child born into the human race, would destroy the works of the devil, including the havoc he has made in the church. This is the first biblical prophecy of the coming of Jesus.

As promised He came! He paid sins price! His perfect blood covered our sin! Those who accept Him and His sacrifice can again know beauty within their homes, families and churches. Freely He offers to restore our churches! He wants to bring us back to His favor.

That can only be experienced when we acknowledge our sin and place our trust in Jesus Christ's perfect sacrifice on Calvary for deliverance from the eternal condemnation, which our sin deserves. It can only come through the doorway of repentance. (Matthew 3:2) Repentance means to come to an end of doing things our way. Realizing all that we are because of sin! Thinking on the evil of our doings! Be heartfelt sorry and making a decision to turn away from all that has been! To turn to the Lord with all of our hearts! It can only come along the avenue of total surrender of all. It's not turning a new page. Rebirth only comes when the decision of man embraces the promises of God.

The Bible is full of stories about loving relationships not just this one. Parallels can be drawn from everyone to relationships today. Successes and failures are contained in its pages. Plots that unfold with every page turned! Stories of the struggles of men and women as they come to that place of absolute surrender. The saga of Adam and Eve is played out again and again as man journeys back to the perfection of Eden. Their symphony of love will carry us across time and space until we come to the greatest marriage feast that will ever take place! Evidence that edify and build up that help us make the right choices in life! Testimonies to help us come to that place of peace and oneness. Options that lead us beyond Eden. Past the Cherubim's with a flaming sword who guards the way to the Tree of Life.! Come on! Let's journey together to the eventual marriage supper of the Lamb! To that great hallelujah chorus. First, though, let's make a brief stop in the life of Peter.

Surrendered Sea Music

Often people say they have been to one meeting after another or to some great conference. 'I went to the altar and made a new commitment in my life,' their claim's ring out. Later they report that nothing was lasting. A few days later they returned to their old ways. Their experience faded like some dying flower. Soon it was all gone! So, they go to another meeting or another conference hoping to get it all back again. This happens because of the many wrong things we have been taught in our churches. Things like, repentance is a few words so some sinner's prayer, recited at the altar.

When God begins a work of absolute surrender in us, and when the Lord, has accepted our surrender, then He holds Himself bound to care for us and to keep us. "He is able to keep that which we have committed to him against that day. (2Timothy 1:12)

Our story, our adventure on the sea of love begins with repentance. It starts the very moment we come to the end of ourselves. This, we've been told time and time again, but we were never really told what that means. Let's take a look at the doorway into the Kingdom!

"Repent: for the kingdom of heaven is at hand." (Matthew 4:17) We must understand that repentance is not a bad thing, it's the result of God's goodness to us.

"It is the goodness of God that leads us to repentance. (Romans 2:42) It's not being beaten up or brought under condemnation by some heartless preacher. I once heard a preacher say: "If someone lives in a garbage dump there is only one thing they want to know. How do I get out of the dump?" He was saying that real repentance is expensive and manifests as a result of the goodness of God being manifest. It is a willingness to forsake all.

"And saying, the time is fulfilled, and the kingdom of God is at hand: repent ye, and believe the gospel." (Mark 1:15)

Repentance is the only way to life in the Kingdom. That applies not only to the individual it also applies to the church or to a nation. Righteousness exalts a nation. (Proverbs 14:34) To repent we must first be convinced that we stand in the need of that repentance. We need to know that total surrender has been absent from our life and from sermons preached. If we feel that we are not in need, the Kingdom cannot be entered.

When the great men of God such as Evan Roberts of the Welsh revival preached, he spoke of love. The goodness of God showed up and repentance roared. People began to break under the mighty hand of God. They wept, some screamed out for mercy. Others shook for hours or days after falling to the floor. When they got up their lives were totally transformed. Their surrender was complete! Where is it today?

Over the years the message of repentance has been watered down for the convenience of our generation and to fit into man's experience. We were told that repentance is when one stops going in one direction and turns around completely and walks in the opposite direction. That's true, yet it is only the very outer edge of truth. Here again the emphasis is placed upon what man can do and not what the Lord has already done. Upon closer examination we see that such a feat is really impossible to man.

Perhaps you can tell me how does anyone stop and turn around when all their lives they have been headed to hell? Why did they not just stop at some other point in their journey? It almost gives the impression that this can be done at will. Repentance, real repentance is a gift from God. Without that supernatural ingredient we will never repent. Real repentance comes at the end of a process of the Lord working upon our hearts. It's a miracle that comes after endless hours of someone kneeling in prayer for us. It comes by faith when the act or decision of man, embraces the promises of God. It comes in answer to love! Every manifestation of God is found in His Word. If a pattern is not found in Scripture toss it out, it's not the Lord. So, what is repentance supposed to look like in the Bible? Let's ask Peter!

"And the Lord turned, and looked upon Peter. And Peter remembered the word of the Lord, how he had said unto him, before the cock crow, thou shalt deny me thrice. And Peter went out, and wept bitterly." (Luke 22:61, 62)

That was the turning-point in the history of Peter. However, earlier Jesus said to him: "Thou canst not follow me now." (John 13:36) At that time Peter was not in any condition to follow Christ, because he had not been brought to an end of himself. He didn't know that he was far from the Kingdom and he therefore could not follow Christ. When he did come to a place where he could follow the Lord, he went out and wept bitterly. Remember Jesus said to him: "When thou art converted, strengthen thy brethren." (Luke 22:32) Up until this moment Peter was unsaved.

"And when he thought thereon, he wept." (Mark 14:72)

When Peter came face-to-face with his sin, his denial, he wept. He saw his need and bewailed his actions. It was the goodness of God that led Peter to repent. In revival, deep sobs of anguish are heard in the church, on the street and in the workplaces. The more love that is poured out, the more repentance is evidenced.

Let me ask a question about when we came into the Kingdom. For how long did those tears flow down our faces? Was it for one hour, six hours, one day, six days, or even six weeks? For years I wondered why I had wept so much when I came to Christ while others around me barely shed a single tear. I thought back across my terrible life and remembered the many whom I had hurt because of the lifestyle I led. I wept night after night. Some said that I had much more needing forgiveness, but they were wrong. Sin is more a matter of who we are, than what we have done. The reason I wept was due to the love I experienced.

To understand Peter a little more we have to look at four aspects of his life. Peter as he lived the life of self; followed by Peter's repentance. Peter the devoted disciple and lastly, at what Christ made of Peter by the Holy Spirit.

Jesus called Peter to forsake his nets, and follow Him. Peter did it at once. Later he is recorded as saying: "We have forsaken all and followed thee." (Matthew 19:27) Everything on the outside spoke of total abandonment. He left his earthly treasures behind, yet his surrender was not complete.

Peter was also a man who knew obedience. You remember Jesus said to him, "Launch out into the deep, and let down the net." (Luke 5:4) Peter the fisherman, knew there were no fish there, for they had been toiling all night and had caught nothing; but he said: "At thy word I will let down the net" (Luke 5:5). He submitted, but was that compliance without doubt? I wonder was he able to hear the music of the sea, drifting across Galilee calling him away to a new future. Did he hear the Lord's orchestrated sound that penetrated to the very depths of the Sea of Galilee? A song from the heart of the Master, calling out to Peter pointing him to tomorrow!

He was a man of faith. When he saw Jesus walking on the sea, he said: "Lord, if it be thou, bid me come unto thee;" (Matthew 14:28) and at the voice of the Lord he stepped out of the boat and walked upon the water. Then, the very second he took his eyes off the Lord he began to sink under the waves of his circumstances. Obviously his surrender was not complete! In this, he was no different from many of us today. We claim that our submission is complete, but is it really? What are we willing to give up?

Let's look at his self-will! You will recollect that just after Jesus asked him who did he think He, Jesus was. Peter replied. "You are the Christ!" Then, Jesus said to him: "Flesh and blood hath not revealed it unto thee, but my Father which is in heaven," Then, the Lord began to speak about His sufferings, and Peter dared to say: "Be it far from thee, Lord; this shall not be unto thee." Then, the Lord rebuked him:

"Get thee behind me, Satan; for thou savorest not the things that be of God, but those that be of men." (Matthew 16:22-23)

There was Peter in his self-will, trusting his own wisdom, strength and actually forbidding Jesus from doing what He came to do. DIE! Where did such thinking come from? Peter trusted in himself and his own thoughts about the things of God. Later on, when the disciples questioned as to who would be the greatest in the Kingdom, Peter was one of them. He thought he had a right to first place. (Matthew 18:1) He sought his own honor even above the others. The self-life was strong in Peter. He had left his boat and his nets, but not his old self.

"If any man will come after me, let him deny himself, and take up his cross, and follow me." (Matthew 16:24)

This statement made to the disciples was directed straight at Peter. His self-life had to die. Self-death is the very essence of abandonment. Without it we can never say, 'it is not I that live, but Christ in me!' (Galatians 2:20) Nor can we rise to the heights of the Kingdom, the Lord has prepared for us. We would fail miserably in any mission entrusted to us!

Self must be utterly denied. What does that mean? When Peter denied the Lord rather than himself he did it three times. "I do not know the man." In other words: I have nothing to do with Him; we are not friends; I deny having any connection with Him. (Matthew 26:72) The Lord told Peter that he had to deny his self-life, not the Lord.

That is the real foundation of true discipleship, but Peter did not understand it, and could not obey Him. So what happened? When the last night came, Jesus said to him: "Before the cock crow twice thou shalt deny me thrice." Even then with great swelling self-confidence Peter said: "Though all should forsake thee, yet I will not I am ready to go with you, to prison and to death." (Mark 14:29; Luke 22:33)

Peter meant it honestly, and Peter really intended to do it with all of his strength; but Peter didn't know anything about his strengths and weaknesses. He didn't believe he was in as much error as Jesus said he was. No one in error, truly knows the depth of error in which they stand.

In all of these Scriptures the word deny is used twice. If we do not deny the self we will deny Him. There is no other choice! Without total abandonment we will always make the wrong choices in life.

Now let's look at Peter's repentance and see what is around us today. Let's see if there is a difference. Over the years I have been honored to be present when some of the generals of the pulpit in our day made altar calls. As the people came forward I noticed a difference in faces. There were some who were quiet, without tears. Others came smiling obviously delighted they were there and the man or woman of God was to pray with them. Even others were chatting back and forth as they stood at the altar. I even saw many Christians go forward. When I asked them why they had responded to a salvation call they told me that they just wanted the celebrity to pray for them. Out of all of them, very few seemed to be deeply sorry for their sin. Next to none needed help get to the altar because their grief was so overwhelming. Once I saw a bride who had to be helped remain on her feet at the altar. She was so overwhelmed by love. When the love of God is present a firestorm of emotions rages.

What I saw in many of those meetings was to say the least confusing. I felt that perhaps there must be a Biblical pattern discoverable in Scripture dealing with repentance. If I could discover that pattern, then I may better understand what we are seeing at our present day altars. Where the Lord led surprised me!

In the book of Matthew, Jesus shared with His disciples a parable about the wheat and tares (Matthew

13: 24-30). It is generally understood that this passage deals with the children of the Kingdom and the false brethren who crept in unawares. The word tare used in this passage is actually the word darnel meaning false grain. The reason that these are to grow together with the wheat is because it is so difficult to tell them apart. It was hard to tell where Peter stood before he was eventually converted as the Lord promised.

These darnel, may be so convincing that if it were possible they could deceive the very elect. They dispense all the right words, charm people by their graces. They seem so very real, yet they are filled with utter darkness. They are so cheery, but devoid of all real light. Such are found in the church during what they call renewal meetings today. They are more interested in the external and not the internal where the Lord does the work. Nor do they care they stand in the presence of the eternal. All they are interested in are so-called manifestations or some new manufactured teachings floating around.

I'm convinced that they have no idea that they are not genuine. Alas this is the state of the church today. They are bones that need to be broken again and reset. Since they are not genuine then their emotions are not real either. Some will want change some will not! However, along with these days of darnel comes real gifts of God and real emotions. Wholeness will reign in the Kingdom heart, but fragmentation is the darnel state.

"Satan marvelously transforms himself into an angel of light." (2Corinthians 11:14) (LITV)

Naturally many will be missed in the church that is geared to seeing only the external and not the internal. Of course, in their own defense many with broken emotions masquerading as whole will point the finger at others and declare them to be the ones who are broken. Only those who are attuned to the Lord will be able to effectively identify them. These will call good evil and evil they will declare as good.

"Woe to those who call evil good and good evil, who put darkness for light and light for darkness, who put bitter for sweet and sweet for bitter." (Isaiah 5:20)

We are living in a time when the Lord has been resurrecting emotions to those who have never surrendered the pain. As they come out of many deep dark places these wonderful people are learning to live again. For some, just like Peter, it's like peeling an onion. Later they will discover that their new whole emotions, they too are to be surrendered at the cross where they take on Christ's emotions. This must take place before we can shout:

"For in him we live, and move, and have our being." (Acts 17:28)

Is this why we are seeing such confusion at our altars? Is what we are seeing in churches, false emotions, false repentance or false commitment? Possibly, but I think there is much more to it. When real repentance comes, miracles take place! Miracles of transformation that we have long ago quenched as mass-produced doctrines abound.

"And when he thought thereon, he wept." (Mark 14:72)

The remembrance of sin committed, is the Holy Spirit's constant method of bringing humanity to weep over our wrongdoing, our wrong being and to turn from it. Maybe if we looked a little deeper into this story of Peter we may discover some more eye opening truths of what he thought about.

The instant that Peter heard the cock crowing he thought, on the truth that he had actually done what Jesus had said he would do. He remembered that he had denied his Lord. His self-life had reigned supreme! What to Peter's character had seemed impossible to him had been done three times. It's another vote to abandon, all that we think about ourselves and search for Christ's view. Peter didn't believe Jesus, when the Lord told him that he would deny him. Does this sound familiar?

As Peter's eyes met the Masters, truth without mercy crushed him as he gazed into the excellence of Jesus. The lover of his soul he had denied. Is it any wonder tears rolled down his face? He had denied heaven's best, the most loving, the loveliest, the gentlest, the most generous, the most merciful, the most compassionate, the most self-denying, the most pure, the Prince of Peace. How could he have done anything else, but cry an ocean of tears? Yet, why are the eyes of Christians so dry when we commit the same sin every day, then go to church as if nothing was wrong? Why do we Christians not cover our faces in shame? Why do we not abhor our actions?

As we think of our sin, think of this. Peter in addition to denying his Master, told a down right lie, and repeated it again and again. He said to the damsel:

"I know not what thou sayest" (Matthew 26:70, Luke 22:60) and twice he said, "I know not the man." It was bad enough for Peter to deny that he was Christ's disciple, but to say, "I know not the man," was a grievous sin. If that was not enough then, "he began to curse and to swear." (Mark 14:71)

Liars abound and I include in that all those who use the term half-lies to justify their manipulative ways.

There is no such thing as half-truths just in the same way as we cannot have half a hole or be half whole. We either speak truth or lie, we have a hole or no hole at all. We are either whole (*Sozo*) or we are broken. (Mark 5:34) We are either alive or dead. We are either going to heaven or hell. There are no half measures! It's surrender of all or not at all! It's one or the other. There are only danger and destruction for the society that lies anywhere in between.

Liars seem to think that they will not be believed and they fancy that, if they swear, then they will be believed. This was Peter's story!

Others will tell you that they are not lying that they just did not reveal the whole truth. Every time they laugh their heart hardens just a little more. Charles Finney many times refused to preach telling the crowd that his preaching would only serve to gospel harden them even more. It's recorded in history that ninety nine percent of all that Finney led to the Lord remained faithful until death. Why has such power disappeared in our day? It's time for the church to come clean.

Have you ever heard the expression have the courage of your convictions? Well Hitler, Mussolini, Asama Ben Laden, Saddam Hussein, all had the courage of their convictions, but not one of them had the courage to examine their convictions, or to change them, which is the true test of character. These tests are the anvil upon which real character is forged. Tyrants are bred from within the ranks of those who justify what they call half-truths. It's time for the church to embrace, the truth, the whole truth and nothing, but the truth and repent.

It's hard to understand the depth of humiliation to which Peter finally felt. It was, however, the turning point in his life. His self-will was gone swallowed up in the love and acceptance of the Lord. Later by the Sea of Galilee Jesus asked him: "Lovest thou me?" His response devoid of all half measures, stands testimony of a life transformed through total surrender "Lord, thou knowest all things; thou knowest that I love thee." (John 21:17)

The transformed Peter preached on the day of Pentecost and thousands were added to the Kingdom. Although great and wonderful as that was something infinitely more powerful reaches to us from the pages of the Book of Peter.

Peter's whole nature was changed. The work that Jesus started in Peter was perfected only when he was filled with the Holy Spirit. Let his own words speak volumes of the transformation that came, to him who was so afraid of what would happen to him, if others identified him with Christ.

"If ye be reproached for the name of Christ, happy are ye, for the Spirit of God and of glory resteth upon you" (1 Peter 4:14)

When standing in a court and challenged to obey the rule of man, he boldly said: "We must obey God rather than men." (Acts 5:29) Peter was utterly changed; the self-pleasing, the self-trusting, self-seeking, full of sin, continually getting into trouble Peter, the once foolish and impetuous, was dead on the ground of absolute surrender. His story is prophetic of all that belongs to everyone who will follow him as He followed Christ. (1 Corinthians 11:1) His testimony tells us that we can be eager and devoted for the things of God, yet we may remain full of self. Peter before he denied the Lord cast out devils and was seen to heal the sick. (Luke 10:17)

Coming to that place of surrender was not an easy road for him. His life was filled with so many life lessons. Let's take an even closer look at his heart as he searched for love in all the wrong places. To do so, we have to go back to the sea with Peter, go fishing one more time and encounter the ballad of Galilee.

Ballad of Galilee!

"And it came to pass, that, as the people pressed upon him to hear the word of God, he stood by the lake of Gennesaret,

And saw two ships standing by the lake: but the fishermen were gone out of them, and were washing their nets.

And he entered into one of the ships, which was Simon's, and prayed him that he would thrust out a little from the land. And he sat down, and taught the people out of the ship.

Now when he had left speaking, he said unto Simon, Launch out into the deep, and let down your nets for a draught.

And Simon answering said unto him, Master, we have toiled all the night, and have taken nothing: nevertheless at thy word I will let down the net.

And when they had this done, they inclosed a great multitude of fishes: and their net brake.

And they beckoned unto their partners, which were in the other ship, that they should come and help them. And they came, and filled both ships, so that they began to sink.

When Simon Peter saw it, he fell down at Jesus' knees, saying, depart from me; for I am a sinful man, O Lord.

For he was astonished, and all that were with him, at the draught of the fishes which they had taken:

And so was also James, and John, the sons of Zebedee, which were partners with Simon. And Jesus said unto Simon, Fear not; from henceforth thou shalt catch men." (Luke 5:1-10)

This is one of the most fascinating passages in the entire Bible dealing with his partial and total surrender. It's a search for love in all the wrong places. Peter, early in life was always in the wrong place. The amazing thing about this scene is that the wrong people seem to be close to our Lord, and likewise the right people seem to be at a distance. You would think that Peter and Andrew, James and John, who had spent much time with Jesus, would be those in the inner circle, closest to the Master. Instead, the crowds pressed in upon Jesus, and the disciples were at a distance, tending to business, washing their nets. They undoubtedly looked on with some interest as they worked, but they were surprisingly detached from the Master and from the crowd.

According to Luke's Gospel, this was not Simon's first encounter with Jesus. Jesus had already been to Simon's home in Capernaum and healed his mother-in-law. (Luke 4:38-39) Perhaps that explains Simon's willingness to let Jesus use his fishing boat as a floating pulpit. In contrast, he knew the miracle working power of Jesus, so why was he so taken up with making a living?

The dissimilarity between Peter and the crowd is striking. He who had experienced the power of God in his own home was busy making money. The people on the other hand couldn't get close enough to Jesus. With them, there were no thoughts of worldly things! They were completely surrendered to the Word of God that poured out of the Master's mouth. They hung on every single sentence. They thought nothing about food, being at their place of work, being with families, they pressed in on Him. Thirst because of the heat, bouncing of the Sea of Galilee, didn't bother them. They were thirsty for the rivers that poured forth from the Fountain of Living Waters. They abandoned themselves to every word.

When Jesus finished teaching the people from the boat, He instructed Peter to launch out into the deep and he would catch fish. The fishermen had toiled all night, still they abandoned all their years of experience gained from fishing the lake. Peter's words, stand out in the passage.

"Master, we have toiled all the night, and have taken nothing: nevertheless at thy word I will let down the net." Peter submitted to the invitation of the Lord. We all know the rest of the story. So many fish were caught that the gill net began to break. They called for a second boat and that too was filled with fish. Here is the result of total surrender to the Master's word. It was not Pater, Andrew, James or John who were abandoned, to the will of God. It was the fish who were surrendered!

God created them; and are they not all absolutely surrendered to Him? Jesus summoned the fish to the net and they obeyed immediately. They allowed God to work in them and do everything He pleased? They couldn't do anything other than live in complete surrender to His desire and will.

What type of fish were they? There are believed to between eighteen and twenty-four different species of indigenous fish in the Sea of Galilee. Since this story ends with fishing for men, can you see the comparison between the types of fish and multi-ethnicities' of people around the world? In actuality the majority of the fish were likely Tilapia. Back then they were called, "Musht." It was not just one or two fish that surrendered themselves to the net at the command of the Lord. They came by the hundreds or perhaps in their thousands.

Think of it! He gathered the fish from all over the lake to a place where none had been the night before. Therefore, this miracle began hours before Jesus even got to the seashore. The fish gathered for Jesus and surrendered their lives even unto death. Was that not what Jesus would do when He surrendered Himself at the cross?

Now let's look at the idea of the Lord telling the fishermen that He would make them fishers of men. I think there is, in these few verses, a hint of true evangelism. A real harvest is when the masses come to the cross in total abandonment. People who just like the fish are prepared to lay down all of their lives to take on new life in Christ. The surrender must be absolutely complete. It's a place where we come to the end of ourselves. What power, what great love, brings us to a day when we are willing to die to self? When we answer love's serenade, we are able to boldly shout. "I am crucified with Christ." (Galatians 2:20a)

Let's turn our attention back to Peter. When he saw the miracle what did he do? "When Simon Peter saw it, he fell down at Jesus' feet, saying: "Depart from me; for I am a sinful man, O Lord." On the outside this looked wonderful, but he was far from totally surrendered. In last chapter, we learned that for Peter total surrender didn't come until the night he denied the Master. Jesus, knew Peter's heart! He knew that Simon did not go all the way to the grave. Sill Jesus said nothing.

That's the wonderful heart of the Lord at work. He takes us just the way we are, all that we are without ever demanding change. The choice of total surrender is always left to us. How many times have we gone to an altar, when total abandonment was the furthest thing from our heart? How many times have we at church stood amazed, in the presence of the King, tasting His power and came away still stubborn and self-willed? Peter did! His self-will didn't die the death until the night they took our Jesus. Let these words from the book of Romans sink in deep!

"God has been kind to you. He has been very patient, waiting for you to change. But you think nothing of his kindness. Maybe you don't understand that God is kind to you so that you will decide to change your lives.

But you are so stubborn! You refuse to change. So you are making your own punishment greater and greater. You will be punished on the day when God will show his anger. On that day everyone will see how right God is to judge people.

He will reward or punish everyone for what they have done." (Romans 2:4-6) (ERV)

Through submitting to Christ as Lord, obeying His commands, we will find even our smallest efforts are blessed with much fruitfulness. Still we must get away from the shore, get into the unfathomable waters, develop a deeper relationship with Him, and allow Him to use our resources. This prepares us to be effective fishers of men!

The joys of fishing have filled my life many times. When I was a boy, after school, I had the privilege of working on a small fishing boat out of the port of Donaghadee in Northern Ireland. Daily we took out fishing charters. Then, smiles on the faces of people, filled my world as they hooked into a fish. When they landed their catch excitement exploded into cheers of joy. These were line fishermen. They caught only one or two at a time. Later I would see them as small, "e," evangelists!

Other boats took to the St. George's Channel who fished with gill nets. To me they became the big, "E," Evangelists. These are the ones who throw the net out into the deep to rescue those who willingly surrender themselves to the desires of the Master Fisherman.

Have you ever considered what a net is? It is a bunch of nothings tied together by the cords of His love. The net is the church that the Evangelist throws out into that sea of humanity and by love scoops them up. Before Christ, we were nothing and He is always everything. Only, in His hand do we become successful fishers of men!

Ah! The beauty and the joys of fishing that I knew as a lad! Soon it was all traded away for the excitement of fishing for precious men! Why don't we linger here just a little longer? Would you like to go on just one more fishing trip with the Master Fisherman?

"After these things Jesus shewed himself again to the disciples at the sea of Tiberias; and on this wise shewed he himself.

There were together Simon Peter, and Thomas called Didymus, and Nathanael of Cana in Galilee, and the sons of Zebedee, and two other of his disciples.

Simon Peter saith unto them, I go a fishing. They say unto him, we also go with thee. They went forth, and entered into a ship immediately; and that night they caught nothing." (John 21:1-3)

Jesus had told them before His crucifixion that after He had arisen He would meet them in Galilee. (Matthew 26:32) (*Tiberias is also called Galilee*) Obviously they had forgotten what He had told them. Despite the fact that the Lord had appeared to His disciples even after the resurrection, Peter and the boys were distraught. When the Lord was no longer with them, they had no means of support so they by good intentions did what may have been the proper thing and return to their profession as fishermen. The reason John records that seven men were fishing is probably because the other disciples had other means to provide for themselves. However, I think there might have been a little bit more to Peter's reasoning.

Simon Peter's decision to go fishing is as if he was trying to generate some energy. 'Well, I'm going fishing. I'm not going to just sit around here and be depressed.' The others then said, in effect, 'All right, we'll go with you.' So they, went out and fished all night and caught nothing.

The atmosphere of discouragement would have been heightened by their inability to catch any fish. This is what always happens when we try to accomplish things with the arm of flesh. It's similar to what many do when they feel the Lord distant from them. They turn back to the things they knew in the world.

When the Lord showed up, He called to them while they were out at sea. Was it a supernatural call? Perhaps! However, voices carry a long distance over water and we don't want to spiritualize everything that we miss the rest of the story. What the Lord said to them was nothing more than what we can hear people ask of fishermen fishing of some pier. "Did you catch anything?" (John 21:5)

Their reply in one simple word speaks volumes of their discouragement. "NO." It was then the Lord told them to cast their nets on the right side of the ship. (Verse 6) In compliance they were amazed as a boatload of fish came in. Once more we see fish coming in total submission to the purposes of heaven. Again, we see fish surrendering themselves to death. In this, we are given yet another glimpse into Peter's Bible College as Jesus taught him about evangelism. Why-oh-why has the church abandoned the message of total surrender today. If it was preached the fish, (*humanity*) would again gather for Jesus.

At first, Peter had no idea who had called to them. When the Lord identified Himself, Peter, covered his partial nakedness. The next thing he did was to jump into the sea in a mad dash to get to shore. (John 21:7) How typical! We often try to cover our nakedness when the Lord comes on the scene. It was the very same in the Garden of Eden. (Genesis 3:7) Peter was learning the road to submission!

The rest of the fishermen dragged behind the boat a net loaded with fish to the shore. When Peter made it ashore, he found the Lord by a fire with both fish and bread cooking in the coals. The Lord didn't need the fish they had supernaturally caught. He already had the meal prepared. (John 21:9) Here we can see that there was a greater lesson for Peter to learn.

Then, comes something really interesting. The fishermen counted the fish they had caught. They totaled 153 big fish! To get the significance of this we must take a look throughout the New Testament.

The book of Mark records Christ, on a total of three occasions, personally blessed three people. These events were the healing of a man with an unclean spirit, (Mark 1:23) healing a man who was deaf (Mark 7:32) and making whole another who, was blind. (Mark 8:22) Matthew, however, writes that on 23 occasions Jesus blessed a total of 47 people. Some of those upon whom He bestowed God's grace included a leper, (Matthew 8:2) a non-Israelite woman and her daughter, (Matthew

15:22) Mary Magdalene, (Matthew 27:56) and Joseph of Arimathea. (Matthew 27:57) Luke writes that on 14 occasions 94 people were blessed. They include the seventy disciples sent out to preach and heal, (Luke 10:1) ten lepers cleansed at the same time (Luke 17:12) and Zaccheus. (Luke 19:2) Lastly, the apostle John, bears record of eight incidents where nine people were helped by Jesus. Nicodemus, (John 3:1) the woman accused of adultery (John 8:11) and Lazarus (John 11) are among those personally touched by the Savior of humanity. All told, the Lord directly blessed a grand total of 153 people in these 48 separate incidents! One hundred and Fifty three people, 153 fish in the net!

The bread on the coals is also significant. Jesus the Bread of Life experienced the hot coals of God's judgment for our sins. The fish, an early Christian symbol called the Ichthys stood for, "Jesus Christ, Son of God, and Savior." All of Jesus, in total surrender, faced the coals of God's fiery judgment in our place. When Jesus invited them to, "Come and dine," He was not just speaking about a breakfast. (John 21:9) After they enjoyed their meal together, Jesus turned to Peter to discuss his ultimate surrender in much more detail.

"So when they had dined, Jesus saith to Simon Peter, Simon, son of Jonas, lovest thou me more than these? He saith unto him, Yea, Lord; thou knowest that I love thee. He saith unto him, Feed my lambs." (John 21:15)

To understand this portion of the narrative we have got to understand that often English is not enough to explain what, is going on. In English there is only one word for love. The Greek language (*the language of the New Testament*) uses three different words to describe and define love. This, we discovered in the first chapter.

The first one is "agape." This love is represented by God's love for us. It is a non-partial, sacrificial love probably best exemplified by God's provision for our rebellion:

"For God so loved (agape) the world that He gave His only begotten Son, that whoever believes in Him should not perish, but have eternal life." (John 3:16)

Then, there is brotherly love described by the word, "phileo." It is a soulish (*connected through our emotions*) kind of love, something that can be experienced by both believers and non-believers. This is in contrast to agape, which is love extended through the Spirit. Then, there is "Eros," the love of a friend.

The first time Jesus asks Peter, "lovest thou me," He is asking do you love me more than your friends. He uses the word, "agape," in this He is asking, Peter as God do you love me more than these others? Jesus knew exactly where Peter's heart lay. Peter's reply went right to the core of the issue. "Yes Lord you know I love, (Phileo) you! His reply was clear. You know I love you with the love of a brother. Despite the fact that Peter's love relationship with the Lord was lacking the Master commissions him. It seems that Jesus was trying to get Peter to understand that he must love Him unconditionally in order to be the leader God called him to be.

"Feed my lambs." Literally this means, tend, pasture my little ones. He's talking about the process of the future growth of the disciples. He was telling him to set an example for the rest who were young and easily, influenced. Jesus knew the degree of influence Pater had over the other disciples. Remember Peter had gone back to his worldly ways of fishing and the rest followed his example. No one can ever become more than their pastor. If all we know is, "phileo," brotherly love, for the

Lord that is what those around us will know. They follow our example! Three times Jesus speaks and three times Peter replies.

It's possible that by His repeated questions Jesus was subtly reminding Peter of his three denials. There's no doubt of those denials and how he felt when Jesus turned to look at him. That moment, was seared deeply into Peter's mind. (Luke 22:54–62) It wasn't lost on Peter that Jesus repeated His question to him three times, just as Peter previously denied Him three times.

"He saith to him again the second time, Simon, son of Jonas, lovest thou me? He saith unto him, Yea, Lord; thou knowest that I love thee. He saith unto him, Feed my sheep." (John 21:16)

Again when Jesus asked him the question He again uses the word, "agape." He is asking, Peter do you love me with a self-sacrificing love? Agape carries the meaning of intense, complete, devoted, surrendered love that he would need in the days and years ahead. The Lord was moving towards revealing to him the cost of service and how he would be called to surrender all just like the fish. Once more Peter replies using the word for brotherly love, "phileo." Peter was essentially saying, 'Well, Lord, all I can commit right now is that I like you like a brother.'

Continuing His call to service, the Lord instructed him to, "feed my sheep." Jesus was emphasizing tending the sheep in a supervisory capacity, not only feeding, but ruling in the Kingdom of love. The reference to sheep rather than lambs show that the disciples would grow and that would bring with it an ever-changing responsibility. This would not be like pushing the feed from the back of some truck or slopping the hogs.

"He saith unto him the third time, Simon, son of Jonas, lovest thou me? Peter was grieved because he said unto him the third time, Lovest thou me? And he said unto him, Lord, thou knowest all things; thou knowest that I love thee. Jesus saith unto him, Feed my sheep."

Verily, verily, I say unto thee, when thou wast young, thou girdedst thyself, and walkedst whither thou wouldest: but when thou shalt be old, thou shalt stretch forth thy hands, and another shall gird thee, and carry thee whither thou wouldest not." (John 21: 17-18)

Just like a sail boat in the wind Jesus changes tack. This time Jesus does not use the word, "agape," He uses the term, "phileo." "Peter do you love me as your brother?" Peter's reply is filled with truth. He recognizes that the Master knows everything about him. He said, "Lord you know I, "phileo," you. At this time, Peter's attitude changed and he appears upset. He was grieved because the Lord was persistent in his questioning. He was not doubting Peter's love for Him because He knew everything about Peter's heart. Rather, He had allowed Peter to confess his love for every wretched denial he had made on that dreadful night. One final time Jesus commands him to, "feed,' (*tend*) my sheep."

Contrary to popular opinion, true shepherds are not made in seminaries. Neither do men ordain them. They are birthed on the anvil of crisis. Everywhere in the Bible we see those who were used powerfully of the Lord were molded in the birth canal of pressure.

Verse 18, calms Peter and brings him to the doorway of the prophetic. The Master said that his mistakes were made because he was young and did what he thought was right in the face of the circumstances. Now that he was growing, the Lord, was showing him clearly that in the years ahead he would have to surrender all. In the days before him, he, Peter would also die on a cross just like the fish died in a net.

"This spake he, signifying by what death he should glorify God. And when he had spoken this, he saith unto him. Follow me." (John 21:19)

Obviously the Master was able to trust the Apostle with this revelation. He knew that Peter would not run in the battle. Just like many before him, who had surrendered themselves in the storms of circumstance, he would abandon himself to the will and purposes of God. He had learned that submission would be a daily choice even as the circumstances grew in intensity. What a transformation. A wonderful miracle had taken place. In the space of just a few days Peter went from denial to a confidence of his love for the Master.

Within a very short time Peter, stood in Jerusalem, filled with the Holy Ghost, preached to multitudes, and carried the standard of the Cross in the very forefront of the battle. The bravest of the brave! When Peter died he died a martyr and some history books record that he asked to be crucified upside down because he felt unworthy to die in the same position as his Lord. So intense was his loyalty to Jesus! Now that's a ballad of Galilee worth singing! Are we prepared to surrender everything to the plans of God no matter what? What are we willing to go through so that others may know the heart of love?

Symphony in "A" Minor Prophet

Have we ever entered a relationship knowing things would not be smooth sailing? Did we hope to change our partner because of the love we held for them? After a time we had to realize, the impossibility of our task. No one, other than God can change people and then only when they want change. If we have gone down that long road of betrayal, we will certainly identify with the agony of Hosea.

The sundial in the garden marked the hour in which Hosea lived. Jeroboam II was on the throne of the northern kingdom of Israel. His military victories had extended Israel's borders farther than they had been since the days of Solomon's kingdom. Tributes from subject nations poured into the national coffers. It was a season of prosperity and a time of peace.

Far too often people think that if they just had money, things in their life would somehow be different. Without financial pressures a marriage will stand forever. Not so! In fact, the divorce rate is greater among the affluent.

Unfortunately when peace and safety abound, sin raises its ugly head. Secularism and materialism capture the hearts of people! After being blessed, Israel again fell into spiritual adultery. The list of their wrongs reads as though the prophet saw into our day. Lying, killing, stealing, adultery, drunkenness, perversion, perjury, deceit, and oppression, grieved the heart of the Father. The thing that grieved the heart of God more than anything else was the sin of idolatry. (Hosea 4:12-13, 13:2) The golden calves set up by the first Jeroboam about 150 years earlier had opened the floodgates to every evil expression of Canaanite idolatry, including drunkenness, religious prostitution and human sacrifice.

Since the Lord viewed Israel as His wife, He viewed her worship of other gods as spiritual infidelity. The Old Testament speaks frequently of Israel whoring after or playing the harlot with other gods. (Deuteronomy 31:16, Judges 2:17) The Father had told Israel from the beginning that He would not share her with others. "You shall have no other gods before me." (Exodus 20:3) Nonetheless she persistently ignored His command, and by the days of Jeroboam II the situation was intolerable. In one last attempt to reach the heart of Israel the Lord raised up the prophet, Amos. Despite the fact that he trumpeted a warning of impending judgment his people turned a deaf ear. The nation paid little attention! So God spoke again, this time through the prophet Hosea! His name means, "Salvation!" He was not salvation however, his whole life's symphony spoke of the salvation that would come through Jesus.

Hosea was a young preacher in the nation of Israel, the northern kingdom. Being a minister is no guarantee that marriage does not end in the divorce courts. Thirteen percent of all preachers today have visited the divorce courts.

People were polite to the young prophet's face, I suppose, but they sneered behind his back. He found that he was being given the nice-and-harmless treatment. They hoped that he would just go away. Solomon said, what was, will be again. In some churches today, board meetings are the lair of schemes designed to isolate and ostracize young preachers who stand for no compromise. To this end they do nothing to help, encourage or promote their ministry. That is what people usually do to preachers that make others uncomfortable. They turn a blind eye thinking that without their support he/she will never amount to anything. These think little about the discouragement their actions or lack of them brings.

The preacher Hosea, knew his source of supply, encouragement and guidance came the Lord. That was vital for his survival because sooner or later the numbers who came to listen to him diminished.

Hosea was discouraged and in the opening chapter of his book we read a personal note about him. He went to the throne room and the Father told him to do something strange. God said, "I want you to get married." I have often imagined the very young man thinking. "I'm God's man of faith and power for the hour. A prophet of the most, High God. Certainly I can have my pick of the girls in the city."

"Hold it, hold it, Hosea! Come on back to reality!" God said, "I have a girl picked out for you already." His excitement must have peaked when the Lord revealed to him her name. Now that is hearing from God! When God speaks it contains specifics. He doesn't speak in warm fuzzy feelings. Nor does He expect us to rely on our senses. He gives names, addresses and a timeline. (Acts 9:11) It was then the Lord revealed to Hosea that there is a cost that comes with the prophetic office. The price is surrender of all.

God said to him, "I want you to marry a prostitute! She will be unfaithful to you!" I would give anything to have been a fly on the wall listening to that conversation. At first silence must have filled the air before he burst out. "But God?" Then, he might have suggested that he had got the voices mixed up. "Hosea, I want you to marry her anyway." (Hosea 1:2)

Of course, Hosea was very perplexed by God's strange command just as Abraham was puzzled by God's instruction to take his son and kill him. God does strange things at times, things we don't always understand! Things we can't categorize! Things that don't fit into what we think we know of Him! Things that require obedience far beyond the understanding of mere man! Things that without complete surrender would be impossible to even consider. This was one of those idiosyncratic commands to a peculiar man. (1 Peter 2:9)

As a man of God he was expected to hold to a certain standard of living. There was a code of conduct acceptable by the church. In our day he would likely have been stripped of his credentials and tossed out onto the street. What would people think? What would be said of him? What would they say about the church that associated themselves with a man who married a prostitute? They wanted little to do with him anyway and here was their excuse to excommunicate him.

A whole lot of people today say that God does not work in these ways. They play the grace card and claim that being under grace removes from us the possibility of such things in our day. The same group quickly claims that God is the same yesterday, today and forever that is if it suits their purposes. (Hebrews 13:8) He is either the same yesterday, today and forever or He is not! One is either saved or headed for hell. One is either healed or not! Delivered or bound! There are no half measures. He is the absolute Christ!

As a prophet he had to deliver object lessons. Just as Ezekiel had to take a clay tablet and draw a picture of

Jerusalem on it and then lie on it for over a year. (Ezekiel 4:1)

The shock to Hosea's system was not yet over. The Lord told him that he was going to have children by this woman. Two boys and a girl! These were also to be object lessons and prophetic in every aspect especially their names. To the Jews names were very important. God often used the meanings of names to teach Israel certain truths. God was also planning to use this entire family as deterrent examples for His people.

Right off the bat you just know this marriage was not going to be a bed of wine and roses. Imagine going to the altar knowing that your spouse was going to cheat on you. What kind of a man would marry someone who was going to betray him? The kind of man who knows real love. Who has a deeper love for the Lord more than all else. Hosea loved the LORD enough to embrace the pain. He was totally abandoned, to the plans and purposes of God.

With no roses in hand, Hosea went courting. His first date must have been awesome. Have you ever thought what life would be like without candy? What no, chocolate chip cookies, ice-cream, spaghetti, pizza, bagels, waffles, french-fries, potato chips, pudding, Jello and Coca-Cola? None of these Hosea knew. Did he invite her home for dinner? Did they eat out? We are not told. What we can accept is that they had likes and dislikes.

The diet that would have been acceptable to them would have been something ordinary and in accordance with Mosaic Law. Bread (*this was the most important food of all*), olive oil (*this took the place of butter*), milk and cheese from the flocks, and fruits and vegetables from the orchards and gardens. On special occasions they might have meat. In any event, romance was not absent. Grandeur filled the night air. No matter what the surroundings human love can be blind at times.

Gomer was attracted to this shy young man, and at length he summoned up the courage to ask her to marry him. To his great relief or expectation, she said yes, and they were married. At first it was heaven on earth. Hosea loved her, despite knowing all that was to come. That takes commitment.

Gomer came by sexual promiscuity through her family line. Her father's name was Diblaim, whose name signified "double layers of a grape cake." This speaks of one completely given up to sensuality. (*Talmud*) With such a father we can understand why Gomer became a woman of sensual pleasure. The Moral Law states that "the iniquity of the fathers comes upon the children unto the third and fourth generation." (Exodus 20:5, *Paraphrased*)

You can't read this prophecy without seeing how much in love Hosea was. During the honeymoon they must have been wonderfully happy together, and then they had their first child. The midwife announced. "It's a boy!"

Hosea's heart was filled to bursting, and he went to God for the name he would give to the lad. "What should we name my boy?" To his surprise, God picked the name Jezreel. (Hosea 1:4-5) Now, Jezreel means "God will sow." Once more Hosea must have been shaken right down to his boots. It was also a name associated with death and destruction! (2 Kings 10:7) In the future it will again be associated with even more death and destruction! (Joel 3:11-13) Then, God was saying that He was going to destroy Jehu in the valley of Jezreel.

Nevertheless that was the name that God picked. Through Hosea's oldest boy, the LORD was warning His people: they too would be castaway if they didn't recognize the folly of their actions!

Israel had left the Lord their God, falling into spiritual fornication by embracing idol worship. The Father however, was going to speak in grace, through this object lesson before judgment fell upon them.

"For the children of Israel shall abide many days without a king, and without a prince, and without a sacrifice, and without an image, and without an ephod, and without teraphim:

Afterward shall the children of Israel return, and seek the LORD their God, and David their king; and shall fear the LORD and his goodness in the latter days." (Hosea 3:4-5)

Without a king: They would lose all political rule! Without sacrifice or sacred pillar: They would be without religious practice! Without ephod or household idols: The people would be without true or false religious practice. (2Kings 23, Ezra 2:63)

The years passed and another child, a daughter, was born to Hosea. This one was named, Loruhamah," which means "not having obtained mercy, not pitied." Mercy is the element of God's love that eliminates us from having to face the consequences of our sin. Israel had refused to embrace perfect love and therefore couldn't experience mercy. They would bear the full weight of their sin.

Imagine naming your little baby girl "void of mercy or not pitied." It meant that God would no longer have pity on His people if they continued in their stubborn rebellion. His patience was wearing thin. After some hundreds of years of trying to reach this stubborn people, He was now warning them that they were nearing the end.

A, "Final Warning," is again being announced in our day! The day of grace is fast coming to an end. A time will come, when He, by our choices will be unable to keep us from what is coming, upon the world. In the days of Hosea, judgment came in the form of invading armies. *(See my book, "Final Warning." ISBN: 978-0-9939070-7-4)*

When this little girl was weaned Gomer, quickly got pregnant again. Her third child was another little boy. This one God named Loammi, "not my people," for God was saying, "You are not my people and I will not be your God." (Hosea 9:1) By then, Hosea must have started to adapt to his role as a prophet. He understood that God never speaks in judgment without an offer of hope and grace.

"Yet the number of the children of Israel shall be as the sand of the sea, which cannot be measured nor numbered; and it shall come to pass that in the place where it was said unto them, ye are not my people, there it shall be said unto them, ye are the sons of the living God." (Hosea 1:10)

Though God casts off the ten tribes, yet He in His sovereignty will gather them again. This is happening in our day! In the interim we the church, were grafted in and in a great day in the future we shall stand Jews and gentiles alike. No longer strangers to the covenant of promise, fellow-heirs together. (Romans 9:25-26; 1 Peter 2:10)

Some might say that after Gomer had her third child she experienced postpartum depression. That, they say was the reason for her fall into extra marital relationships. Hosea knew that it was coming and that it had nothing to do with the baby blues. With post-partum depression mums describe it as like living in a fog, feeling numb inside, with no laughter or excitement in what can be (*but is not always*) one of the best times in their life. Many women say they cry a lot, and feel overwhelmed by feelings of anxiety and incompetence. The situation can be compounded by guilt that they feel so low, despite having a "beautiful baby." These women may also have a sense that they are not "good enough" to be a mother. None of this is evident in the life of Gomer. She resorted to old behaviors present before marriage. She was a prostitute.

I bet, Hosea felt that because of the love he showered upon her that she would stay with him. He hoped that somehow he could make a difference in her life. Maybe he hoped that what God had said somehow might have been averted. Alas, God knows the end from the beginning. A short time after the birth of their third child, Gomer went back to her old ways. Just like the church after the first Great Awakening, after the second, even after the sixth and seventh the church returned to her wallowing.

It didn't just happen overnight. It was a very gradual retreat to the very gates of hell itself. One night Gomer didn't come home. When she disappeared the second time she was gone for a little longer. Finally, one night she walked out of their home and didn't come home again. Her husband, her babies, her friends, her future, all were abandoned.

What a heartbreak it must have been to this young preacher as the whispers began to circulate about his wife and about what happened when he was away on preaching trips. Perhaps even his own children may have unconsciously dropped some remarks about the men who visited when daddy was away. What terrible agony he would have carried all his life waiting for that hour, if he had not been surrendered to the Lord? What excruciating pain would have filled his every waking moment, if he had not given it over to the Lord?

Is this what caused the change in tone that came into Hosea's preaching? He still warned of the judgment to come and the fact that God was going to send the Assyrians down across the land, but no longer did he announce it with thunder. He spoke to them with tears. (Hosea 6:1) He spoke of a day when love would at last triumph! When after the bitter lesson was learned. When they understood that the way of the transgressor is hard, Israel would yet turn back to the God who loved her. Instead of "Not Pitied," she would again be called "Pitied," instead of "Not my people," she would be named: "The Apple of His Eye." (Deuteronomy 32:10)

Poor Gomer by choice she was passed from man-to-man, until at last she fell into the hands of a man who was unable to pay for her food and her clothing. Finally, she was found, naked as the day she was born and about to be sold as a slave.

When the news reached Hosea he raced to the marketplace. He pushed his way through the crowds and reached Gomer who lay at his feet. He looked down at her where their eyes met. She pleaded with him to let her come home as a hired servant. (Hosea 3, Luke 15:18)

I can picture Hosea removing the robes of his holy prophetic office and covering her nakedness. He then raised her to the safety of his arms. He was not interested in her being a servant. He restored her to her rightful place as the love of his life. That day Gomer came home again.

Gomer's story is the epitaph of the backslidden church. Real intimate times with the supernatural dwindle and are soon gone, swallowed up in ritual. Pastors pretend that all is well when the whole counsel of the Word of God is forced to give way to entertainment. So-called manifestation, clouds of glitter replace the cloud of His presence described in the Bible. The instantaneous is replaced by session after session with Sozo teachers. In the end, numbers in the churches, full offering plates are the idols they worship.

It is also the story of many lives. The intimate moments with the Lord grow fewer and fewer. We go to church and pretend all is well. Our study of the Bible dwindles and we end up just reading less than a chapter each day. Some, even less than that. Prayer, conversation with the Lord is reduced to a few un-intimate words at night. We then try to live from Sunday to Sunday with the very little Word we get at Church. At length we end up relying on preachers to tell us what the Word says.

At days end we must assuredly realize that we like Gomer are poor, wretched, naked and blind. We need to realize that we must be set free from the lust of the flesh, the lust of the eyes and the pride of life. (1 John 2:16) Jesus is the only one who can do this for us. Only, He can resurrect a broken marriage! Remember we are married to the Lord.

Why, He has already killed the fatted calf. From a great distance He sees our coming. A new ring He will place on our finger. (Luke 15:22) Now, in His robes of righteousness, we can rise to new life in Christ. Perhaps we know this and just as Israel, put off answering His call of love to another day. It's a day that may never come!

The story of Hosea and his wayward wife Gomer has been told and retold. It is one of the most magnificent stories of redemption and unbounded love in all of literature. It is a classic ongoing drama and a symphony of romance that was that is, and that is to come, played out before angels and men.

In this Biblical literary creation the Lord showcases the divine romance between Himself and His covenant people. It's an account of Israel's idolatry, her scatterings, and her subsequent amnesic wanderings. The life and legend of Gomer is not just an outline of Israel's past history with their idolatry, their captivities and dispersions, and subsequent wanderings. The story of Hosea and Gomer shine a light on mysteries yet to unfold.

The final scenes in this saga show the eventual redemption and restoration of Gomer. This is a prophecy that is now being fulfilled. Gomer finally remembers her true husband and in repentance returns to Him. In rediscovering YHVH-God she comes to her ultimate moment of epiphany. She remembers who she really is. This is a foreshadowing of the corporate salvation of all Israel including the House of Judah.

"The magnificent conclusion to this romance showcases the final restoration of the whole State of Israel." - Gavin Finley MD endtimepilgrim.org

Dr. Finley reminds us that this is our story and it's for our day and time. So many times we try to satisfy ourselves with the lying idols of self-importance, of wealth or a good time. Ours is a blindness like Gomer's that cannot distinguish between lust and love.

We try to run from God and drown our miseries in empty pleasures, in drink, work or social life, but as surely as we think we have escaped, God touches our sleeve. In love He whispers! "My child! My name and my nature are love and I must act according to whom I am. When you tire of all your running, you're wandering and your heartbreak, I'll be there to draw you to myself again." This is His' symphony in, "A" minor prophet as seen in Gomer, in Israel and us!

That is the story of the Bible isn't it? At Bethlehem God entered the slave market where the whole human race was putting itself up for auction, prostituting itself for a cheapened life. But on the cross, the Lord Jesus paid the price, the full price for our freedom, and bought us back. This is the story of God's love and God's heart!

Have we been cheated on? Then, we know what God felt, what He still feels when we cheat on Him. Have we been lied to? Then, we know what God feels when we lie to Him! Have we felt violated? Then, we know what God feels when we violate His trust! Have we felt used? Then, we know what God feels when we pray and find answers only to abandon Him the moment the storm lifts!

What story does our marriage tell? Does it tell of the love of Jesus? Does it speak prophetically of all of the wonderful things about to take place all around the world? Does every part of God's orchestra play a symphony of love in our life? His halleluiah chorus is coming! To get there we have to discover that surrender is only found in the heart of faith!

Lyrics of Power!

As we journey through the New Testament we discover story after story of people experiencing the joys of being totally abandoned to the Lord. Tales filled with both tears of joy and sadness as the characters struggled to come to that place of surrender. As we boldly adventure down that abandoned highway we will be challenged to come to the place where they found power. Power to heal, to change and power that transforms. Each miracle that Jesus did, points the way for us to be able to discover how to walk in the fullness of the Kingdom. Let's join the search of one great man who messaged the greatest man of all.

"Now when he had ended all his sayings in the audience of the people, he entered into Capernaum.

And a certain centurion's servant, who was dear unto him, was sick, and ready to die." (Luke 7:1-2)

These first two verses tells us much about the Centurion's character. Things that are often missed as we race through this wonderful story. The centurion posted to the Capernaum garrison, (*Walled Village*) was far more than just a military officer.

He is deeply moved by the sickness and imminent death of a beloved servant. "Servant" sounds good to eastern readers, but he was actually a "slave. The Greek word used to describe this servant is, "Doulos," slave. While many slaves were treated horribly this man was loved beyond measure. We are not told if that love eventually brought about his release from slavery. If not, then the love received from man was not so unconditional. Such is the case with all human love, only, "agape love," the love of God is unconditional and given expecting nothing in return. When the young man fell ill, his condition was diagnosed as terminal. By his actions, we can see the Centurion's longing to see his servant well again. Matthew's describes the slave as being paralyzed and in terrible pain. (*Tormented*) What the condition was, we do not know for sure. However, it changed his life. (Matthew 8:6) The search for healing was engaged.

From the stories of many families around that search for a cure for the children we can glean insight of what the Centurion may have gone through. Parents of kids with Acute Myeloid Leukemia exhaust themselves looking for a suitable donor for an immediate Bone Marrow or Stem Cell transplant. They start with having their family members tested for a suitable match. When this fails they turn to friends. Often a call goes out over television for a donor within their ethnic grouping. The days and sleepless nights roll by as the clock ticks away at an ever increasing rate. Finally, for the parents comes the thought, "what if?"

"And when he heard of Jesus, he sent unto him the elders of the Jews, beseeching him that he would come and heal his servant.

And when they came to Jesus, they besought him instantly, saying, that he was worthy for whom he should do this:

For he loveth our nation, and he hath built us a synagogue." (Luke 7:3-5)

The centurion was deeply respected by the religious community in Capernaum. Even though he was not Jewish he was solicitous to the Jewish faith. "He loves our nation," the community elders told Jesus, "and has built our synagogue." Obviously this man was well to do financially and shared his wealth in love. What a wonderful statement. "He loves our nation and he built for us a synagogue." We all need to take careful note of that statement. If we love our nation we will build the church! Spiritually, financially, no matter the size of the gift. Of course the prerequisite of such building depends on us being first built up in the faith. The future of our nations lies at the doorstep of the church.

For a non-Jew to get the leaders of the synagogue to "plead earnestly" with Jesus on his behalf says a lot about the esteem in which they held him. Jews were often so proud that they had no association with a non-Jew. This centurion was clearly an exception to the rule. He was a seeker after the God of the Jews. They could see that and admired him for it.

The Centurion is depicted as a deeply humble man. Centurions didn't lead by being bashful or self-effacing. They had a commanding authority in everything they said and did. Yet, this Centurion never actually appears personally before Jesus to plead his cause. Instead, he sends others in his place, not as a tactical move in order to get Jesus to agree to his request. Clearly it is because of a sense of personal unworthiness. Right from the beginning of his story we can see his actions saying; "I am nothing He is everything."

"Then, Jesus went with them. And when he was now not far from the house, the centurion sent friends to him, saying unto him, Lord, trouble not thyself: for I am not worthy that thou shouldest enter under my roof:

Wherefore neither thought I myself worthy to come unto thee: but say in a word, and my servant shall be healed." (Luke 7:6-7)

Instead of going himself, his friends are told to say, "Lord, don't trouble yourself, for I don't deserve to have you come under my roof." No doubt the Centurion knew the pious Jew's common refusal, to enter a Gentile home. That brings us to a, "Selah," (*Just pause and think about that*) moment! How grateful should we be! Jesus a Jew not only visits our homes, He lives in our homes. Not only does He visit our temples, He lives within us and we are Gentiles.

There is much more to this story! The Centurion has a very clear sense of whom Jesus is, and what His level of authority is. His humility is grounded in a profound respect for Jesus' position. Since he sees himself as undeserving, he is all the more aware of the pure grace within, which Jesus operates.

I love the fact that the Centurion gets this! He says, "I understand chain of command. I rule over a hundred soldiers, and you, you're in a completely different rank." God became a man! He holds complete authority. He is the one and only sovereign ruler.

This must carry us back to our days in the military at least it did for me! On a patrol when an order is given there must be immediate compliance. To hesitate means you could be killed. There must be total and complete surrender of the will to those set over us. This is what basic training is all about. Many times men and women have lost their lives because they hesitated. When the ping, ping of flying bullets explode all around, there is no room for our opinion or ideas. The officer commanding gives the orders not with the view of getting us killed. Rather, each order is to promote safety and get the mission accomplished. At least that is how it is supposed to work.

In the battle of life to many Jesus is just a helper, a counselor, a comforter, a friend. He's not Christ. A perfect example of this comes from Bethel Sozo in Redding, California. They say: "A Sozo session is a time for the Sozo team to sit down with you and with the help of the Holy Spirit walk you through the process of freedom and wholeness." Just a helper. They need to get the same revelation that Centurion had.

He was not the ruler, he was not the commander Jesus was. He is Lord, Savior, God, King, and Judge. This man, the soldier, he understood who Jesus is. "I understand chain of command. You're at the top. Creator, that's who you are." That's who Jesus is.

"Then, Jesus went with them." (Luke 7:6a)

He was on His way. He was going out to do what He came to do! He was going to love, heal and forgive! He was going to preach, teach, and manifest the Kingdom of love.

Unlike religion, where we go looking for God, Christianity is about God looking for us because we're lost, and He's not. People can be heard to say, I found the Lord. No they didn't. When I got saved, Love found me lying on the scrap heap of humanity with my hopes, my dreams my worth all gone and my life at an end.

Some of us don't know it, but Jesus is looking for us. He is actively seeking us. He knows us. He loves us. He died for us. He's pursuing us. He's a humble initiator. He doesn't owe us anything, but He pursues us in His lyrics of power.

"He was not far from the house when the centurion sent friends to say to Him: "Lord, don't trouble yourself, for I do not deserve to have you come under my roof. That's why I did not even consider myself worthy to come to you. But say the word, and my servant will be healed. For, I myself am a man under authority, with soldiers under me. I tell this one, "Go," and he goes; and that one, "Come," and he comes. I say to my servant, "Do this," and he does it.

When Jesus heard this, he was amazed at him, and turning to the crowd following him, he said, 'I tell you, I have not found such great faith even in Israel." (Luke 7:6-9 *Paraphrased*)

The centurion understood clearly that a person in authority has the power to delegate authority to accomplish his purposes. He doesn't have to do it himself in person. Parents learn gradually to assign chores to their children to get the housework done. Office managers organize the staff to accomplish the work. An army captain assigns a lieutenant a mission to accomplish under the captain's orders. The lieutenant issues his orders to the sergeant, who, in turn, issues orders to his men. Each man in the chain of command is acting under orders from above. Along with the responsibility to fulfill the mission, comes the authority to prosecute it by whatever authorized means are necessary.

Jesus He too, was acting under instructions from the Throne of Glory. He said in John 5:19, "Verily, verily, I say unto you, The Son can do nothing of himself, but what he seeth the Father do: for what things soever he doeth, these also doeth the Son likewise."

The Centurion saw Jesus as a commander like himself. He knew Jesus didn't have to come into his servant's chamber, and lean over him, lay hands on him, and personally raise him up. He certainly didn't have to meet with the slave week after week for session after session.

Why do we think we have to get the sick to the church or into a prayer line for them to be healed? The Centurion recognized that Jesus has authority in the spirit realm to heal. We have delegated authority in the spirit realm to heal, to set people free! Period! By whatever means and by whatever agency necessary and the healing will be instantaneous. The Centurion knew that all Jesus had to do was to speak the Word and it would be done. He turned his faith loose! "But say the word, and my servant will be healed." (Luke 7:7)

Luke doesn't record Jesus ever spoke a word. However, in all likelihood He did speak in order to satisfy the Centurion's friends who had come bearing this message full of faith. "Then, the men who had been sent returned to the house and found the servant well" (Luke 7:10).

The servant was up and fit and healthy. He was completely healed the consequence of a Centurion, who abandoned himself to Christ!

Sometimes in our powerless self-thought life we mumble something about, 'If Jesus were here in the flesh and were to lay His hands on this person he would be instantly healed.' This can be termed faith, but it's only a beginner's level of faith. It's like the woman with the issue of blood who said to herself, "If I may, but touch his garment, I shall be whole." (*Sozo*) (Matthew 9:21)

Her faith was focused in her personal ability to touch the hem of Jesus' garment. Jesus accepted her just the way she was without asking for change.

We're like that sometimes. We want a great name present. 'If only the pastor were here, he could accomplish this.' 'If only Billy or Franklin Graham or John Wesley or some other general of the faith were here.' We look to the personal instrument of the healing rather than to the Healer who can accomplish the task with just a word. This same power, He delegates to us so as we are empowered to accomplish our mission.

The Centurion's insight is that Jesus' delegated word of authority can span distance. It doesn't matter if the person being ministered to be in the next room or miles away. He has power in the spirit realm to speak a word and His word is accomplished. Here, the Lord is teaching us that a life surrendered to heaven in the timing of God can do the very same things. He said: "Verily, verily, I say unto you, He that believeth on me, the works that I do shall he do also; and greater works than these shall he do; because I go unto my Father." (John 14:12)

I have seen this happen time and time again when I have conducted healing meetings over Skype to Pakistan. This is His delegated spiritual authority in action. Nothing has changed. He is the Captain, we are the private, corporal or sergeant, and we carry out His orders with His full authority and power backing us up, to accomplish the task by any authorized means. Any authorized means, is after the fashion contained in the Word as it lines up with the calendar of heaven. If it's not in the Bible it is not authorized.

Why do we not see this more often? I guess it's because we really don't believe He can delegate His power for the instant to us. Our faith limits His power largely to the thirty-three years of His life in First Century Palestine. This is an insight often denied us because of the lack of spiritual eyesight. The Centurion's insight, his faith, astounded, Jesus. "I tell you, I have not found such great faith even in Israel." I don't think Peter or the other disciples grasped these truths at that time. I doubt that few in our own day grasp it either. That's why we come up with substitute theologies that pigeonholes faith into our experience. Real faith, requires a total abandonment to His will!

We see Jesus in this story serving Jew and Gentile, rich and poor. We see him serving slave and free. We see him serving the Roman and Jewish people alike. Unlike some religions that tell us that their God loves their nation, their people, their tribe, their tongue, their heritage, and their tradition more than others. Jesus loves all people equally whether or not they accept His love. Christ is for all nations, young, old, black, white, yellow, brown, rich, poor, Jesus is for all. He is so tremendously wonderful. One God, one Savior, one answer, Jesus and none, but Him.

Why did Jesus go towards the Centurion's home that day when He knew the circumstances before they unfolded? The Lord always responds to the voice of faith. It's what arrested Him on His way to raise Lazarus from the dead. The touch of the woman with the issue of blood arrested Him and commanded all of the attention of heaven. The touch of faith is something that is internal which manifests on the eternal. Religion always looks at the external. Did you give? Did you tithe? Did you pray? Did you read? Did you serve? Did you cry? Did you go? Did you experience the glitter cloud? Did the oil drip from your hands? Did you see the angel feathers or orbs of light?

Jesus, He looks on the heart! "Do we love Him?" Has the love of God been shed abroad in our hearts? When the roll is called up yonder we are going to be seen not by what we have done, but by who we have become. Who we are deep down inside, the very essence of our being is going to be laid bare. "Do we trust Him? Do we believe Him? Do we have faith in Him? Do we belong to Him? Are we living in total surrender to Him?

What magnificent grace He gave to that servant who suffered. I have often wondered; when He healed that servant what was in the Lord's mind? Were His thoughts about the day, when He, would give His all, as the faithful suffering servant? I wonder how much did that servant knew about Jesus? Did he ever set eyes on the one who healed and raised him up?

What of the grace shown to the Centurion? He was a believer and in the end probably turned from Judaism to the Master. What about the crowd that heard this story as Jesus used this man's faith as an example? Our God is a grace giver. He lives to give. He's the giver of every perfect gift. (James 1:17)

There is another aspect to this story that is often missed. A reality that only a few with military experience may pick up on. He was a Centurion. The Centurion's job was to go into battle and if necessary, lay down his life so that others may live. In battle we always engage the enemy for our brother or sister next to us. They are the ones we fight for and not for some cause or flag. We fight for those around us. These are the ones we are willing to lay down our lives for.

At an appointed time Jesus, would die that others might live! He as our substitute gave His life in our place to secure our freedom. Jesus is a greater Centurion. His war was against Satan, sin, poverty, sickness and death. He is a Centurion that carried the scars of battle, on His hands, on His feet and in His face. The very weight of our sin disfigured Him. He is the warrior of warriors. Unselfishly He offered Himself in total surrender to the

Father. He abandoned Himself to fulfil the demands of the Law. That's our Jesus. That's the real Jesus, the commander of love. How do we come into such surrender as demonstrated by the Centurion, Peter, the fish or Hosea? Let's experience firsthand His eternal symphony of love and follow Him by His example through a harmony of romance.

Harmony of a Romance

When it comes to expressions of love, there are few things more poignant than sacrifice. It's inherently romantic to tell someone, "I want you to be happy and I don't care what it costs." Of course, the greater the sacrifice, the greater the expression of passion and love. Before we leap into the romance of the centuries, we need to understand a little about types and antitypes of the Bible.

Typology is a special kind of symbolism. A type is something, someone, a relationship or a family which represents something or someone else. The type is the action whereas the antitype is the fulfillment of the lesson in type in Jesus.

We can define a type as a "prophetic symbol" because all types are representations of something yet future. More specifically, a type in Scripture is a person or thing in the Old Testament which foreshadows a person or thing in the New Testament. This is vital to understand as we explore Rachel's harmony of romance. It's a symphony teeming with lives and love surrendered.

As the younger daughter, it was Rachel's task to go to the well and draw water for her father's sheep. It was no mere coincidence that she went that day when Jacob arrived. She might have been sick or indisposed, and if Leah her sister had gone for the water, what a different story might have been written of Jacob, as well as of the history of Israel. (Genesis 29)

Fleeing from his home to Haran, Jacob met with the supernatural at Bethel. He had been ensured that the Lord would be with him and direct his steps. "I am with thee, and will keep thee in all places whither thou goest."

(Genesis 28:15) Immediately he met a bunch of shepherds who told Jacob of Rachel. (Genesis 29:6)

The meeting between the couple, was of God, and was His providence that ordered their first glimpse of each other at the well. Jacob went to the well and took the large covering stone from its mouth and watered her sheep. The very next thing that takes place may leave some questioning. Genesis 29:11, tells us that he kissed her and then wept. No he was not being forward. She was his cousin and hugs were an acceptable custom in the east in those days. Did he smooch with her? Definitely not! Jacob was becoming a gentleman and no longer a manipulator. Laban also kissed him in Genesis 29:13.

It was no by chance meeting. Their steps were ordered by the Lord, directing them right into each other's arms. Today we sometimes forget that the most seemingly ordinary incidents in life are as much of the divine plan as the smallest parts of a watch. The tiny parts of a plan are the foundation upon which all the others depend. Our steps, when ordered by the Lord, lead to the greater things in life. (Psalm 37:23)

That was certainly the case with Jacob. He fell in love with this woman named Rachel. In fact, he'd been in love with her since the moment he first laid eyes on her. (Genesis 29:1-14) Love at first sight is possible. In fact, he was so in love with Rachel that he took the first opportunity he could to express his feelings to her. He was evidently not a reluctant lover. (Genesis 29:18)

Probably the tears Jacob shed, were those of gratitude to God for bringing him to his mother's relatives, and also tears of joy because he knew instinctively that the lovely maiden he embraced would be his wife. Jacob acquainted her with his story, and was taken home by an excited Rachel where he was hospitably welcomed. This couple had no real idea what prophetic messages they and their children would carry down to the end times.

He worked for Laban her father and as is customary in the east when he presented his proposal of marriage; it was given to her father. Laban was a foxy old character and saw an opportunity to get some work out of Jacob.

Seven years he had to work if he wanted the hand of Rachel. Seven in Hebrew is the number of completion. Six days the Lord took to create the earth and on the seventh He rested. (Genesis 2:2) Six days shalt thou labor and do all our work, but the seventh is a day of rest. (Exodus 20:9-10) For Joseph there would be seven years of plenty and seven years of famine for Egypt! (Genesis 41:29-30) In the book of Revelation there are, seven churches, seven spirits, seven candlesticks, seven seals, seven horns, seven eyes, seven trumpets and seven thunders! Certainly it's all connected. (Revelation 1-2)

Seven is all around us, even in music, the seven notes repeat, with the eighth key a higher octave of the first as you go up (*or down*) the keyboard. All other minor notes, sharps and flats, fit within the structure of the basic seven musical notes. A harmony of romance was being formed!

We are distinctly told that "Jacob loved Rachel," and that the seven years he served Laban for his daughter, "seemed to him, but a few days because of the love he had for her." (Genesis 29:18, 20) I can see a very anxious bridegroom, pacing up and down waiting for his bride at the altar. I wonder did his wedding party fuss with his clothes. They would have wanted him to look just right! He nervously looked around and perhaps asked someone to check the sundial for the time. It was a day of happiness that was not to be! Laban deceived him! Instead of being married to Rachel, Leah showed up in a veil. His heart sank when he lifted the veil and saw that he had married Leah. (Genesis 29:24) Obviously Rachel went along with the deceit. Why?

The trickery perpetrated by Laban upon Jacob added color to the record. Laban cunningly beguiled Jacob into marriage with Rachel's elder and less beautiful sister Leah. Jacob had accepted Laban's terms to take no wages for his labor in his fields and at the end of the seven years, waiting expected to receive Rachel. In the gloom the bride appears closely veiled, according to custom.

The ceremony was performed and the wedded pair retired to their bridal chamber. In those days the veil was not lifted at the altar of the church. In the light of early morning Jacob discovered Laban's duplicity! A treachery in which Leah had a part. It also brings question to Jacob. We know he knew the embrace of Rachel. How was it he didn't realize the one holding him that night was not Rachel? When the veil came off there was the plain-looking, undesired Leah instead of the face of his dearest Rachel. Why?

Leah, by her father's deceit, had stolen her sister's blessing. Isaac had blessed Jacob, believing him to be Esau, and now Jacob marries Leah believing her to be Rachel. In the moment of his surprised discovery did Jacob remember how he had stolen his brother's birthright by covering himself with a hairy skin, a venison-smell, and making himself appear as Esau? (Genesis 27) Was this a retributive providence, for his own deception of his blind and dying father? What we sow we reap! (Galatians 6:7) Was this the only reason this took place or was it perhaps in some way prophetic?

Laban condoned his unrighteous act by declaring that in those times the younger daughter should not be given in marriage before the first-born. He should have told Jacob this when he covenanted to serve the first seven years for Rachel. At the very least it should have been mentioned well in advance of the wedding.

Rachel then faced a great dilemma. She could fight for her right to wed Jacob as promised, expose the plot, humiliate her sister in public and bring great shame to the entire family. Putting her sister's honor before her own, she went along. This speaks volumes as to her character and of a heart coming to surrender to the Lord.

Even after Jacob found that he had been deceived by Laban and had been given Leah he served and waited for Rachel another seven years because "he loved her more than Leah." (Genesis 29:30) Here exposed in his heart, is his road to abandonment to the plans, purposes and timing of God!

Rachel was Jacob's choice for a wife, yet the real choice was not Jacob's, but God's, no matter how that choice was dictated to by the games of men. So why did the Lord permit him to end up with Leah? There are the three wills of God! The good! The acceptable and the perfect will of God. (Romans 12:2) Obviously Leah was not God's perfect will. In his second marriage, Rachel only received half of Jacob, the other half had been given to her rival sister. Have you ever had to share your partner with another? Some have to share their mate with a hobby, a car, a job or in some cases another person.

Jacob was then involved in two marriages, which were not deemed unfitting in an age when polygamy was tolerated even by godly men. For another seven years

Jacob toiled bravely on! True love enabled him to persevere until Rachel was his. What interests me is the nagging thought of the absence of any recorded protest on Rachel's part against her father's deception! Why did she not cry out to her father, when she saw that Leah, instead of herself, was being given to Jacob? What greater truths are available to us in this story?

God loves His chosen people, the house of Israel. From Rachel and Leah would come all the twelve tribes of Israel! Do you remember what happened in the Garden of Eden? Adam and Eve were also deceived! Jacob, later called Israel, was deceived by Laban as history repeated itself.

Prophetically this tells us that the people of Israel would also be deceived. To this day they do not accept Jesus as the Messiah. One day Rachel would weep over her children! (Matthew 2:18) Rachel always symbolizes the nation of Israel. Because of the deception, Leah was if you like, grafted in. In that Leah is a type of the church.

Rachel was first desired, as was Israel, but due to circumstances, Leah was married first, as was the church. The beloved wife was barren, while Leah bare many children. The church has brought forth fruit while Israel remains barren. The beloved wife eventually would bear children, being visited by God. So shall it be in the parallel revival of the end times. Israel shall bring forth fruit that shall remain.

In Isaiah 54:1, God speaks to Israel, who the beloved and barren Rachel typifies. He says "Sing, O barren, thou that didst not bear; break forth into singing, and cry aloud, thou that didst not travail with child: for more are the children of the desolate than the children of the married wife, saith the LORD."

It is also worth of noting that Jacob's name was changed to Israel when he was returning home with his wives and offspring. When Christ returns to the earth with His armies, which is also His bride, He will then bear the name, Word of God, a sword! (Revelation 19:11-14)

If Rachel had resentment at the hour of the marital vows between Jacob and Leah, she must have suppressed it. Why was she so placid amid such a calamity? What did she know? The day she had longed for came and was swallowed up in deception.

All couples speak tenderly about their coming wedding day. Who would attend? How many invitations are to be sent? What life would be like for them beyond the wedding day? How many babies? Rachel longed for a family! Why, why, why no protest? Is there even more to her story than what we have already discovered hidden in the pages of the Bible?

Unmurmuringly, she went on waiting for another seven years. In the interim, she had to share Jacob with the woman who soon would bear him many children. Can you imagine what raced through Rachel's heart every time she saw Jacob and Leah together? The thought of her lips touching his! Holding his hand or sharing his bed would have been extremely unpleasant. Why would she go through such agonies if there was not something more to this story?

Think about how God has waited longingly for Israel, the apple of His eye. Think of His pain and tears and how He watched them fall by deception. (Joel 1:12) Be mindful of the many times Israel fell into spiritual adultery. Think of His feelings as Israel caressed idols of wood and stone. Contemplate His tears as she lay on that bed of sin. Consider the thousands of years that have passed and how the Lord has waited for Rachel to be fertile and to come to Him.

While Leah might have had the keys of Jacob's house, Rachel held the keys of his heart. Leah seems to have influenced his judgment: Rachel never ceased to hold his love. Leah bore Jacob six sons, Rachel was the mother of only two: but the sons of Rachel were dearer to him than the sons of Leah. Rachel will never be without the affection of the King of Kings. Leah, the church, will never be without His tenderness and devotion. At an appointed time the Father will bring us together at the cross of Christ. The seed of Abraham is coming home! (Galatians 3:29)

Leah, too, despite experiencing the pain of being Jacob's unloved wife, whose only consolation was bearing his children, must have known agony! All her life she knew she played second fiddle in his orchestra of love. Not so with the church in the heart of the Lord.

Leah's heart cried out in sisterhood while her head looked for her identity in a man. After three times of counting on a baby, to secure her man's attention, she didn't get it. She refocused her loves hunger from Jacob to Jehovah; from her husband to her Heavenly Father.

There are many today who have been disappointed by a partner; hurt by a spouse. As a result, frustration and bitterness became their lot in life. If you're a woman, maybe you've been hurt by a father whose love or approval you could never seem to win, or maybe a boyfriend or a husband has let you down. Or maybe you've been abused or betrayed and abandoned! It could be that we've had a positive relationship with the partner in our life, but they still, haven't been able to be all we need. Rachel eventually hated her sister Leah. (Genesis 30:1-2) That hatred turned into something equally more devastating. She introduced her maid to her husband's bed. (Genesis 30:3-6) She was bitter, jealous, deceitful and a conniving woman. She was a chip of the old block! Soon greater conflict broke out between Rachel and Leah. (Genesis 3:15-16) Leah was broken out of hand as she looked even more for her identity in Jacob.

"And Jacob came out of the field in the evening, and Leah went out to meet him, and said, Thou must come in unto me; for surely I have hired thee with my son's mandrakes. And he lay with her that night."

Rachel had sold her husband. She prostituted him to Leah. "In Hebrew dudaim, it means "love-plants," and occurs only in Genesis 30:14-16. It has been called the "love-apple." The Arabs call it "Satan's apple." It contains narcotic properties. It still grows near Jerusalem, and in other parts of Palestine." – Bible Study Tools

Deception always breads deception. At this point in their lives both were seeking their approval from a man. Their jockeying for position for the heart of Jacob brought them nothing but trouble and served to widen to gap between Rachel and Leah.

No one was ever meant to derive their identity and worth from the approval of others. Leah finally said, "I'm going to turn to the Lord." (Genesis 29:33) Maybe we ought to do that! All are headed for disappointment and chronic insecurity if they try to define themselves by someone else. It's a liberating day when we discover that no man or woman, no child, can do for our worth what the Lord can do.

God loved Leah; her man didn't. The Lord gave her His divine blessing when her man wouldn't give his. Let's learn from Leah. Don't waste time trying to find our identity in the fickle, fragile love or approval of people. Look beyond them to Jesus', real Love. Start drawing on Him for all our needs.

Does a jealousy still exist between Israel and the church? There are people out there who ascribe to a replacement theology. They feel that because of sin, all the promises, all the blessings granted to Israel have been revoked. They say that they now all belong to the church. It's amazing what jealousy will do! Nothing could be further from the truth! Israel and the church are two distinct groups just as Rachel and Leah were two distinct people. History clearly shows that God has not abandoned Israel. History also shows that God has not abandoned the church because of our sin either. Rachel and Leah were sisters. Israel and the church are sisters in Him. The sin of one or the other does not make that any less true.

Were they able to hold their relationships together? It's a horrible day when a spouse interferes with sibling love and rivalry ensues.

Despite their enormous compassion towards one another at the beginning, the sisters had very different personalities representing two entirely different planes of reality, which in later times developed into rivalry that divided. Even in our day there has been rivalry between the church and Israel.

The great gulf that divided their respective worlds not only affected their own lives, but continued as a rift into the lives of their descendants. The sins of the father are visited upon the children to the third and fourth generation! (Exodus 34:7)

Whoever said relationships were easy? In the end times, we will again come together as Israel comes home. We had better make room in our heart for Rachel!

For a moment let's ponder the rivalry between Joseph (*Rachel's child*) and his brothers. (*Primarily Leah's children*) They sought to kill him, but instead they were calmed by selling him as a slave to a passing camel caravan. (Genesis 37:28) This has continued throughout the centuries. Attempts to kill the Jews by those claiming Christianity has always been with us through the epochs of time. Let's recall that Rachel clearly typifies Israel and Leah the church. (*Christianity*)

When the Nazis came on the scene in Germany professing they were believers, they were able to draw upon the legacy of Christian anti-Judaism. Biologically-based anti-Semitism went well beyond classical Christian anti-Judaism by arguing for the annihilation of the Jews rather than only for their misery and marginality. Christian anti-Semitism provided an indispensable seedbed for the success of Nazism on the popular level. It was birthed because of the cheap-grace message that filled the churches. It led some Christians to embrace the Nazi ideology and many others stood on the sidelines as masses of Jews were exterminated. Dietrich Bonhoeffer, the great German pastor stood up against cheap-grace. To the church he was a wave maker disturbing the status quo. To Hitler he was dangerous. Absolutely surrendered to Jesus and his love for the church he was hanged by the neck until dead.

Even here in Canada we followed the line of Joseph's brothers by surrendering Jews into captivity. In May 1939, nine hundred and seventy Jews set sail from Germany aboard the steam ship St. Louis, in search of freedom. Like Joseph, they had been stripped of everything they held dear and tossed out of their country. When Cuba would not accept them they made for Canada. Here, Prime Minister Mackenzie King turned them around and thereby selling Joseph into bondage. This has been a blight upon Canadian history. Several years ago, Canada assembled the few remaining survivors of that ship and publically apologized to them and repented before the Lord.

I wish I could tell you that the church in Canada and around the world ended their animosity against Israel at the end of World War II. Far from it. The Salvation Army, the Assemblies of God, (*the USA counterpart to the P.A.O.C*) the Baptists, Lausanne Congress on World Evangelization, based in Vancouver, the Presbyterians, the Methodists and the United Methodists the Church of Scotland, the Lutheran Church and the Episcopal Church, to name a few. All have taken a clear stand to intentionally disenfranchise Rachel.

In the Bible this division surfaced in the time of Moses. It was Moses, Leah's descendant, who redeemed the people from their slavery in Egypt, but only Joshua, a disciple of Moses and Rachel's descendant, who was able to lead the nation, into the Promised Land. The type continues to unfold throughout the pages of Old Testament history. The antitype is clearly revealed in the New Testament. Let's go back to Rachel!

Once Rachel became Jacob's second wife, her continued barrenness created impatient anxiety. Seeing Leah's many happy children made her jealous. Absolute desperation settled over her. What terrible anguish is wrapped up in the words! "Rachel was barren!" (Genesis 29:31) What terrible anguish should descend upon the church of our day as we consider our plight? We are barren, just as Rachel, without children! The sounds of multitudes of new born babies are nowhere to be heard at our altars.

Rachel would taunt Leah on not having the love of her husband, while Leah would find revenge in the childlessness of her rival. Rachel's whole being was bound up in the desire to become a mother, so she cried to Jacob, "Give me children, or else I die." (Genesis 30:1) Her words resonated hundreds of years later by the Scottish Evangelist John Knox who cried: "Give me Scotland or let me die. His sorrow over the barrenness of the church in Scotland resounded from the pages of Scripture. Revival resulted.

Rachel's statement, "else I die," reverberates the findings of doctors in our day that study infertility in marriage.

"Women may feel angry at not being able to have children and hold resentment towards other pregnant women. They may have feelings of guilt, regarding their infertility as punishment. A diagnosis of infertility will often lead to feelings of grief associated with the loss of control over reproductive capabilities, plans and goals. Some women may become uncomfortable around children and start to isolate themselves from family and friends with children. This isolation can leave women without social support networks to help overcome the feelings of depression and frustration commonly associated with infertility. Occasions such as Christmas, Mother's and Father's Day can become painful reminders of their infertility. A woman may develop feelings of inadequacy, perceiving her body as dysfunctional." - Women's Health Queensland Wide Inc.

Similarly, a woman's sense of femininity is often closely associated with fertility. Infertility may therefore have a serious impact on a woman's sexual identity, leaving her feeling less sexually attractive or asexual. Infertility and attempts to overcome it can lead to a loss in perspective. Women may put everything else in their lives on hold, putting all their energy and time into getting pregnant. They may delay making changes in everything from their careers to their current housing situation, deciding to wait until after they have 'had the baby. Infertility can place women on an emotional roller coaster of hope and then despair. Women may go through a cycle of hopefulness leading to one disappointment after another. Even in this, there is a parallel to the church!

O, how I would to God that the church in our day knew a positive desperation. John Knox of old, showed us the way to bring spiritual children to the birth. Rachel, however, directed her petition to her husband and not to the throne room. God always answers the cries of desperation no matter how misdirected they may be.

Rachel should have cried to God instead of Jacob whose anger was kindled against her for her impossible request. (Genesis 30:1) Certainly Jacob loved Rachel! Still, his righteous indignation kindled like a fire. She saw Jacob as the cause of her bitterness. He should have thought of that bitterness, caused by Rachel's disappointment, and quietly pointed out to her the wrongdoings. His anger, went from righteous to wrongful. Was heaven without answer for her even though her request was misdirected? I think not!

Poor, childless Rachel was not forgotten by the Lord for He remembered her and opened her womb. (Genesis

30:22-24) She gave birth to a son, and thereby the Lord took away her reproach. The grateful mother was moved in the prophetic and she called her baby Joseph, which means, "The Lord shall add to me another son." It was not merely the language of desire, but the prediction of a seer.

Of all the children of Jacob, Joseph became the godliest and greatest. Renowned as the savior of Israel he stands out as the most perfect type in the Bible of Jesus who was born of woman, to become the Savior of the world.

The time had come for Laban and Jacob to part, company. Laban had learned by experience that he had been blessed because Jacob had been with him. Our employers are blessed for our being in their service. They are prospered because Jesus is in us, although they usually are unaware of that fact.

Due to his wives, children and rich possessions Jacob could no longer live at Haran. So, he set out for his old home, and took with him all that God had given him. Laban was angry at losing his business partner who had worked with him so faithfully for twenty years. While Laban was absent for a few days caring for his many sheep, Jacob gathered all his family, cattle and possessions and secretly left. Returning home, Laban found Jacob gone and he set out after him. When he caught up with the caravan, Laban took Jacob to task not only for leaving so secretly, but also for stealing some of his household goods and gods. (Genesis 31:30)

It was this accusation that revealed Rachel, lovely as she was, in a very dim light. Be sure you sin will find you out! (Numbers 32:23) Rachel the heir to God's promises evidently was a secret believer in heathen practices. This again is proof positive that surrender may be not always be absolute. She stole the household idols, and when Laban sought for them she hid them beneath her. In her cunning, she hid the small images, in human form, used for divination. (Deuteronomy 18:10) Rachel manifested something of her father's deviance. She remained a chip of the old block! (Judges 17:5; 18:14, 17, 18, 20)

Given to deception she kept her mouth shut. It was not until Jacob returned to Bethel that he buried those strange idols under the oak at Shechem. Those lifeless deities, the size of a miniature doll, were regarded as indispensable evidence as to the rights and privileges of family ownership. Hence, Laban's query, "Wherefore hast thou stolen my gods?" (Genesis 31:30)

Spiritually adultery lay in her heart. There was a professed relationship to the God of Israel, yet at the same time she was married to idols. (Genesis 30:23-24) She was a thief the moment she carried away that which did not belong to her. Obviously her years of being barren resulted in her turning to idol worship. It was also prophetic of Israel's future.

It would not be the last time that Rachel, (*Israel*) would fall into idolatry. The Father reminded Ezekiel that He had repeatedly warned Israel that their dead bodies would be found in some valley. They would lie at the foot of their idols and altars. They would be gripped in the clutches of death with their hope almost gone.

"And I will lay the dead carcasses of the children of Israel before their idols; and I will scatter your bones round about your altars." (Ezekiel 6:5) They would be scattered from one end of the earth to the other. (Deuteronomy 28:64)

The church today needs to be careful! We need to understand that false teachings, false worship, strange fire are in the house. They are hidden in the hearts of believers and expounded from the pulpits of the world. (Leviticus 10:1, Numbers 3:4, 26:61)

Rachel would weep yet again! Matthew 2:18, says: "In Rama was there a voice heard, lamentation, and weeping, and great mourning, Rachel weeping for her children, and would not be comforted because they are not."

Some say this is reference to the slaying of the innocents at the time of the birth of Jesus. There is much more to this verse than that very narrow interpretation permits. The Lord went on to promise a regathering of Rachel's children in our days. (Ezekiel 37:21) The State of Israel was born on May 14th. 1948. Does it end there? Far from it!

Sadly in Rachel's harmony of romance, there lies the first recorded instance in the Bible of death in childbirth! How horrible is it to realize that not all of Rachel's children will come to the birth. Equal are the tears for the children of Leah, (*the Church*) for not all of hers will come home either. Matthew tells us that a day is coming when the Lord will gather the nations. He will then separate us into two groups. One on the right hand the other on the left. To some He will say: "Come you blessed of my Father inherit the Kingdom that has been prepared for you from the foundation of the world." (Matthew 25:34) Others on that fateful day will learn that not all who call Him Lord will enter in. (Matthew 7:21)

Some, in fact, will hear Him say: "away from me I know you not!" (Matthew 25:12) Not all who call Him

Lord will make it to the greatest coupling of history. Tears once more will fall from the face of Rachel.

"In Rama was there a voice heard, lamentation, and weeping, and great mourning, Rachel weeping for her children, and would not be comforted, because they are not." (Matthew2:18)

This Scripture has reference not only to the Babylonian captivity as described by Jeremiah. (Jeremiah 31:15) It also refers to the death of the first born at the time of Christ. (Matthew 2: 13-23) It is also possible that it references a day at the end of time thus making it a typological prophetic utterance.

During the course of her life, Rachel had surrendered her idolatry into the valley of the shadow of death. She was a woman who knew transformation in her life. Young Joseph's great reverence for the Lord testifies of Rachel's godly training in his boyhood years. She had gone from idol worship to loving the one true God! Jacob he too had been transformed throughout his life! Jacob's love for her and his stronger faith was used of the Lord to help mold her character. She lived on long after the death of her first son. They both knew many ups and downs in their lives. Every circumstance they went through, the Lord used to bring them to surrender of all. It was the Lord, who caused them to rise to the crest of the waves on the sea of life and by love come to complete abandonment.

It was time for Rachel to go to her eternal home in glory. Before leaving her precious husband, in fulfillment of the prophetic word she had spoken, Benjamin was born. How often the brightest dreams of life are clouded by the gloom of the grave! Rachel prayed for children, but the beginning of her second son's life was the ending of her own. What travail and anguish are described in the words, "Rachel travailed, and she had hard labor ... she died." (Genesis 35:16, 18) Facing death she called her son, Benoni, meaning "son of sorrow." Suffering had brought her to the gates of life and death. The very gift she coveted turned out to be a crushing burden under which she sank.

Soon Jacob chose another name for their child and called him Benjamin, signifying, "the son of the right hand," and he showered much affection upon the motherless child.

The last cry Rachel uttered as she died was "Benoni," son of sorrow and it is in the spirit of this, Benoni that the Bible portrays Rachel. When Jacob came to die in extreme old age, he spoke sorrowfully of the loss of his beloved Rachel who through her years had been caught in a web of much sorrow and unhappiness. He loved her at first and ever afterward.

Broken, Jacob buried Rachel on the way to Bethlehem, and set up a pillar over her grave. I can imagine him visiting the grave regularly with flowers, his gift of love. In "his heart that grave remained evergreen, and he never ceased to deck it with flowers." In a previous grave at Shechem he had buried Rachel's idols, and with them her pagan beliefs. The headstone he erected was a sad token of his broken heart.

For Rachel, to everything in her life there was a season, and a time to every purpose under the heaven: There was that wonderful day when she was born. She knew times of planting and times of harvest. There were times when she broke down and times of healing. A time when her love relationship with the Lord was built in beauty. Often she knew times of weeping and times of rejoicing. Times when she spoke loudly and times when she kept silent. All too soon with a broken heart her time to die had come. (Ecclesiastes 3)

Leah and Rachel had helped build the house of Israel. (Ruth 4:11) One day Rachel's precious dust will be revitalized as she steps out of the valley of dry bones. (Ezekiel 37:5-6) In her new glorified body she again will sit down with Jacob, this time in the kingdom of heaven.

As life takes its twists and turns, as the storms of life blow we need to learn that the only way to overcome is through total and complete submission. The only way to live is to die! Remember, its surrender of all or not at all!

Oratorio of Ruth

Life takes amazing twists and turns at times, especially in relationships. We plan, we grow moving steadily towards our dreams. We think that life goes on forever! Most people work and save towards the day when they retire. Traveling, taking long walks together and spoiling the grand kids are all part of our dreams. Every day the bank account grows and with every passing week we know that we are one step closer to our goal. Every night when we tuck into bed, we discuss with our partners the coming day. How we will spend some tender moments together? What special things we want to get for each other? When will the mortgage be paid off? All adds their tender touches to our quiet times.

Suddenly in an instant illness and death shatters all our dreams! We never took those circumstances into account. We're launched into a world, we know little about. Funeral arrangements, caring for the kids on a new level! All alone, the sting of death hits home. When the relatives and friends leave after the funeral, loneliness delivers one more blow.

We long for familiar sounds! Our nostrils sniff the air, longing to grasp the scent of our partner, even for a fleeting moment. At night we listen for the front door to spring open! A sound calls out to us! Perhaps it's them and we will finally awaken from the long nightmare! We wonder how on earth, we will be able to move forward! What if life's sledge hammer delivers even more agonizing blows? Will we ever know peace again? Will we ever be happy again? How can we find the Lord in any of this?

If that has been our story, we will identify with the characters in the Book of Ruth. Their tale, maps a way to submission through a multitude of circumstances they faced. In our day some read it and take advantage of their saga of love and find benefit. Others turn a blind eye to the challenges, patience, faith and victory declared for the end times.

It's the twists and turns of life that brings us to new day. Ruth experienced this and in the end she found a greater happiness than she had ever knew before. Her happiness was found in the heart of real love, Jesus! Alone and lonely she was accepted into a new family. Warmed by the love of a mother-in-law and her husband Boaz, she dreamed many dreams. Let's go back to the beginning of her oratorio and travel with her through the kinks and curls in her life.

The book of Ruth has long been revered as a work of great literary genius, even among secular scholars. The way the book is written, every word is significant as it relates to the overall storyline. Every sentence has a multiple of meanings, ranging from the obvious surface meaning, to many 'hidden' surprises.

"Long ago, during the time when the judges ruled, there was a famine in the land, and a man named Elimelech, left the town of Bethlehem in Judah. He, his wife, and two sons moved to the country of Moab." (Ruth 1:1) (ERV)

When Elimelech and Naomi started a family together they didn't plan on a famine happening in Judah. None of us ever plan for such things! This was not any ordinary famine though. The famine came upon the land because the people had fallen into sin. They had turned from the one true God and worshiped idols. Judgment always comes upon such nations. It wasn't God jumping on them when they messed up. Within the Bible there are both blessings and curses. (Deuteronomy 28) The choice in which we live is entirely up to us.

For Naomi, grace was poured out and she and her family, (*husband and two sons*) finally moved to Moab. There, life would be much easier or so she thought. They could get on with their plans for retirement together. They set about building a home in the hills of Moab. (*Jordan*) (Ruth 1:20) (ERV) The view must have been spectacular! Hills and valleys, from arid to green lands, overlooking the Dead Sea, Moab was an artist's paradise. As the days passed and the weeks rolled into months life seemed to be getting better. Then, it happened!

Death struck with its iron fist and Elimelech was gone. Conquering the storm that tried to swamp her, Naomi with her two sons gathered up the pieces of their lives. Soon the boys married two Moabite women, Orpah and Ruth. Ten years later the hammer of death fell again. This time both of Naomi's boys were gone. If the loss of her husband was not enough to deal with, now her kids were taken. (Ruth 1:4-5) (ERV)

The narrative says that Naomi was left alone. Deep inside an emptiness, tried to pull her under the waves of despair. Have you ever noticed when the loss of a loved one is present then wave after wave of emotions rolls in? What was she going to do? Not only was she left alone, she lived in a land with strange customs and culture.

Soon Naomi learned that the famine in her homeland had passed and she wanted to go back home to Judah. (Ruth 1:6) Praying for her daughters-in-law, Naomi suggested that they return home to their families. She was saying, 'I can't look after you and you have to make a life for yourselves.' (Ruth 1:8-9) When Naomi kissed the two girls they both began to cry. Have you ever wanted a mother-in-law like that? She was so close to the girls. Obviously Naomi had accepted and loved them as her own. Their relationship was far from what many know today.

Some feel alienated by their in-laws. Rather than acceptance as equals, some are embraced by indifference. Some dads at the wedding say: 'I'm not losing a son rather I'm gaining a daughter.' In some cases it can be said of these that, if their mouth is moving, they're lying.

The few words; "they lifted up their voices and wept," gives us clear insight into the heart of this mother. (Ruth 1:9) By her gentleness, patience and understanding she had found a place in the hearts of the widows. Mom, reminded them there was nothing she could do for them. She saw no future for them with her. Her desire was to place their welfare ahead of her own.

Of the many beautiful things that can be attributed to this verse, I think the beauty of the motherhood of Naomi is, by far the best. It is a beauty that's been around since time began. A beauty that some men are not able to see. In her we see the wonders of God's love. From her we can see and live again the beauty of faith as seen in Sarah, the attractiveness of Rachel. The beauty and purity in the Shulamite bride. The courage of Esther! The tender watchful heart of Miriam! Ah, the splendor of love as seen in Ruth herself the result of the influence of Naomi. A mother's love is a symphony that must ring it's melody in our hearts every day. In Naomi, we see the devotion of Eunice and Lois as we are launched onto the sea of faith, a faith to change. What more, shall we say about the lessons of motherhood we learned from Deborah? The beauty of motherhood is alive; it grows, resembling the progression of light in the heavens and in our hearts. It's a heavenliness that unfolded in the hearts of Naomi's children with every passing day.

Mere physical beauty grows until it reaches full flower and then starts to languish. Not so with the pulchritude of God as seen in mothers. It grows brighter and brighter through the years. It's a wonder that defies all the ravages of time, care, and disease. It's an unconscious charisma.

A mother gives of herself, again and again. Late at night, early in the morning her devotion is fresh and alive. Who makes the lunches? Who is it that's usually last to bed at night and first up in the morning?

Mothers give and impart, even to the point where she might lose her health. Her beauty shines through the darkness and her sincerity to others defies comprehension. Often she is excessively engaged in her caring and faithfulness, to ever be mindful of her own beauty. Humility rises from the depth of her being. Here, lies the legacy and the oratorio of Ruth.

At length Orpah, hugged her sister and left. She wanted to go back to her family and the gods of Moab. (Ruth 1:12-16) (ERV) Ruth on the other hand took an entirely different direction. What terrible pain that, would have brought to the heart of God. Orpah, could have made better life choices as did her sister. Still the LORD would use her choice to speak to the church in the last days.

Ruth's choice launched her along the highway to abandonment. Elimelech and Naomi had influenced her by the lifestyles they led. "Whither thou goest I will go!"

She was prepared to leave her own country and perhaps never see it again! "Where you lodgest, I will lodge!" She didn't care where she would live, in a castle or a tent. "Thy people shall be my people!" She was saying that she would fly the Star of David over her home. No longer would the standard of Moab be waved.

Ruth was unlike many immigrants today who claim the benefits of our lands, but want to continue to fly the standards of another. "Thy God, my God." In all of this she shouted from the hills of Moab that for her it was to be all of God or none of God. (Ruth 1:16, 18) Seeing the strength and courage of Ruth's commitment, Naomi agreed and soon they were on their way towards an appointment with destiny. They were on their way back to Bethlehem. The birthplace of the Messiah!

When they arrived in the city, excitement filled the air. Naomi was recognized. However, the joy of the people was greeted by the sadness of her heart. She told them don't call me Naomi anymore, call me Mara! (Ruth 1:20) How amazing, how wonderful that even in the midst of so many circumstances she embraced truth. According to Strong's, Mara means to be angry or bitter, to be burdened down. Of course these things that tried to settle over her are natural at times. What is supernatural however, is that Naomi was going to rise above her feelings.

When Ruth met her father-in-law's family she met Boaz. Was it a per chance meeting? Hardly! Her steps were being ordered by her destiny. Boaz was very close to Naomi and Ruth accepted him immediately. (Ruth 2:1)

Ruth understood the rules of common sense when in a new country. She went nowhere without first telling

Naomi. She was off to the fields! It was the time of the barley harvest! Her goal was to find someone who would permit her to glean. (Ruth 2:2) This tells us that Ruth had a keen understanding of the customs of Judah. Leviticus 19:9, says:

"When you cut your crops at harvest time, don't cut all the way to the corners of your fields. And if grain falls on the ground, you must not gather up that grain."

Gleaners, picked of the crops designed for those in need. Ruth knew this and was about to take advantage of it. Her heart was to provide in whatever way she could for the family. Following the harvesters she learned that part of the field was owned by Boaz.

In the process of time Boaz came to the fields to greet his workers. That in itself tells us a great deal about his character. He was not looking for personal gain or riches. Rather, it speaks loudly of his care for those in his employ. (Ruth 2:4) His first words to them were; "the Lord be with you!" Strong's tells us that by extension this phrase means: "The Lord overshadow you!" His desire was that his workers be safe while working the fields. Their response to him equally gives evidence of their heart. "The Lord bless you or grant you abundance."

Instantly, Boaz caught a glimpse of Ruth. "Whose girl is that?" (Ruth 2"5) (ERV) Romance was in the air! Her oratorio had begun in-depth! (*Oratorio – a piece of music for multiple voices with Scripture at its heart*)

One of his workers identified her. The foreman also told Boaz that she had only taken shelter from the sun for a very short period of time. In short, her work ethic was excellent. Boaz on the other hand perhaps had other things on his mind. He told her that she did not have to work in the other fields. In fact, he suggested that she follow his female workers daily in his fields. (Ruth 2:8) (ERV) In verse nine, he told her that he had instructed the young men not to bother her. He was impressed by the fact that she loved Naomi and that she had left behind all that she knew and held dear. He also indicated that he did this because she had turned to the Lord with all of her heart. What wonderful things come when our life's journey is given over, completely to the Lord! (Ruth 2:11-12) (ERV)

Their first date was in an old field. The table was set with bread, vinegar and roasted grain! Boaz was playing things by the book! When Ruth was full, she returned to work in the fields. (Ruth 2:14) (ERV) Ruth was to glean the corners of the fields and anything the harvesters dropped by accident. Boaz however, ordered his workers to drop full heads of grain for her. (Ruth 2:16)

After laboring all day, she made her way to the local market to sell her wares. On the way she stopped with Naomi and gave her some food that she had left over from her lunch with Boaz.

Then, Naomi and Ruth came up with a plan! Romance continued to blossom. Somehow, someway, Ruth had to meet up with Boaz for some private time. Naomi told her where Boaz was going to be that evening. She told her to wash and put on a pretty dress. She told her to go to the threshing floor and to watch where Boaz lies down for the night. Then, when asleep, she was to go to him and uncover his feet and lie down by him.

Immediately many jump on this as an act of seduction. It was far from it. This couple, their integrity was beyond reproach. To understand this, we have got to uncover the culture and customs in which they lived. Then, we must be carried even further into the typology that the characters of this story represents.

"Uncover his feet, and lie down!" (Ruth 3:4) Some might think this was a provocative gesture, as if Ruth was told to provocatively offer herself sexually to Boaz. This was not how this gesture was understood in that day. In the culture of their time, it was understood as an act of total submission. It was a submission not demanded or required of her. She gave it freely because Boaz had earned it.

In that day, it was understood to be the role of a servant to lie at their master's feet and be ready for any command of the master. So, when Naomi told Ruth to lie down at Boaz's feet, she told her to come to him in a totally humble and submissive way. It's in this same way we must come to our Redeemer.

Don't lose sight of the larger picture: Ruth came to claim a right. The Law of Moses permitted if a family member died another in the family could claim the widow as his wife. (Deuteronomy 25:5) Boaz was her goal, her kinsman-redeemer, and she had the right to expect him to marry her and then raise up a family to perpetuate the name of Elimelech. But Naomi wisely counseled Ruth not to come on as a victim demanding her rights, but as a humble servant, trusting in the goodness of her kinsman-redeemer. She said to Boaz, "I respect you, I trust you, and I put my fate in your hands." (Ruth 3:1-9 *especially* 9)

Now let us begin to look into the typology. Boaz was a type of Christ hence he is called her kinsman-redeemer. The type seen in Naomi follows the history of Israel exactly. Her sojourn in the "land" is a picture of Israel's existence in the land of Israel for a period of time. The dispersion of the family of Naomi by famine, to the land of Moab, is a picture of the spiritual poverty of Israel at the time of Christ.

Now, this is where things really get interesting. Notice that Naomi could not redeem her land until Boaz took Ruth as his bride. (Ruth 4:3-4) Scripture tells us that the Church is the (*gentile*) bride of Christ. (Revelation 19:7) Only when the full number of gentiles has come in (Romans 11:25), will God redeem His land, Israel, and establish the promised throne of Messiah in Jerusalem.

Ruth is seen as a partial type of the Church. Ruth is typical of the faithful members of the Church who are the bride of Christ at the end of the age. It's Ruth who clings to Naomi even in her poverty-stricken condition.

Orpah she too is a type of part of the church. She went back to her Moabite family, a type of the gentile world system and Israel's dispersion into the gentile nations in 70 A.D. with the invasion of Israel by the Roman General Titus.

The sufferings and trials of Naomi in gentile Moab follow the exact pattern of God's prophecies about Israel's persecutions among the gentile nations. (Isaiah 53) The return of Naomi at the "Good News" of the restored fertility in the land has been experienced by the nation of Israel since 1948 and up to the present time.

Just as Naomi had returned to the land, but does not receive her inheritance until after the harvest, Israel is in her land, but she does not yet hold complete possession of it. In the days to come Israel will totally possess the land after the harvest of the Church is complete, (the *rapture*) and the dark night of threshing (*the tribulation*) is completely over. The land that God gave Israel includes the Sinai Peninsula, Syria, part of Iraq,

Jordan and Saudi Arabia, so Israel is still dispossessed of most of her land and the church of our day continues to oppose the resettlements in the land of promise. Most of the land including the oil wealth of the Arab nations will again belong to Israel when she receives her full inheritance.

Ruth and Orpah together prefigure the complete Church. As gentiles under the curse and estranged from God, both are brought into the family of God through the "exile" or Diaspora of Israel. Both believe in Naomi's God and both follow Naomi out of the land of exile toward the land of promise. It is Ruth who crosses over the Jordan River into the land, but Orpah turns back before she crosses over Jordan.

Crossing over Jordan is a type for entering the spirit-filled life, so only Ruth enters the spirit-filled life. Orpah fails to do so. This does not negate the fact that Orpah was still part of the family of God, even though she turned back to the world. Consequently, Orpah typifies the unfaithful members of the church who are spiritually saved, but do not go on into maturity in the faith.

Some have been snared by false teachings and manifestations of the external that appear appealing. The lust of the flesh, the lust of the eyes and the pride of life never changes as the world seduces the unfaithful in the church. (1 John 2:16) They will miss out if they do not turn back in total surrender.

The heart of Oprah's heavenly Father must have broken in a thousand pieces by her choice. Still the choice was hers to make. With hidden tears flowing He continued to do what He could for her. Nonetheless, He had to let her go. Such love, such wondrous love the LORD in silence shows to us every moment. Day after day He knows we will make wrong choices. Like Hosea who knowingly, waited for the day when his bride by her choice would not come home to him. The Father waits for the hour we chose to sin, then stands firm and longs for the moment of our return. Blessings flowed to Ruth while Orpah went her own way.

When Ruth went to the threshing floor at midnight and lay at the feet of Boaz, he agreed to take Ruth as his bride, but it was not until daybreak. Following the typology! It's time for the bride of Christ to go and lie at the feet of Jesus until that new day dawns and light breaks onto the world's stage. The harvest, the rapture, the parallel revival, stands at the door. When will the end come?

Interestingly, in the plot line Naomi never actually meets Boaz just as historically, on the whole, not all the Jewish people will come to know Yeshua as Messiah.

Intriguingly, Boaz gives Naomi, through Ruth, six measures of Barley. (Ruth 3:17) Then, Naomi said to Ruth in 3:18:

"Sit still, my daughter, until thou know how the matter will fall: for the man (*Boaz*) will not be in rest, until he have finished the thing this day." (*Parenthesis mine*)

Finish what thing? Making Ruth his bride. God did not rest until the seventh day when the LORD finished His work of creation. (Genesis 2:2) Jesus will not finish gathering in His bride until the time of the end! When will that be? What is the Lord waiting for?

"Be patient therefore, brethren, unto the coming of the Lord. Behold, the husbandman waiteth for the precious fruit of the earth, and hath long patience for it, until he receive the early and latter rain." (James 5:7) The harvest!

What else can we learn about the plans for earth's history and the end of the world from Ruth's oratorio of love? Let's take a look back again to Elimelech and the famine that drove them into Moab!

Famine is a picture of God's judgment upon disobedience. The exit of Elimelech with his wife Naomi and two sons from his land is a picture of the Diaspora of the Jews from the land and their sojourning in the nations of the gentiles. It was because of Israel's rejection of Jesus Christ and disobedience that God allowed the Roman General Titus to come into the land and disperse the Jews. The vision of the valley of dry bones also depicts this death and resurrection of the entire nation of Israel. (Ezekiel 37)

Even the death of Naomi's husband speaks volumes to every heart and every marriage. (Ruth 1:3) Death brings separation! This is what sin does, it separates us from all the blessings of God. It's a death in every way! The people divorced or separated themselves from God during the Diaspora! He did not divorce them! He loved them dearly. Their spiritual adultery landed them in a place alien to their culture. Just as Naomi would remain in a strange land so the children of God would languish in a strange land of death. It was during this time that Orpah and Ruth became members of the family of God. (Ruth 1:4) This was the grafting in of the church. The Lord commenced a very long process to restore Ruth and Oprah to each other. The gospel since the beginning of time is for all the nations.

The name Orpah comes from a word meaning, "stiff-necked." She speaks to us of those in the churches who are saved, who fall back or decline into the ways of the world. The word for Ruth means a friend, companion, or associate, and by extension means one who tends or feeds a flock. In this Ruth typifies those in the churches who are faithful to the full counsel of the Word of God and remain faithful to the nation of Israel. Here is where all believers should stand. Today very few Christian organizations are rising up with the spirit of Ruth to help feed and rebuild Israel.

On the other hand, there are those who claim Israel has been replaced by the church. These enemies of the cross have birthed within the church an apathy towards what the Lord is doing in our day. They say they bless Israel, but few rarely do. One would think we would be excited to get in on what the Lord is doing in our day by reaching the Jews. Sadly we are not.

A remnant, has remained faithful through the ages. Israel and the church are two distinct entities, yet at an appointed time we shall be one.

Since Naomi typifies the nation of Israel, which returns to the land and receives the inheritance, Mahlon and Chilion her sons, typify those among the divided nations of Israel and Judah who perish or are destroyed in the wilderness. Remember these two died in the land of Moab. (Zechariah 13:7, 13:8-9, Ruth 1:6)

Naomi returns to the land! In the history of the nation, Israel has been totally devastated by wars and abuse of the land. One group after another have tried to destroy and wipe her off the face of the earth. All failed miserable as the LORD's protecting hand covered His sinning child. Despite her choices and since 1948, she is now becoming a fertile land with an abundance of trees and crops of fruits and vegetables. It's the goodness of God that leads us to repentance. (Romans 2:4) As promised the Lord has returned His people to the land just as

Naomi returned. He will surely bring to pass the rest of His promises.

As the final curtain of the oratorio of Ruth begins to descend we find the happy couple were married at the city gates. In the days ahead Israel and the church will stand in oneness second to none. Those today who do all they can for Ruth, to help build her, is prophetic of that union.

The marriage between Ruth and her kinsman-redeemer also prefigures the marriage of the Lamb in Revelation. Then, comes something even more interesting.

"So all the people and elders that were near the city gates were witnesses. They said, May the LORD make this woman who is coming into your home like Rachel and Leah who built the house of Israel. Become powerful in Ephrathah! Be famous in Bethlehem!" (Ruth 4:11)

Rachel and Leah! You will recall we learned that Rachel typified Israel and Leah the church! The restoration of Israel and the church would never die out. The fact that the elders were present again serves to remind us that Ruth and Boaz had acted appropriately with each other back at the threshing floor.

Ruth delivered a son and their neighbors named him Obed. (Ruth 4:17) The moment the child came into the world he was greeted by the prophetic. (Ruth 4:14) (ERV) The women prophesied that the lad's name would become famous in Israel. This in itself is somewhat amazing. Bethlehem was in Judah not Israel. Bethlehem is today in the occupied territories. Part of what is claimed to be Palestine, not Israel. Here, perhaps Ruth's story reaches into the end times. To the day when Israel, would again possess all of the Promised Land. To the hour of the coming parallel revival in the last days. Ruth loved the child deeply. Her ability as a mother stands evidence of her deep relationship with the Lord and the high esteem in which she was held by others. Obed was the father of Jesse who was, the father of David. If you follow the linage all the way down you come to Jesus.

Life does take its twists and turns! Sometimes when we don't understand, we have to trust that the Lord is working all things out for good to them that love Him who are called according to His purpose. (Romans 8:28)

So many things in this wonderful love story speaks prophetically. Let me ask you! What does our love story say to those around us or to the world at large? Everything in the New Testament and we still live in the Acts of the Apostles. Everything about us, our lifestyles and our relationships, all are to speak prophetically of the coming Kingdom. Does our marriages speak of the wonderful marriage supper of the Lamb? Can people see in us, all the glories of the coming Kingdom?

There is nothing broken there! There is no more death, no sorrow and in the Kingdom of love every tear will be wiped away from our eyes. Is this where we live? Does our relationship's direct people to the Creator of love? To the beautiful gift of grace the Father gave us in Jesus?

Let the dance of destiny continue through you and me as we race towards the last great wedding day! Let the symphony of His love, call us onward, ever onward. Deeper within His heart, where melodies play eternal. Can we hear those fresh chords of music created just for us call us forward! Sweet harmonies that embrace the tempo of our hearts! Will we heed the trumpets call to eternal pleasures? Can we see His hallelujah chorus assembling on the walls of glory? Can we feel His heart beating within our breast? A flawless balanced melody radiating from our oneness filling the air. The music intensifies to a trembling crescendo! We shake in His presence! The music of our trembling calms as He whispers three simple words. "I love you!" It's a symphony of love that reverberates throughout the universe and down the corridors of eternity!

Ah, but are we ready for that hour? When we leave this earth we will be asked to lay down mortal flesh and move into eternity in a glorified body. Are we ready or do we want just one more day to this life? Are there still things that we need to be willing to lay down?

Anthem of a Throne

One of the most awe-inspiring women of the Bible is Esther! Only two women have a book in the Bible that bears their names. Ruth and Esther! Esther was an ordinary woman that God chose to use for His purposes.

The events recorded in Esther take place fifty years after King Cyrus had decreed that the exiled Jews in Babylon could return to Jerusalem and twenty-five years before Ezra's return to Jerusalem to rebuild the temple. She lived in Persia in the reign of Ahasuerus, whose kingdom extended from India to Ethiopia. His palace in Shushan was an architectural ornamental beauty. It was located in what today is Iran.

The king liked to flaunt his wealth. He lived the high life and hosted one party after another. Those events lasted for days on end. (Esther 1:4) His wife Vashti, was used to his drunken gatherings at which he displayed all his processions. One night he commanded that she present herself before the crowd. She was aware that to the king she was nothing more than another one of his collections. Vashti, refused and the king flew into a rage. After consulting with his cronies, he stripped her of her role as queen. His next move was to host a beauty contest to find another procession to replace the queen. (Esther 2:8)

Of course Esther won hands down and the road to her surrender was engaged.

Her physical beauty added to her intelligence, integrity, courage and her queenly character claimed the day. Ahasuerus, gave her seven maids to tend to her needs and tossed her into the house of women to join his other property. (Esther 2:9)

Esther was no different from any other young lady of her day. She had the same desires and feelings every woman possessed. Her early life probably mirrored that of many women today. She was orphaned at a young age and raised by her male cousin, Mordecai. It's a traumatic thing for a child to lose their parents and this can result in life-altering affects. Her life and attitudes while unsurrendered were certainly affected by her status as an orphan. (Esther 2:7) However, just as anyone struggling with a devastating obstacle in life, this was a barrier that Esther had to overcome. Every life is filled with challenges that can be surmounted by total and complete surrender. Her pain, the wounding of her heart, her sorrow and grief had to be given over totally to the Lord. Perhaps akin to her story did the Lord inspire Isaiah to later write? "Surely he hath borne our griefs, and carried our sorrows." (Isaiah 53:4) The moment these are abandoned they are gone. Jesus took them and nailed them to the cross.

Dealing with the baggage of losing her parents are not all she had to deal with. Her physical beauty, her place in social circles and the inferiority of women within the culture all added its weight to an already aching heart. The Lord divinely placed her as a leader and tool for His glory. Sometimes we think that our circumstances come to break us rather than to make us. Only God can equip and establish a person as an instrument to accomplish His will. God chose Esther to be such a means.

If God can use an unlikely candidate like Esther, surely He can use anyone who desires to surrender themselves to His plans and purposes. God can use anything or anyone to accomplish His will; even if one does not have faith in Him. We have seen this time and again throughout history. Wesley went off to preach in America while still unconverted. It doesn't matter how little one has to offer God, He takes whatever is given and makes it enough. It's not what we possess, but who desires to possess us that constitutes the difference.

Esther found herself entwined in a life she knew nothing about. How often have we said, 'Lord I don't know anything about what you're asking me to do? I know nothing about such a task, how can I?'

Esther went from being a carefree young girl in Mordecai's household to the courts of the king. We also go from the insignificant to the courts of glory to rule and reign with Jesus as kings in this life. (Revelation 5:10) Like Esther we are in unfamiliar territory.

Many times, as leaders, we find ourselves engulfed in unfamiliar territory trying to do and accomplish things we have never done before. We must, like Esther, learn how to be flexible, adapt, and have the assurance that God is present and working regardless or our situation. We have been formed by God and we must continue upon the characteristics He instilled within us at the new birth.

Esther was always respectful of others and humble, even though her social position in life had changed dramatically. (Esther 2:15) Respectfulness of others and sincere humility are qualities that come on the road to abandonment and they propel us to places beyond what we can imagine. God uses many things to form a surrendered heart. The culture, our Christian community, years spent in the Word, all have a profound effect on our future years. Many times attitudes are formed and instilled during early years and these can either benefit or hinder our accomplishments as a believer. It's evident that Esther didn't allow the fact that she was an orphan to determine the outcome of her life.

She chose to rise above her less-than-perfect situation. As the church in our day, we must learn to overcome our past circumstances and difficulties through surrender. We must not allow what is behind us, to dictate our future. All must be given up. Esther is a prime example of this type of overcoming attitude. She was more than a conqueror through Him who loved her! (Romans 8:37) Throughout her book we can see that she was "persuaded that neither death, nor life, nor angels, nor principalities, nor powers, nor things present, nor things to come; nor height, nor depth, nor any other creature, would be able to separate her from the love of God." (Romans 8:38-39 *Paraphrased*)

Esther was content with life in Mordecai's house and then became content with the day-to-day concerns of life in the courts of the king. She never set out to serve God in any grand manner or be used as His instrument. However, God had strategically placed Esther to be His divinely placed resource even though it was not sought after or understood by her.

Far too often we seek for things that are not for us. We need to be surrendered to His purposes and calendar for our life. When we reach for His destiny we find our own. It is the unlikely who accomplish the most amazing. The reluctant usually turn out to be the most effective, just ask Moses, Joshua or any one of the prophets.

Perhaps we have not set out to be in ministry or have any high and lofty aspirations, but God knows why He has created us and what He has ordained as the purpose our life will fulfill. We may not feel that we have any unique skill sets, gifting, talents or qualities, but whatever God has developed and poured into our life is more than enough to accomplish the task when anointed by the Holy Spirit.

Bigthana and Teresh, the king's chamberlains who were also eunuchs, became angry with the king and sought to bring harm to him. Mordecai, learned of the plot and told Esther what was, going down. She in turn told the king. (Esther 2:21-22) Following an investigation both were promptly hanged. At that time the king raised up Haman to the role of Prime Minister. (Esther 3:1)

It was required that all prostrate themselves before Haman. Mordecai flatly refused to bow to him giving the reason that he was a Jew. (Esther 3:1-4) There was good reason why Mordecai did not bow. Haman was probably an Amalekite, and God had expressed himself as being at war with Amalek "from generation to generation."

"For he said, because the LORD hath sworn that the LORD will have war with Amalek from generation to generation." (Exodus 17:16) (*Amalek was the descendant of Esau who sold his birthright.*)

It was a matter of integrity to God and not a political issue on Mordecai's part. This angered Haman and he sought retribution not from Mordecai, but from all the Jewish people. Ethnic cleansing is not something knew. Anti-Semitism was alive and well in 474 B.C. Haman offered the king 750,000 pounds of silver to order the holocaust. His offer was refused, but the king told him to commence the cull.

The would-be butcher, Haman sent letters to all the regions of the Kingdom. From India all the way to Ethiopia. "The letters were the king's command to ruin, kill, and completely destroy all the Jews. This meant young people, the old, women, and little children as well none would be exempt. The command was to kill all the Jews in a single day." (Esther 3:13) (ERV) The victims were supposed to be stripped of everything before being marched to their death. This was Haman's "Final Solution." Everything about his desires was prophetic. Little did anyone realize then, it would happen under Hitler in 1933-1945. When the command went out Haman and the king sat in the palace and got drunk. (Esther 3:15)

The Jewish people lived in a constant state of tension. Their hearts burst with pain. Every time someone came to their homes it was terrifying. The slightest noise outside froze the blood in their veins. A real sense of helplessness tried to drown them.

All over the land they were found lying on the ground in sackcloth and ashes. (Esther 4:3) When Esther heard about the proposed ethnic cleansing she sent clothes to Mordecai. Consumed with grief he would not be comforted. In turn, he sent a message to the queen asking her to go to the king and beg for mercy. Esther reminded him that death awaited her if she went to the king without being summoned. (Esther 4)

Mordecai reminded Esther not to think because she lived in the palace that would save her. Her reply was ordained by heaven. "Have the people fast for me, I will go," she responded. Her request didn't come from some survival instinct. She knew that there was only one fast the Lord has chosen. When Isaiah spoke of this fast it was not something new. (Isaiah 58:6) He wrote about a fast to break the bonds that bind us. A fast that is governed by giving unselfishly to others.

Esther knew that perhaps some issues still existed and they had to be laid down if she was to become abandoned. Esther needed freedom to be able surrender her life if need be.

Our miracle comes when we stop thinking about ourselves. When we are willing to let go off our rights and are willing to deny ourselves, we have reached the point of surrender. When God's work takes priority above our interests we have abandoned ourselves to God.

Esther was an unlikely warrior in God's army. However, God chose and divinely prepared and established her to fill the assigned place, He had ordained. He could only do His work through a surrendered vessel.

Just as He used Esther, He is able to use anyone that surrenders themselves to Him. She was a sleeper agent in the king's court. Patiently she waited until the appointed hour of her rising.

Are we agents of glory in waiting? There is a time and a purpose for our being placed where we are! When the hour of our rising comes, how submitted will we be? Sufficient to if necessary lay down our life for the glory of heavenly nation?

After three days Esther made her way to the King's Hall. She was ready to trade the anthem of the king for the anthem of God's throne. When the king noticed her he offered her his golden scepter. This symbolized she would not be killed for appearing before him without invitation.

Ahasuerus, noticed that something was wrong. "Then, the king asked, "What is bothering you queen Esther? What do you want to ask me? I will give you anything you ask for, even half my kingdom." (Esther 5:3) The king had planned another one of his parties that day for Haman. Quickly the king called for the Prime Minister so as all could learn what the Queen's request would be. As the wine began to flow the king asked her again what she wanted and he promised to give her anything to the half of his kingdom. (Esther 5:5-6) Perhaps she thought he was under the influence of the alcohol, in any event she told the king she would prepare another party for the following day where she would make her request.

Haman's blood lust for Mordecai boiled even more. His wife suggested that he have some of his friends build a hanging post, seventy five feet high, on which to dispose of Mordecai. (Esther 5:14) That night the king could not sleep. He ordered that the book of the Chronicles of the Kings be brought and read to him. The delivering hand of God was at work.

The passage that was read spoke about: "Bigthana and Teresh, the two King's Chamberlains, the keepers of the door, who sought to lay hands on King Ahasuerus. It was the time when Mordecai saved the king's life.

The king said: "What honour and dignity hath, been done to Mordecai for this? Then, said the king's servants that ministered unto him. There is nothing done for him." (Esther 6:2-3) (ERV) Obviously Mordecai never sought recognition for saving the king's life. What the Lord sees in secret He rewards openly. (Matthew 6:18) (LITV) Sometimes the things we think hold little significance, do not get past the LORD.

Esther risked her life to save the Jewish people. Esther took on a responsibility that few would have been willing to accept. Consider the emotions she felt as she chose to violate the order of the court. She knew that death awaited her if she entered the throne room without being summoned. I wonder did she think that all of her plans for her future might be shattered. I wonder how much fear gripped at her heart.

Think of our plans, our dreams, and our goals. Aspirations that we have thought about for years; things we want to do, places we want to see. Would we be willing to set them all aside for the glory of God? Some too quickly say yes, I'm willing whatever it costs. Are they really?

Let me pose a question to you! With the thought of a "Daesh," I.S.I.S., combat knife ready to decapitate us if we don't renounce our beliefs, would we respond just as quickly as Esther? Picture us, on our knees in an orange jumpsuit, waiting for the cold steel of that knife to sink deep into our jugular vein. The propaganda cameras are rolling! How will we die? Will we go kicking and screaming for all the world to see? Come on, place yourself in that situation, that's what Esther did! Will we be at peace because we are totally surrendered to the plans and purposes of God even if we don't understand why we have to die?

Haman showed up at the palace before the party began. He came to ask the king to hang Mordecai. The king asked his Prime Minister. "Haman, what should be done for a man the king wants to honor?" Haman thought to himself, 'Who is there that the king would want to honor more than me? I'm sure that the king is talking about honoring me.' (Esther 6:6) (ERV) Haman's reply came swiftly. "Do this for the man the king loves to honor. Have the servants bring a special robe the king himself has worn and a horse the king himself has ridden. Have the servants put the king's special mark on the horse's head. Let a leader put the robe on the man the king wants to honor. Then, let him lead him on the horse through the city streets. As he leads him, let him announce, 'This is done for the man the king wants to honor!'" (Esther 6:9) (ERV *Paraphrased*) Give a man enough rope and sooner than later he will hang himself.

"Go quickly," the king commanded Haman. "Get the robe and the horse and do just as you have suggested for Mordecai the Jew. He is sitting near the king's gate. Do everything that you suggested." (Esther 6:10 ERV)

There they went through the streets. Haman walking and Mordecai riding high upon the king's charger as humiliation drowned the villain. I can only imagine all that went through the mind of Haman. Right after he headed home to get some more poor advice from his wife and friends. While they were still taking together messengers from the palace came and summoned him to the court.

Esther's party entered its second day before Ahasuerus asked the queen what she wanted. "King, if you like me and it pleases you, please let me live. And I ask you to let my people live too. I ask this because my people and I have been sold, they are to be destroyed. They are to be killed and wiped from the face of the earth. If we had just been sold as slaves, I would have kept quiet, because that would not be enough of a problem to bother the king." (Esther 7:3-4 ERV *Paraphrased*)

Would Esther really have settled for second best? Would she have accepted slavery if death was taken off the table? Perhaps that was not her intent. It does, however, pose a thought. How often do we settle for less than God's best?

Then, King Ahasuerus asked Queen Esther, Who did this to you? Where is the man who dared to do such a thing to your people? Esther replied: "The man against us, our enemy, is this wicked Haman." (Esther 7: 5-6)

Haman was filled with terror before the king and queen. To say the least the king was steamed. Finally, something had drawn him away from his wine. He walked out and went into the botanical garden. Haman remained with the queen pleading for his life. He knew that Ahasuerus had already made up his mind to kill him. To top it all off, as the king re-entered the room he saw Haman falling on the couch where Esther had been laying. Finally, she was resting.

"Will you attack the queen even while I am in the house?" As soon as the king had said this, servants came in and killed Haman. (Esther 7:8) A servant, Harbonah said, "A hanging post 75 feet tall has been built near Haman's house. Haman had it made so that he could hang Mordecai on it. Mordecai is the man who helped you when he told others about the evil plans to kill you." The king said, "Hang Haman on that post!" (Esther 7:9 ERV *Paraphrased*)

Because of the actions of this young Jewish girl, an entire group of people's lives were spared. Esther's surrendered life is inspiring Thirty years after Esther's actions saved the Jewish people, Nehemiah rebuilt the walls of Jerusalem. This would never have happened without the intervention of Queen Esther. God always finds a way to accomplish His will. Looking at this situation through human eyes, it would appear that without Esther there would not have been a Jewish nation for the Messiah to come from. "Esther paved the way, unknown to her, for the coming Christ. Satan had tried to prevent His coming.

Throughout Scripture Satan has tried to stop the coming of the Lord. Every time his schemes, his plans ended in failure. Then, one day another tree was prepared. That tree was an old rugged cross. It was Satan's greatest mistake when, we by our sin, when his henchmen condemned Him to that tree. Out of death came life for you and me. It was the ultimate self-sacrificing act of love, in the history of humanity.

Surrendering to God means to be self-less to the work of God. There is no room for selfishness in the Kingdom of God. Surrendering to God means to place the utmost faith in His Ways, even though we cannot see the end from the beginning.

We were all created by God for a mission, but if we don't embrace our true mission, we'll embrace a "shadow mission," drifting toward the pursuit of things, paths, or goals that aren't really what God designed for us. When we miss God's mission, we miss God's best for our life. Still the choice is ours to make. What are we willing to surrender for the glory of God? Natural devotion, our spouses, or children, our hopes and dreams, our entire self-life, our reputation or life itself? They are ours to give. Esther risked it all and the effects of her story came down through the years to us and raises the curtain on the Canticle of Mary!

Canticle of Mary

When Mary was born, the golden age of Israel's history was long gone. King of David's family who had ruled in Jerusalem for well over five hundred years had no one on the throne. Centuries of upheaval resulted in the branches of the royal family being scattered into oblivion. As proud as the Jews were of their glorious past, they were looking for an even more glorious future. Every believing heart in Israel longed for the Messiah to come.

Mary had reached her early teen years! She was beautiful and caught the eyes of every eligible bachelor around. Her parents in accordance with custom began to plan for her marriage to a suitable young man. Then, marriages were arranged and the search was on!

If you had to arrange a marriage for your daughter, how would you go about it? What or who would you look for when your daughter's happiness is at stake? The thought of; would the person be able to keep her in the way she was accustomed too might come to mind. What is his belief structure? Does she like any of those around her? Do you like any of the available potential suitors? What would you need to know about the person's family? What's his employment situation? Is he stable and of good reputation within the community? What's his likes and dislikes? Is he tender and understanding? Is he a good fit? For the Jews his linage would top the list. A million questions ran through the hearts of Mary's parents.

Her folks chose, wisely. Their daughter was promised to a man who was a carpenter. Joseph was a gentle hardworking man, committed to the Lord. (Matthew

13:55) A tradesman with a fine family pedigree in the line of the patriarch Joseph. Soon the announcement was made in the synagogue that Joseph and Mary were officially engaged. Family and friends showered congratulations on the young couple, and preparations began for the wedding one year later. Engagements in the east are as legally binding as any marriage contract. They also require a divorce to dissolve the relationship should anything go wrong. The couple was in love and looked forward to their very special day!

Within a few months, however, circumstances would dramatically change for all concerned. God would break in on their lives with astonishing news. News that would alter their lives forever and shake their community, right to its foundations.

In Nazareth, Gabriel spoke to the very young Mary. She was still a child when she began to move in the realm of the supernatural. The absolute brilliance of the presence of the Lord surrounded her. Gabriel, the messenger's first words are startling: "Greetings, you who are highly favored! The Lord is with you." (Luke 1:28) The word translated "favored" means to receive grace. Later Gabriel will add, "Mary, you have found favor with God," or "you have become the recipient of God's grace." (Luke 1:30) She was saved!

Before we get too far into this love story let's understand. Mary was not chosen by God to bear His Son because of something inherent righteousness of her own. Gabriel made it crystal clear that Mary was chosen by God as an act of grace. God's grace upon her was not from some intrinsic goodness of her own. Mary later confirmed with her own testimony that she like every other human being, needed a Savior.

"And my spirit hath rejoiced in God my Savior." (Luke 1:47)

God chose her among all the other women on earth to give birth to Jesus. By the same token God chose you among all the women on earth to give birth to your child.

When Mary visited her cousin Elizabeth she sang a canticle that reinforces the fact that she was not chosen because of some righteousness of her own.

"I praise the Lord with all my heart. I am very happy because '<u>God is my Savior</u>.'

'<u>I am not important</u>,' but he has shown his care for me, '<u>his lowly servant</u>.' From now until the end of time, people will remember how much God blessed me.

Yes, the Powerful One has done great things for me. His name is very holy.

He always gives mercy to those who worship him.

He reached out his arm and showed his power. He scattered those who are proud and think great things about themselves.

He brought down rulers from their thrones and raised up the humble people.

He filled the hungry with good things, but he sent the rich away with nothing.

God has helped Israel - the people he chose to serve him. He did not forget his promise to give us his mercy.

He has done what he promised to our ancestors, to Abraham and his children forever." (Luke 1:47-55) (ERV) ('*Underline mine*')

Even Mary's response to the angel's greeting, demonstrated her humility and sense of unease. Luke writes, "Mary was greatly troubled," not at the angel's presence, but at the angel's words. (Luke 1:29) When the angel said, "You, Mary, are greatly favored with the grace of God," her response in essence was 'Why me? I have nothing good in me to offer God. Why would He choose me?' Troubled, I guess she was troubled. Wouldn't you be?

Gabriel senses Mary's surprise and concern and reassures her, "Do not be afraid, Mary." Then, he makes an incredible announcement:

"You will be with child and give birth to a son, and you are to give Him the name Jesus. He will be great and will be called the Son of the Most High. The Lord God will give him the throne of His father David, and he will reign over the house of Jacob forever; His kingdom will never end." (Luke 1:31-33)

The emphasis of Gabriel's message was on the child, not on Mary. Mary was the vessel chosen by God to bear His Son, and therefore she was greatly blessed. But far overshadowing Mary was the character of the child she would bear. This child would be all that the Old Testament prophets said He would be. He would reign as the greatest King Israel had ever known. Greater and mightier than even King David. David reigned for forty years and then died. In the last years of his reign one son after another rose in rebellion to claim the kingdom as his own. Mary's child will reign forever. His kingdom will never languish under the limitations of earthly kingdoms.

This promised son would be much more than a great man; He would be called the Son of God. In the Jewish mind, to say that a person was "the son" of someone meant that the person shared the same inherent nature as the one called Father.

Gabriel added a stunning promise: "For nothing is impossible with God." A literal translation of that sentence explains, "For no word from God will be empty of power." Gabriel was assuring Mary that God will do everything He promised to do. Everything spoken of in the prophets, in the love stories of Adam and Eve, Hosea and Gomer, Jacob and Rachel, Ruth and Boaz, and even in Esther would come to pass. Gabriel's theme was the same as it was when God spoke to Daniel and to Zechariah: God keeps His promises!

Can you imagine what thoughts must have gone through Mary's heart as she listened to Gabriel's announcement about the child she would conceive? The first question out of her mouth shows logic. "How shall this be, seeing I know not a man?" (Luke 1:34)

What other thoughts might have run through her mind? She was the kind of person who pondered things carefully. She took in all the facts and then thought deeply about the significance of those truths in her life. (Luke 2:19) Mary listened to the angel and wrestled with the consequences that would come into her life if she accepted God's call. The choice to accept was hers and hers alone!

She was willing to pay a high price in order to submit to God's purposes. The moment she said yes, life as she knew it was over. All the rest of the events in her life, her place in Scripture and her place in God's plan can be traced back to this one momentous decision to follow the Lord no matter what the cost. Obedience to God always costs dearly.

What thoughts would go through our mind if this had been us? How am I going to explain this to my man? What will he think? Would he even believe me? Let's consider that for a moment!

"Mom, Dad, I'm pregnant!" No matter how close we are to our parents, we're going to wonder how they will react or will they respond. It's, one thing if our parents think we're having sex, it's another thing if their customs and culture forbid us to have premarital sex. Such, is completely against their values and beliefs. In our day because of sin, some parents have pretty liberal values, but they're still shocked to think their teen had sex.

Mary's parents' personalities would also have played a part in how they reacted or responded. Some parents are easy to talk to or calmer in a crisis. Some are more emotional, more easily stressed out, more likely to get upset or angry, to yell or cry, or express themselves loudly. These react rather than respond.

Perhaps they wished to be supportive of their daughter who, is pregnant even if they wanted to become angry or upset at first. Some parents don't show how they feel at first. They may take time to absorb the news. Others react quickly and there's no mistaking how they feel. Others will listen and be sensitive to the teen's feelings. Some parents will spring into action, taking charge, telling her what to do. It's impossible to really know for sure how her parents responded. We are not told. Two things we can assume is that her statements must have shaken them down to the ground and because of their faith they responded.

A ton of emotions must have raced through their hearts. Naturally the thoughts for some would be, 'just you wait until I get my hands-on that Joseph.' 'No Dad! It wasn't Joseph!' That must have hit like an earthquake. 'What?' May have been their only response! The silence would have seemed deafening. 'Then, who Mary?' Her announcement must have floored them. 'The Holy

Ghost!' Go on try this with your dad and see his reaction. The silence of the Word regarding her parents' response speaks volumes.

What would be the reaction of the neighbors or the villagers? She still had to explain it to Joseph! Would he put the wedding plans on hold? How would Joseph handle the seemingly impossible news? How would she break the news to him?

A list of names appears in your local newspaper almost daily. Just below the names of those just born and those who passed away, there are other names of couples filing for divorce. Maybe our name has been on that list. Certainly we have had a family member or friend who has gone through the pain of a broken marriage.

It's pretty shocking to open the pages of Scripture and find one of the Bible's heroes contemplating divorce. When Joseph makes his first appearance in the biblical story, that's exactly what he is doing. His marriage to Mary had only been promised. The engagement period had already lasted a number of months, but now new information had come to light. News that crushed his heart and drove him into the extreme.

Guys, what would be the extreme for you? We love the girl. We have worked many long hours. Sacrificed and saved for the day when we would give her the wedding of her dreams. We have kept ourselves pure waiting for our wedding night. Suddenly the news comes that she is pregnant! Not only that, but she is blaming it all on God! At first he might have thought she was cracking some sick joke.

His relationship with Mary had been carried out in full view of her family and the close-knit community surrounding them. Mary at first seemed not to have been the person Joseph thought she was. One of the things that had attracted Joseph to Mary was her humble desire to live a transparent life before God and the community. After one brief conversation, Joseph felt his perception of Mary was destroyed! He thought his life lay in shambles.

When Joseph wanted to know who the father was, Mary probably said that an angel of God had spoken to her and told her that she would conceive miraculously. Her son would be the promised Messiah, and God's Son. She said it so calmly, and with confidence. How could Joseph believe such a story? He left the garden without saying another word and went back to his home. In all likelihood he spent some time in shock as his tears cascaded to a cold uncaring ground. Divorce seemed to be his only solution.

Local opinion was harsh and most people told him to divorce her openly in a public condemnation before the religious leaders. That would bring shame and reproach upon his Mary. In those days an adulteress was stoned. Since she was not stoned we can see, the grace, the protection and the keeping power of God. His only other option was a private divorce. Two or three trusted friends would stand by as witnesses. Following the statutes laid down by Moses, Joseph would write out a bill of divorce and give it to Mary. (Deuteronomy 24) No reason for the divorce was needed other than her questionable character.

Joseph realized that he loved Mary more than any other person he had ever known. He couldn't pay back her apparent betrayal with more betrayal. Public humiliation was out of the question. He decided to divorce her privately and to do it quickly. (Matthew 1:19)

The townsfolk would find out only when people recognized that Joseph and Mary no longer sat together in the courtyard. They would also see Mary's figure change as the baby grew within her.

Once more grace was manifest. He would arrange it the very next day, and before the coming of the Sabbath. He would be forced to go on in life alone. If that had been the case he might have nursed the wounds of betrayal most of his life if not surrendered. Have we been there? Has our dream's been shattered by betrayal? Has our hopes, our dreams of a wonderful future crumbled into the dust beneath our feet?

His decision made, Joseph fell sleep and that likely brought on by exhaustion from stress. That night he began to dream. It was then God opened up to Joseph an option he had never considered. That's how God often works in our life. When we are at the end of our rope, the Lord opens the door of new possibilities. A door that requires absolute confidence in God alone!

The supernatural entered into Joseph's world of brokenness. Before he could complete the divorce an angel showed up. The angel told Joseph that Mary's story was true. She was carrying the Messiah. She had not been unfaithful to Joseph. The conception was a miraculous work of God as the Spirit overshadowed her. The child was God himself in human flesh. (John 1:14) If Joseph could only believe his ears the weight of the world would fall from his shoulders.

Matthew in his account of the story added further confirmation of the supernatural conception. Joseph was aware of the prophecies dealing with the coming Messiah. "All this took place to fulfill what the Lord had said through the prophet: A virgin will be with child and will give birth to a son, and they will call him Immanuel, which means, God with us." (Matthew 1:22-23)

Joseph demonstrated his righteous character by responding to the angel's message with immediate obedience. Wakened from sleep his life was back on track. All thoughts of divorce were gone. His tears of sadness turned into shouts of joy and happiness. Before long the wedding day came. I bet the entrance to the synagogue was filled with onlookers. Some delighted that a new day was bursting onto the pages of Israeli history. Others to look at the baby bump and perhaps ridicule. After the ceremony a new chapter in their lives began. What was their wedding night like? It was not like yours or mine!

No consummation of the marriage took place until after Jesus was born, but Mary's companionship was an immediate, satisfying reality in Joseph's life. (Matthew 1:25) Proof positive that real love has nothing to do with sex. Real love is about being one with your partner without the physical. The physical comes as an extension of commitment, friendship growing in to love, emotionally and spiritually. All through her nine months she faced doubting hearts, scowling faces and tongues as sharp as a razor.

When their special day came! Yes their special day! Too often we forget that Joseph was chosen from all the men in the world to be the baby's step-father. He was selected not because of some inherent works that he did. He had no special qualifications. The choice of Joseph was also a magnificent work of grace.

It was time for the midwife to come. Such was the case all through the pages of the Old Testament. For Mary, they were not summoned. God, the Father delivered His own Son into the home of two people whose hearts were fully His. The delivery room was a stable because there was no room for Love. Let's ask ourselves a question! What risk are we prepared to take to be fully obedient to the Lord?

The whole story of Jesus' birth is a story filled with trust! Mary and Joseph had to trust each other. They had to trust God and rest in His promises. Consider how vulnerable they both felt. All their lives they walked in difficult times. Despite it all, quietly and courageously, with the tenderness of a father, Joseph demonstrated his faith by risking everything to obey the Lord. When he walked down the street some may have laughed behind his back. They would have thought he had been taken in by Mary. Obviously Mary had been promised to the right man! He was God's choice and not the selection of Mary's parents. Both were willing to give up their reputations if that was what God asked of them. Are we?

Eventually the couple came together and they had other children. James, and Joses, Juda, and Simon were His brothers. (Mark 6:3) He also had sisters, exactly how many we don't know for certain. (Matthew 13:56) Growing up would also have been tough for the other children.

Kids in the community can be cruel at times. The raging comments about their illegitimate brother would have been all over. Such brutal attacks against the family would have come from the religious dead. The chorus of gossips from the time of Solomon remained faithful to their idle rubbish. Remember not all would have accepted the truth of the Master's birth. If God didn't have a firm grip on their emotions the roller coaster ride would have been horrendous. It would be thirty years before Mary and her family were vindicated. Joseph, tradition holds passed away before that vindication came. Obviously he didn't need it or he would have been there when it came down from glory. Perhaps the cause or timing of his death is not nearly as important as the strength of character he displayed. Jesus and Joseph were very close. So close in fact that the Lord, followed Joseph into the family carpentry business.

The days passed and the weeks, at length the years came and went. Then, came a marvelous day! In Jewish tradition when a child reached the age of thirty, the father claimed them publically and gave them a token of their inheritance. When Jesus was thirty years old He came to His cousin John to be baptized. While He was still a way off, John saw Him and said; "Behold the Lamb of God who takes away the sins of the world." (John 1:29 ERV) John knew of His supernatural birth! What happened next was vindication!

I bet that day there were many gathered to see if someone from Joseph's family would in accordance with tradition claim Jesus as the child of Joseph. When Jesus came out of the waters of baptism, the heavens opened! The trumpet of glory sounded. "This is my beloved Son, in whom I am well pleased." (Matthew 3:17) The Father Himself claimed Jesus as His son. Then, the Spirit in the form of a dove descended from heaven and settled upon Jesus. This has been called an earnest of His inheritance. It is the token of His inheritance that fulfilled the custom of His day.

After so many long years, of facing the abuse of the people! After suffering in silence, through day after day of religious dribble! Only after decades of standing faithfully obedient and devoted to the Father.

Vindication for the entire family came! (Matthew 3:17) How long are we willing to wait for vindication?

Jesus, He too would know marriage in time! Not some mere earthly marriage. It would be the wedding to end all weddings. One day His waiting bride, beautiful in every way, will go to Him. He will take His espoused, the church; the bride of Christ to present her before the Father. One day the processional down the halls of glory will commence. In his vision in Revelation 19:7-10, John saw and heard the heavenly multitudes praising God because the wedding feast of the Lamb, literally the "marriage supper," was about to begin. The concept of the marriage supper is better understood in light of the wedding customs in the time of Christ.

These wedding customs had three major parts. First, a marriage contract was signed by the parents of the bride and the bridegroom. The Bridegroom himself would pay a dowry to the bride or her parents. In our case, the dowry was the Messiah Himself. Jesus paid the full price for us when He went all the way to the cross.

This began what was called the betrothal period, what we would today call the engagement. This period was the one Joseph and Mary were in when she was found to be with child. (Matthew 1:18; Luke 2:5) Today you and I, His bride, are betrothed looking towards the day of His arrival.

The second step in the process usually occurred a year later, when the bridegroom, accompanied by his male friends, went to the house of the bride at midnight, creating a torchlight parade through the streets. Remember that we have been told to watch because He may come as a thief in the night. (1Timothy 5:2) The bride would know in advance this was going to take place, and so she would be ready with her maidens. This custom is based on the parable of the ten virgins. Five were wise and went with the bridegroom. Five were foolish. They never prepared for his coming and were shut out. The wise would then all join the parade and end up at the bridegroom's home. (Matthew 25:1-13) The exact moment of the arrival of the bridegroom was not known. He is coming, so that where He is there we may be also. (John 14:13) Exactly when He will come we have no idea, only the Father knows. (Matthew 25:13)

The third phase was the marriage supper itself, which might go on for days, is illustrated by the wedding at Cana in Galilee. (John 2:1-2) All the preparations are in place and very soon He will come! Are you ready? Let the Word bring this together for us.

John's vision in Revelation pictures, the great wedding feast of the Lamb, (*Jesus Christ*) and His bride (*the Church*) this is the third phase. (Revelation 19) The implication is that the first two phases have already taken place. The first phase was completed on earth when each individual believer placed his or her faith in Christ as Savior. The dowry paid to the bride's father God was the shed blood of Christ. The Church on earth today, then, is "betrothed" to Jesus and, like the wise virgins in the parable, all believers should be watching and waiting for the appearance of the Bridegroom. (*The Second Coming*)

The second phase symbolizes the Rapture of the Church, when Christ comes to claim His bride and take her to the Father's house. The marriage supper then follows as the third and final step unfolds.

Attending the wedding feast will be not only the Church as the bride of Christ, but others as well. The "others" include Old Testament saints who are going to be raised at the Second Coming, as well as the martyred dead of the Tribulation together with Jews saved during the Tribulation revival. As the angel told John to write, "Blessed are those who are invited to the marriage supper of the Lamb" (Revelation 19:9). The marriage supper is a glorious celebration for all who are in Christ! What will it be like when Jesus presents His bride to our Father God? What a tremendous joy will echo through all of eternity?

Then, the waiting of the bride and Groom will be over. Just as it came for Mary and Joseph it is coming for us! Have you ever wondered what it will be like? Come with me, let's journey together to that wonderful day. Let's soar across space and through time to that day when we just simply float away to the halls of glory. Before our departure let's take a look at yet another beautiful aria of devotion. An opus of love that will help prepare us for that day of our vanishing.

Opus of Love

When a relationship begins in song and dance many pronounce, it won't last! When a country girl marries a city boy some question the cultural exchange. So it was for the Shulamite in Solomon's Song of Songs. A young dark farm girl, was destined for the throne! Solomon thought that it was to be his throne!

Her journey to Jerusalem must have been filled with ever-changing emotions. She certainly brought out many insecurities in her story. She was in love with a shepherd, but on her way to the city, ordered there by the king. Her skin was dark, she was not black! The Hebrew word for the one who is naturally dark skinned, was not used. She was concerned by the fact that she was well tanned. (Song of Solomon 1:5)

She experienced feelings of self-doubt in spite of the fact that she was beautiful. (Song of Solomon 1:6) Perhaps she questioned if the king would accept her when she was in love with her shepherd boy and sporting well-tanned skin. (Song of Solomon 1) I wonder did they play the race ticket way back then, when a skin tone was slightly different to others. They certainly play it today, when it comes to marriage.

It's a long tiring journey to any wedding day. Solomon wanted to add her to his collection of other women. On the way I'm sure she considered the oneness she and her shepherd lover may never know.

Intimacy in any marriage is much different from plain old sex outside the marriage. Making love is not a neat clean or a surgically-precise process. It's not what we've seen or heard in movies. Movies that we shouldn't have been watching in the first place!

Often on the wedding night some question. 'What if I just run to the bathroom and hide wanting to stay there until I die of old age?' 'What if I trip on my high heels?' In marriage where the love of God is at the helm we are naked and unashamed. (Genesis 2:25)

On her journey I am sure that she thought about the forced ceremony, the guests, the music, the dancing and the food. Above all else she thought about the shepherd she left behind.

What do we do with the pain that comes with relationship? Most marriages bring with it relational pain. It walks hand in hand with intimacy. Afraid of that pain, yet desiring intimacy many go to the strip clubs or buy filthy magazines. They want false intimacy and avoid relational pain at all costs. In this, they cater to their own insanity. Porn movies, perverted practices have no place in the bedroom of the believer. Everything must be pure and sweet. We are told to keep the wedding bed undefiled. (Hebrews 13:4) Solomon had over 700 wives and concubines! He certainly fell into defilement and tarnished everyone he touched. How would it be possible for our princess bride to share herself with so many others? Solomon, he, wanted just another conquest.

There is much more for us to think about. The wedding night is only the beginning of something wonderful. It's not the end of a journey, but the beginning of a new one! Real marriage is not about sex it is about oneness, spiritually, emotionally and least of all physically.

Let's consider the spiritual aspect for a moment. The Word tells us that in marriage the two become one flesh. (Mark 10:8) They are no longer two, but oneness reigns. When we look at the spiritual aspect of marriage we are brought to this verse. "Therefore, I urge you, brethren, by the mercies of God, to present your bodies a living and holy sacrifice, acceptable to God, which is your spiritual service of worship." (Rom 12:1) The spiritual is connected to service and also to obedience and worship.

In the Old Testament all worship was service and service was worship. When we obey the Lord, we serve Him, when we serve Him, we are worshiping Him. Therefore, when we come together in intimacy in a godly marriage in accordance to the Word our oneness rises in obedience as worship. When we come to appreciate this truth we are able to see what the enemy is doing in our day.

For a moment let's accept the premise that a godly union is in some aspects worship, then let's turn our attention to ungodly worship. When a couple gets involved intimately outside a godly union, it remains worship. Worship to who? That needs to be the question. Those involved in just sex, in illicit relationships, whether living with another, or through extra marital relationship the worship is then of Satan. This is why our nations are filled with pedophiles, why incest and why sexual assaults takes place. The enemy is craving worship. Everything about him is in complete contrast to God and godly living. For these reasons we need clear thinking people around us. In the process of life's journey if we do not have a mentor and if that mentor is not Jesus we are in trouble.

Arriving in Jerusalem her adjustment from farm life to living in the palace must have been a challenge. Solomon introduced her to some friends who would help her make the adjustment. They were called the daughters of Jerusalem. (Song of Songs 1) I call them the chorus of gossips!

Once more we find that the Shulamite's story is a type of something yet to come. The shepherd boy typified the Lord whereas the Shulamite typified His bride, the church.

There are many commentators today who fall into overemphasis or neglect when it comes to understanding Scripture. Some allegorize almost every word in the 117 verses of this book. (*Allegorical Theory*) They do this in answer to others who claim that the book should not have been included in the Canon of Scripture. (*Officially accepted books of the Bible*) Both miss a beautiful balance available to us in a choral symphony of love! It is a practical guide for marriage, intimacy, allegorical of Christ and His church and steeped in the prophetic. In those days the church was a secret in the heart of the Father thereby making it prophetic in nature. This is called the typical interpretation.

As the king begin his attempted courtship he showered upon her gifts! (Song of Solomon 1:10) Hold on a minute! Gifts do not relationships make! He was filthy rich! He had a harem not only of wives, but concubines. Obviously he suffered from a sexual addiction! I'm sure at first he viewed the Shulamite as just another acquisition. He was a scoundrel! He had already used his kingly powers and coerced her to the city.

The book of Ecclesiastes lays bare his character! He had turned away from wisdom and became a drunk on his own power. He dismissed, good sense, understanding and foresight. He wanted to be tended hand and foot so his house was filled with servants. The

Shulamite girl from the farm would simply end up as another toy. He filled his world with materialism and it was this, he used to impress the girl. He was without any restraint. Everything he saw he wanted and did everything in his power to get it! (Ecclesiastes 2:3-10)

In no way was this Shulamite having anything to do with such a man. She remained faithful to her shepherd lover. She stood in absolute contrast to where Israel lay, in degradation and sin. The Word of God had been abandoned. Worship was nothing more than formal ritual. Their religion got all messed up with idolatry. Following Solomon's example the people were more interested in their creature comforts than in real values. The more Solomon came on to her the more her mind drifted away to the love of her life.

As Israel languished in the valley of idolatry, the Father, pleaded with her. Throughout the eons of time the Lord's love has called out to the apple of His eye. "Arouse yourself, my love, my beautiful one, and come away." (Song of Solomon 2:10 LITV) Like the concubines of the court, Israel turned a deaf ear to enjoy the pleasures of sin for a season. (Hebrews 11:25) Come away, come out from among them and touch not the unclean thing, He pleaded. (2 Corinthians 6:17) Only deaths dark silence, filled the air. The Shulamite bride pointed the way for them with her words. How she longed to be with her Shepherd lover.

"Let him kiss me with the kisses of his mouth: for thy love is better than wine." (Song of Solomon 1:2)

She compared his love to wine. A new wine that was far distant from the wine offered by Solomon. Having worked her entire life on her father's vineyard she knew a good vintage wine. That was not the king! Fondly she remembered the sweet odors of real love. When she spoke of ointment in the Song of Solomon 1:3, we are reminded of the words of Jeremiah. The prophet spoke of the balm of Gilead! (Jeremiah 8:22) He posed a question, "is there no balm in Gilead. Is there no physician there?" He was asking, is there no healing available? The true balm of Gilead is Jesus.

Only real love could sooth and heal that Shulamite heart. Only Jesus can heal the brokenhearted and bind up their wounds. (Psalm 147:3) Day after day she longed to be with her man, yet she remained captive, held firm by her circumstances. If only her lover would come to the palace she would run away with him. (Song of Solomon 1:4)

Continually the Father uses this love story to remind Israel to walk away from evil and be as the Shulamite, upright. (Psalm 18:25) Like this precious woman, the church, the bride of Christ, needs to radiate devotion to Him. To the people of Israel, Solomon was a type of Satan who tried to get her to walk in unfaithfulness. He is doing it again in our day as he tries to get us to abandon the written Word in favor of some new revelation.

"Love not the world, neither the things that are in the world. If any man love the world, the love of the Father is not in him. For all that is in this world, the lusts of the flesh, and the lusts of the eyes, and the pride of life, is not of the Father, but is of this world. And the world passeth away, and the lust thereof: but he that doeth the will of God abideth forever." (1John 2:15-17)

Those around her put her down because of her dark skin. (Song of Solomon 1:5-6) The chorus of voices never seems to change. These so-called daughters of Jerusalem were vicious. She however, stood her ground. She knew who she was, her worth and value to her shepherd lover. When we have a special relationship with the great Shepherd there will always be those who will try to demean us.

Sitting at the king's table just out of sight was a small sprig of myrrh. (Song of Solomon 1:13) It had been a gift from her far away lover. Myrrh was brought as a gift to the Christ child and depicted His suffering. Sitting at that table she suffered from a heart pining away. In daydream she was a million miles away from her abusive dinner companion. O, how she longed for her bridegroom. How she wanted to feel safe and secure again, nestled in his warm loving arms. Such will come the cry of the church in the end times. To be away from it all! To cast aside earths vain shadows! Soon we will look to the heavens in wonderful expectation! "As the dear pants for the water brooks so shall we long after Him." (Psalm 42:1) While the enemies of the cross in our day prays for the tribulation to come, we will long for the love of our life. Then, one day He will come in answer to the cries of the heart of His church.

Solomon, sly as a fox, tried flattery one more time. He was a smooth talker, be cautious of silver tongued devils. He said:

"Behold, thou art fair, my love; behold, thou art fair; thou hast doves' eyes. Behold, thou art fair, my beloved, yea, pleasant: also our bed is green."(Song of Solomon 1:15-16)

Dove's eyes are a symbol of purity and faithfulness. I choose to think when he looked at her the Holy Ghost was looking right back at him. A person's eyes are windows to the very soul. They reveal much about our character. When he looked at her he saw the character, the integrity and her faithfulness to the Great Shepherd.

Once more her thoughts carried her away from a twisted Solomon. Isn't it marvelous how we can just shut our eyes and the Lord, is right there to carry us away from temptation every time? Solomon, was not one to give up easily! It's too bad the same can't be said for his walk with the Lord. The Shulamite was giving no place to the devil! (Ephesians4:27)

Drifting deep within her heart, her thoughts uttered the prophetic. "He brought me to the banqueting house, and his banner over me was love." (Song of Solomon 2:4) Not only will we one day be seated as the bride at the great wedding feast, we will soon learn that He, Jesus is also the banquet!

The hour is coming when we His Church will go with Him to the place He has prepared for us. (John 14:1-3; 1 Thessalonians 4:13-18) The long awaited marriage of the Lamb will occur, and we will enjoy blessings untold as His Bride.

"And I heard as it were the voice of a great multitude, and as the voice of many waters, and as the voice of mighty thunderings saying, Alleluia: for the Lord God omnipotent reigneth. Let us be glad and rejoice and give honour to him: for the marriage of the Lamb is come, and his wife hath made herself ready. And to her was granted that she should be arrayed in fine linen, clean and white: for the fine linen is the righteousness of saints. And he saith unto me, Write, Blessed are they which are called unto the marriage supper of the Lamb." (Revelation 19:6-9)

Unlike Solomon, Jesus with His own dear hands, will prepare each place setting. He won't leave the task to some servant. Painstakingly He will place a name card at each place. Think of it, a chair has been set especially for you. No other can sit in your seat. Then, we will discover that He is the banquet! Upon Him will we feast! He is the table upon, which will be laid the choicest of fruits, the fruits of the Spirit. Is it any wonder she knew that His banner over us is love! That day is coming, a day in which He will say: "Rise up, my love, my fair one, and come away." (Song of Solomon 2:10)

At long last, the wait for our Shulamite girl was over and she heard from her man. Tears must have burst from her eyes as his words caressed the air. In poetic prose he bares his heart!

"Thou art all fair, my love; there is no spot in thee.

Come with me from Lebanon, my spouse, with me from Lebanon: look from the top of Amana, from the top of Shenir and Hermon, from the lions' dens, from the mountains of the leopards.

Thou hast ravished my heart, my sister, my spouse; thou hast ravished my heart with one of thine eyes, with one chain of thy neck.

How fair is thy love, my sister, my spouse! How much better is thy love than wine! And the smell of thine ointments than all spices!

Thy lips, O my spouse, drop as the honeycomb: honey and milk are under thy tongue; and the smell of thy garments is like the smell of Lebanon." (Song of Solomon 4:7-11)

The shepherd's words enticed her to leave Jerusalem and come back with him to the home they have planned in the country. He described the splendor of Lebanon, especially the majestic view from the top of Mount Shenir, and Mount Hermon. Tenderly he calls her to come away with him. Let's just run away together he pleaded.

The words of his song could only emanate from a heart filled with genuine unbridled love. They had been apart, yet their devotion for each other weathered the storm. True love does not waver even in the most difficult of times. Together we ride out the storms of life with our eyes fixed firmly on the lighthouse pointing the way to safe harbor. Who is that light, why Jesus the Light of the World. Though the road may seem rough He will bring our relationship safely through every storm. "Many waters cannot quench love neither can the floods drown it!" (Song of Solomon 8:7)

No sooner has our girl felt the heartbeat of love and Solomon shows up yet again. His words reveal a heart intoxicated by sensual carnal desire! Every time he showed his face his sexual addiction was manifested. (Song of Solomon 7:1-9) All he can see is her physical appearance! If she were to go to Solomon she would need a writing of divorcement from her shepherd boy. In Just the culture of that early day, an engagement was as legal as the marriage. That was the story of Mary and Joseph. Such custom continues to this very day in Albania. The Shulamite was espoused to her shepherd. (Song of Solomon 4:8) She was having nothing to do with it or Solomon. Turn away, turn away quickly from that one who is trying to destroy, your marriage. Run from the one who would lead our soul into hell.

When we take such a stand others will question, accuse and doubt our fidelity. That is what happened to our heroine in Song of Solomon 8:10-12. Quickly she asserted her purity even in the face of the chorus of the so-called daughters of Jerusalem. Misery loves company and they also incited the villagers against her. She said that, despite Solomon's repeated attempts to seduce her she remained chaste. In short she said, my body is mine and it is only for the one I love.

At last the shepherd in front of all, proposes to her. What a day that must have been. Well, did she say yes?

"Make haste, my beloved, and be thou like to a roe or to a young hart upon the mountains of spices." (Song of Solomon 8:14)

Often I have wondered at the depths of words his heart conveyed that day. If he had only known the full impact that his words as a type would have across the centuries ever since. If he somehow could have considered the thousands of years that have passed as our Bridegroom still waits for us. The clock of grace ticks slowly by! 'My love, my precious bride why don't you come to me!'

Of course she said yes! Will we respond with similar love?

Did she return to Lebanon to be with him? Did they move to Jerusalem? We're not told. One thing for certain though is their relationship conquered every attack of carnality. We can be sure that no matter what came in life, they would remain together through it all. Will we remain faithful in our love relationship with Jesus, no matter what may come?

Of a surety a day will come when we shall leap as a roe or a young hart upon the mountains of His grace. (Song of Solomon 2:17) We shall live on those mountains with no more valley experiences. Can you hear Jesus as you read this book? "Will you marry me?" Well, did you say yes?

Quartet in Surrender

The book of Daniel has got to be one of the most fascinating books of the Old Testament. Its accuracy is beyond doubt, despite the fact that many have also challenged not only its contents, but the writer. The pundits of theological tripe never seem to end their ravings. The book is an accurate discourse to prepare the church in our day to be surrendered and ready for the glorious coming of our King. In its pages, Daniel, prophetically reaches into our day. He readies believers for the most gruesome of deaths in the end times. Into that valley of death, Jesus told us, some will walk in the last days.

It opens to the reader not only judgments that are to come upon unbelievers, also the devoted love of the Father. Daniel is verification that no matter what the circumstances in which we live, trust, peace, blessings and favor are available to all at the moment of our surrender. Let's jump into the pictures he paints!

When we go to church we go looking for a blessing. We search for someone to tell us something positive that things in our future are going to be a glory hallelujah ride. What if standing at that altar, we find out that its God's will that we spend our life in prison? What are we going to do?

Some may argue that we live in the day of grace and such things just don't happen. In the day of grace, Dietrich Bonhoeffer's message of true grace opposing cheap or hyper-grace, got him hanged by the neck until dead. Corrie ten Boom's messages of love, found her in a lice infested Nazi prison camp. Nora Lamb because of her faith, they placed in front of a firing squad. On the command to fire, the guns exploded and she fell to the ground unharmed. The Lord graciously spared her. Many others have paid the ultimate price. Certainly it happens in our day. Submission to such a thing would not come easy! What would we do? Would we hire the best attorneys that money could buy to get us out of prison? What if the sentence of the court was even worse? What then? Daniel immediately said, "Yes Lord, whatever your plans are I want what you want." Here was a call for a life, an entire life, to be abandoned to God.

He was just a lad of sixteen years when that call came to him. His whole life lay ahead of him. I am sure he had many dreams and aspirations. All had to be laid down as he was carried off to a life sentence. Where he would serve that sentence, he had no idea. His was a life interrupted by the destiny of God.

Daniel accepted God's requirement of seventy years in captivity. (Jeremiah 25:12) If he survived he would be eighty six years old before he saw the light of day again.

He wanted God not just in the good times, he wanted the perfect will of the Father at all times. (Romans 12:2) These are some of the reasons that these wonderful heroes are in the Bible and went through so much. They walked and lived in places where many fear and refuse to tread. O, how this message of surrender needs to be restored to the church.

Daniel the young prince was taken by Nebuchadnezzar to Babylon. To serve his sentence the Lord had Nebuchadnezzar bring him to the palace together with others. Even in prison nothing is too good for God's people. Daniel was team player! Three others of his team in particular he referred to were Hananiah, Mishael, and Azariah. (Daniel 1:6)

The Hebrew children were given new names honoring the Babylonian idol-gods. This was not the first time in history, this occurred. Joseph like Daniel, a type of Jesus, had his name changed. Joseph, 'yo-sif-yaw,' Yaw is the name of God. Pharaoh however, changed his name to Zaphnathpaaneah. (Genesis 41:35) His new name meant one who reveals mysteries. Such a move shifted the attention from the gift giver to the gift itself.

The change of their four Christian names was to signify a connection with heathen worship. In the Hebrew, Daniel by interpretation is, "God is my;" Hananiah, "gift of the Lord;" Mishael, "who is what God is;" and Azariah, "whom Jehovah helps." Since these names had some reference to the one true God and portrayed some connection with His worship they had to go.

Bel, meaning lord or master referred to a group of pagan deities. This is who Nebuchadnezzar worshiped. The changed names had definitions linking them to his heathen divinities and worship of the Chaldeans.

Belteshazzar, the name given to Daniel, stood for, "prince of Bel;" Shadrach, "servant of sin" (*the moon god*); Meshach, "who is what Aku is" (*Aku being the Sumerian equivalent of sin, the name of the moon god*); and Abednego, "servant of Nebo."

Hananiah, Mishael and Azariah are names that must be restored to them as we read Scripture and refer to them in our daily lives. Over the centuries we have continued to call them by the pagan names given them. In that we have perpetrated a crime not only against them, but also against God. Their biblical names speak of how abandoned to God their lives would be. Names they carried since their naming ceremonies early in life, spoke prophetically of all they would become in life.

The ministry of Daniel started with determination and it ended in a rapturous vision of Jesus.

"But Daniel purposed in his heart that he would not defile himself with the portion of the king's meat nor with the wine that he drank: therefore he requested of the prince of the eunuchs that he might not defile himself." (Daniel 1:8)

Come what may, Daniel was not going to be defiled by the food or drink attributed to idol worship. The young hero was determined to go all the way with God. He could have experienced all the best that the palace had to offer. All of the gold, the marble, the great ornate pillars, and all the delicacies that graced the king's table were his. Yet, all paled in comparison to being submitted to the Lord. He knew full well that everything around him was tainted by paganism. He was not going to be contaminated. The importance of this move needs to be understood as in these end times, we too must be determined not to be tarnished.

It should not come as a surprise that the word 'Allah.' was not something that showed up with Muhammad or revealed in the Quran. It has been around for centuries before Muhammad in 570 B.C.

According to the Encyclopedia of Religion: "Allah" is a pre-Islamic name, corresponding to the Babylonian Bel.' - Encyclopedia of Religion, I: 117 Washington DC, Corpus Pub., 1979

If you have difficulty with the idea that Allah was an Arabian pagan deity in the times before Islam consider this.

"Allah is found in Arabic inscriptions prior to Islam."- Encyclopedia Britannica, I: 643

"The Arabs, before the time of Mohammed, accepted and worshiped, after a fashion, a supreme god called Allah." - Encyclopedia off Islam, I: 302, Leiden: E.J. Brill, 1913, Houtsma

"Allah was known to the pre-Islamic Arabs; he was one of the Meccan deities." - Encyclopedia off Islam, I: 406, ed. Gibb

The word Meccan sounds very like Wiccan, they are one and the same and both revere the moon god! Wicca is again rampant in our day.

"Ilah appears in pre-Islamic poetry. By frequency of usage, al-ilah was contracted to Allah, frequently attested to in pre-Islamic poetry." - Encyclopedia off Islam, III: 1093, 1971

"The name Allah goes back before Muhammad." - Encyclopedia of World Mythology and Legend, I: 41, Anthony Mercatante, New York, the Facts on File, 1983

In our day the worship of the pagan demon Allah is growing by leaps and bounds. Many seem to think that Allah is the God of the Old Testament. It is not, it is a demon to be avoided.

Along with Allah came a system of rituals touching food and drink. In Islam it remains the same today. Halal food is prepared by ritual where the one doing the slaughter calls upon the name of Allah. In essence, it is offered unto idols. The New Testament clearly tells us to refrain from foods offered in such a manner. (Acts 15:19-20) So the next time you visit the grocery store avoid that isle. It's not harmless, it has been offered to idols.

Daniel purposed in his heart not be defiled in such a way. The prophet was on the road by the way, of circumstance to a day when his surrender would be completed. As a result, God's grace was poured upon him. Nothing other than the grace of God could bring him into the favor with the chief of the eunuchs. (Daniel 1:9) The Lord also established a close bond between the two of them. The chief eunuch went along with Daniel's request for a trial period of eating food that was in accordance with his own belief structure. In doing so Ashpenaz took the risk of being beheaded. (Daniel 1:10) At the end of the ten-day trial the four lads appeared fairer, fatter than all others. (Daniel 1:15) Daniel came out of that time of preparation with a keen understanding of visions and dreams. He began to move in the supernatural!

One night Nebuchadnezzar went to bed. On his mind was his kingdom. That night God gave to the dictator a glimpse into the future. Dreams troubled him all night long and he couldn't sleep. (Daniel 2:1) Not knowing the interpretation of the dream he assembled his court.

"Then, the king commanded to call the magicians, and the astrologers, and the sorcerers, and the Chaldeans, for to shew the king his dreams. So, they came and stood before the king." (Daniel 2:2)

It was a parade of the demonic realm until Daniel entered. The wise men were psychics! Magicians those who cast spells, witches! Astrologers, those who used star charts, fortune-tellers! Sorcerers, those who communicated with the dead, necromancers. (Deuteronomy 18:11) Chaldeans, spiritualists, users of divination and numerology. Are we sure that this doesn't describe our day? Churches today are loaded with occultists plying their evil behind the scenes. Automatic or spirit writing, materialization of angel feathers, orbs of light, Backmasked worship, all hailed by the deceived as the presence of the Lord.

The soothsayers, asked the King to tell them the dream and they would give him the interpretation. (Daniel 2:4) Nebuchadnezzar was having nothing to do with it. His kingdom was loaded with people who would do anything including using religion to hold on to their positions. (Daniel 2:5-6) In every generation there have been the counterfeits to all that is truly spiritually discerned.

Their refusal tossed the king into a rage. He demanded that all the wise men and magicians be destroyed. (Daniel 2:12) The sentence of death also included Daniel and his three companions. When word came to Daniel his response to the news was amazing. He didn't react in panic! There was no fear in his voice as he spoke to Arioch the king's captain. A peace that passes all understanding filled his voice. (Philippians 4:7) Only surrender can bring such peace. There was no fighting to hold on to his life! No fasting from panic! He was resolved to go with God no matter what the cost. In fact, he told the king's guard to take a chill pill!

"He answered and said to Arioch the king's captain. "Why is the decree so hasty from the king? Then, Arioch made the thing known to Daniel." (Daniel 2:15)

Daniel demonstrated his trust in the Lord. After speaking with the King, he went back to his house. (Daniel 2:17) Despite the sentence of death that hung over his head he was at ease. He rode on the waves of circumstance, enjoyed the ride, with the sails of grace unfurled. He was so laid-back that after he convened a prayer meeting he fell fast asleep. (Daniel 2:18-19)

That night the supernatural that Daniel had been used to, sprang into action. In his sleep the Lord revealed to him not only the dream and interpretation he also saw into our day. It's possible that the Lord in that dream translated him through time and space to witness firsthand the events, in our future. The words in verse 22, are striking. He said God changes the times and seasons. When one is prophetically translated they are not just physically translated across space, but through the space-time continuum. An example of that is John on the Island of Patmos who was carried, into the future. (Revelation 1:10. Revelation 4:1) Ezekiel was moved when he measured the tribulation and millennial temples. (Ezekiel 40-48) Einstein's, Relativity and the Space-time Continuum agrees with Daniel. Not that God needed his confirmation, He expounded it long before Einstein.

With interpretation in heart he went to the King.

"Thou, O king, sawest, and behold a great image. This great image, whose brightness was excellent, stood before thee; and the form thereof was terrible.

This image's head was of fine gold, his breast and his arms of silver, his belly and his thighs of brass.

His legs of iron, his feet part of iron and part of clay.

Thou sawest until that a stone was cut out without hands, which smote the image upon his feet that were of iron and clay, and brake them to pieces.

Then, was the iron, the clay, the brass, the silver, and the gold, broken to pieces together, and became like the chaff of the summer threshing floors; and the wind carried them away that no place was found for them: and the stone that smote the image became a great mountain, and filled the whole earth.

This is the dream; and we will tell the interpretation thereof before the king." (Daniel 2:31-36)

The detail is astounding! In just a very few verses the course of the entire history of man is described from Babylon to Jesus, our day and right into eternity. Again, we see Daniel not as some lone wolf in ministry as are many today. In verse 36, he uses the words. "We will tell the interpretation." Evidently his three companions were present. Daniel at no time tried to claim credit for himself, rather he gave all the glory to God and mentioned his brothers.

"Thou, O king, art a king of kings: for the God of heaven hath given thee a kingdom, power, and strength, and glory.

And wheresoever the children of men dwell, the beasts of the field and the fowls of the heaven hath he given into thine hand, and hath made thee ruler over them all. Thou art this head of gold.

And after thee shall arise another kingdom inferior to thee, and another third kingdom of brass, which shall bear rule over all the earth.

And the fourth kingdom shall be strong as iron: forasmuch as iron breaketh in pieces and subdueth all things: and as iron that breaketh all these, shall it break in pieces and bruise.

And whereas thou sawest the feet and toes, part of potters clay, and part of iron, the kingdom shall be divided; but there shall be in it of the strength of the iron, forasmuch as thou sawest the iron mixed with miry clay.

And as the toes of the feet were part of iron, and part of clay, so the kingdom shall be partly strong, and partly broken.

And whereas thou sawest iron mixed with miry clay, they shall mingle themselves with the seed of men: but they shall not cleave one to another, even as iron is not mixed with clay.

And in the days of these kings shall the God of heaven set up a kingdom, which shall never be destroyed: and the kingdom shall not be left to other people, but it shall break in pieces and consume all these kingdoms, and it shall stand for ever.

Forasmuch as thou sawest that the stone was cut out of the mountain without hands, and that it brake in pieces the iron, the brass, the clay, the silver, and the gold; the great God hath made known to the king what shall come to pass hereafter: and the dream is certain, and the interpretation thereof sure." (Daniel 2: 37-45)

Daniel would again repeat this prophetic word to the son of Nebuchadnezzar, Belshazzar in chapter seven. There, the symbolism is somewhat different, the meaning however, remained the same. Belshazzar was the last ruling king of Babylon before their fall to the Medo-Persian Empire.

Each part of the great statue represented the empires of the world. The head of this image was of gold and it represented the Babylonian Empire, the first kingdom of his prophecy. The modern day countries that were involved in that kingdom were. Iraq, Egypt, Syria, Lebanon, Israel and parts of eastern Turkey.

The next kingdom destroyed Babylon. This second kingdom represented by the two arms of the image was made of silver. It was a dual empire, Medo-Persia. Countries involved with this kingdom were. Part of: Afghanistan, Arabia, Bulgaria, Greece, India, Pakistan, Russia, and Ukraine. The Persian Empire also took in all of: Armenia, Azerbaijan, Georgia, Iraq, Iran, Egypt, Israel, Jordan, Lebanon, and Pakistan.

Then, we have the belly of brass, the third kingdom, which happens to be the Greek Empire, Greece! The Bible calls it Grecia. (Dan. 8: 21, 10: 20) After Greece fell apart four rulers took the kingdom, divided it four ways, and ruled it (Dan. 2: 32, 39, and 7: 6: 8, 22). So Greece was divided into four kingdoms each having its own ruler. The Hellenization of most of the world happened under Alexander the Great. Countries owing allegiance to Greece were, Turkey, Palestine, Egypt, Persia, and the Punjab region of India.

Then, came the legs and toes of this image which represent the fourth kingdom. Here is where the enemy jumps into the picture to confuse those living in the last days. The word spoken by Daniel is just too accurate for some theologians to swallow. Many have claimed that this is not a representation of the Roman Empire. They say that because Rome never controlled parts of Asia it cannot be the kingdom referred to. This is incorrect according to Wikipedia who claims Roman involvement within Asia. Furthermore, today in the resurgent Roman Empire there are more than 176,000,000 practicing Catholics in Asia. The old empire consisted of Italy, Spain, Portugal, France, Belgium, Switzerland, Monaco, Syria, Egypt, Turkey and parts of Asia. To understand the Roman view of interpreting Daniel a little better we need to fast forward to the book of Revelation.

Those 10 toes in Daniel are the 10 horns, 10 kings, 10 kingdoms or 10 nations which will also have ten rulers. In the seventeenth chapter of the book of Revelation we see those 10 horns united into one kingdom under the Antichrist. The kings of the earth will give their kingdoms to the beast or Antichrist. (Revelation 16:10, 19:19) This unification will take place during the tribulation period.

Thirteen nations currently make up the European Union. They came out of the lands that were once the Roman Empire. A few more nations will rise and be added. However, during the tribulation period the Antichrist will cause them to drop off. They will not be a part of that kingdom, the empire of the Antichrist. Then, it will consist of only ten. When the Roman Empire is resurrected under a European banner, Scotland and Northern Ireland will have to succeed from the United Kingdom. Neither of those two countries were ever a part of Rome. In fact, in October 2014, Scotland held its first referendum on separating from the Union of Britain.

Let's make clear that the fourth beast of Daniel's dream, is not the Antichrist. That fourth beast in Daniel 7:23, is the same as the fourth kingdom of Nebuchadnezzar's dream, the Roman Empire. (Daniel 2:33, 40) The Antichrist will be its leader.

For argument sake let us recap. The first kingdom was Babylon. (Daniel 2:32, 38) The second was Medo-Persia. (Daniel 2: 32, 39) The third kingdom was Greece. (Daniel 2:32, 39) The fourth kingdom turns out to be the Roman Empire. (Daniel 2:40) Then, the ten toes of the image that represent 10 kingdoms with their 10 kings or rulers will rise in the end times. (Daniel 41-44)

In Daniel's second encounter with these kingdoms some details are slightly different. (Daniel 7) Here Daniel talks about four beasts which happens to be four kingdoms. Daniel also gives a great deal of additional information concerning the little horn, the Antichrist.

Bear with me just a little longer. We need a firm Scriptural base for what I am going to propose.

Put yourself in the Father's shoes for a moment. All through the years he pleaded with Israel to come home. Every time they turned their back on His love. Love is patient and so He has waited. Centuries have passed and still He waits. To Daniel, He outlined all that would come before the love of His life came home. Ages would pass, but in the end she will come home to wide open arms that await. When will Rachel come home again?

Out of the old Roman Empire in the latter days, a little horn will come forth. (Daniel 7:7-8, 21, 24-25) This is the Antichrist. He will come out of one of those 10 nations at the start of the tribulation period. He may already be in the world today! At least we know that his spirit is already here. (1 John 4:3) Daniel 9:27, tells us that there will rise on the world's scene a man of supernatural power who, Daniel reports, "shall destroy many in their prosperity." (Daniel 8:25) This man will come out of the European Union (*The resurrected Roman Empire*) and will offer help to resolve the Islamic/Israeli crisis now raging in Israel. So who is this guy? Why did Daniel tell us about him if we are not to recognize him when he takes to the world's stage? Can he be identified? What does the word say about his identity?

"Here is wisdom. Let him that hath understanding count the number of the beast: for it is the number of a man; and his number is Six hundred threescore and six." (Revelation 13:18)

The first clue in our pursuit is that he is a man, who carries the number 666. He is the son of perdition, meaning the son of Satan. The Bible, tells us to count the number for it is the number of a man. Latin, Greek, and

Hebrew have numerical values assigned to various letters in their alphabets. On the pope's tiara is the words, Vicarius Filii Dei. When we take a look at the numerical values of this title it comes to 666. That in itself is not proof beyond reasonable doubt that the Papacy is the beast. It does however, open the door for further investigation and presents us with a decision to make. (*See my book, "Final Warning," and discover the shocking identity of the Antichrist*)

The very moment Nebuchadnezzar heard of the greatness of the role Babylon would play in the history of humanity, his ego soared.

"Nebuchadnezzar the king made an image of gold, whose height was threescore cubits, (*90 feet*) and the breadth thereof six cubits: (n*ine feet*) he set it up in the plain of Dura, in the province of Babylon." (Daniel 3:1)

At the dedication of the idol, the herald commanded the people.

"That at what time ye hear the sound of the cornet, flute, harp, sackbut, psaltery, dulcimer, and all kinds of musick, ye fall down and worship the golden image that Nebuchadnezzar the king hath set up:

And whoso falleth not down and worshippeth shall the same hour be cast into the midst of a burning fiery furnace." (Daniel 3: 5-6)

Nothing could be any more barbaric. Even today believers in Syria, Pakistan and other places are being burned alive for their faith. The sins of the fathers have come down through the centuries to, "Daesh," I.S.I.S.

Hananiah, Mishael, and Azariah because of their love and surrendered lives would have no part of it. They were fully aware that a price would be required of them. Bravely, they committed themselves to the plans and purposes of God. When they refused to participate in this idolatrous worship Nebuchadnezzar flew into a rage. He ordered that the furnace be heated up hotter than normal.

Given one last chance to recant their faith, Hananiah, Mishael, and Azariah stood defiant in the face of Satan.

"If it be so, our God whom we serve is able to deliver us from the burning fiery furnace, and he will deliver us out of thine hand, O king.

But if not, be it known unto thee, O king that we will not serve thy gods, nor worship the golden image which thou hast set up." (Daniel 3:17-18)

Why did the three not feel it was necessary to defend themselves? Why do we do the complete opposite when faced with a fiery trial? Where did their faith in God's ability to save them come from? How could they so calmly accept the possibility of their own deaths? What was the source of their courage? All came from the fact that the plans and purposes of God were more important to them than life itself. Real love, agape love is a self-sacrificing love. The very nature of the Lord is seen in their words.

When they were tossed into the fire, their would-be executioners died in the process. (Daniel 3:22) The three lads were bound and flung like garbage into an incinerator. (Daniel 3:21) When the king went to look into the furnace he saw a miracle. The three men of God were walking in the flames. (Daniel 3:24) With them, was one like unto the Son of God! (Daniel 2:25) They had been cast in bound, yet they were free and walking. The only thing that was burned away was the bindings that kept them from walking in the fullness of God. Every last ounce of self was burned away in the fiery trial as they abandoned themselves to the Lord. That day all that remained of their self-life died in the furnace of God's blazing love. Their voices in a trio of surrender were about to be added to, by another.

Daniel himself faced a similar trial where he too stared death in the face. He was thrown into a den of lions. (Daniel 6:16) Always before being moved to the next level of ministry there is a time of preparation. Daniel's preparation came in the presence of the jaws of death. After spending a restful night, with the lions in their lair he emerged unscathed.

The years passed, kings came and went as the four continued in their quartet of surrender on a daily basis. At length Daniel's story soared to the heights of glory.

"I Daniel understood by books the number of the years, whereof the word of the LORD came to Jeremiah the prophet that he would accomplish seventy years in the desolation of Jerusalem.

And I set my face unto the Lord God, to seek by prayer and supplications, with fasting, and sackcloth, and ashes:" (Daniel 9:2b-3)

Daniel was a student of prophecy as we should be. He understood from scrolls that God had said Israel would be in captivity seventy years. When he realized that the hour of their deliverance had come he set his face to seek the Lord in fasting and prayer. (Daniel 9:3)

Daniel was praying for Israel, acknowledging the nation's sins against God and asking for God's mercy. As Daniel prayed, the angel Gabriel appeared to him and gave him a vision of Israel's future. (Daniel 9:23) A vision of the Messiah's coming the first time and His second advent. He also gave his readers somewhat of an idea of when these things would take place.

In verse 24, Gabriel says, "Seventy 'sevens' are decreed for your people and your holy city." Almost all commentators agree that the seventy "sevens" should be understood as seventy "weeks" of years, in other words, a period of 490 years. These verses provide a sort of "clock" that gives an idea of when the Messiah would come and some of the events that would accompany His appearance.

The prophecy goes on to divide the 490 years into three smaller units: one of 49 years, one of 434 years, and one seven years. The final "week" of seven years are further divided in half. Verse 25 says, "From the time the word goes out to restore and rebuild Jerusalem until the Anointed One, the ruler, comes, there will be seven 'sevens,' and sixty-two 'sevens.'" Seven "sevens" is 49 years, and sixty-two "sevens" is another 434 years:

49 years + 434 years = 483 years

Let's see if we can understand the purpose of the 70 weeks. Everything the LORD does, He has reason for us to discover.

The prophecy contains a statement concerning God's six-fold purpose in bringing these events to pass. Verse 24 says this purpose is: *1)* "to finish transgression," *2)* "to put an end to sin," *3)* "to atone for wickedness," *4)* "to bring in everlasting righteousness," *5)* "to seal up vision and prophecy," and *6)* "to anoint the most holy."

Notice that these results concern the total eradication of sin and the establishing of righteousness. The prophecy of the 70 weeks summarizes what happens before Jesus sets up His millennial kingdom. Of special note is the third in the list of results: "to atone for wickedness." Jesus accomplished the atonement for sin by His death on the cross. (Romans 3:25, Hebrews 2:17)

This therefore refers of the coming of the Lord and His work at Calvary.

Let's now jump into the fulfillment of the 70 Weeks. Gabriel said the prophetic clock would start at the time that a decree was issued to rebuild Jerusalem. From the date of that decree to the time of the Messiah would be 483 years. We know from history that the command to "restore and rebuild Jerusalem" was given by King Artaxerxes of Persia c., 445 B.C. (Nehemiah 2:1-8)

The first period of 49 years (*"seven sevens"*) covers the time that it took to rebuild Jerusalem, "with streets and a trench, but in times of trouble." (Daniel 9:25) This rebuilding is chronicled in the book of Nehemiah.

Using the Jewish custom of a 360-day year, 483 years after 445 B.C. places us at A.D. 30, which would coincide with Jesus' triumphal entry into Jerusalem. (Matthew 21:1-9) The prophecy in Daniel nine, specifies that after the completion of the 483 years, "the Anointed One will be cut off." (Verse 26) This was fulfilled when Jesus was crucified.

Daniel 9:26, continues with a prediction that, after the Messiah is killed, "The people of the ruler who will come will destroy the city and the sanctuary." This was fulfilled with the destruction of Jerusalem in A.D., 70 under the Roman ruler Titus. He was a type of another who will come at the end of time. The "ruler who will come" is a reference to the Antichrist, who, it seems, will have some connection with Rome, since it was the Romans who destroyed Jerusalem.

Now we step closer to glory as we look at the final week of the 70 weeks.

Of the 70 "sevens," 69 have been fulfilled in history. This leaves one more "seven" yet to be fulfilled. Most scholars believe that we are now living in that time. In the time when Israel begins to come home. Most will return to the Lord during the tribulation. The prophetic clock as it were has been paused they claim. Or has it? Are we now just approaching the final week? The final "seven" of Daniel is what we usually call the tribulation period. A time that stands at the very door.

Daniel's prophecy reveals some of the actions of the Antichrist, the "ruler who will come." Verse 27 says, "He will confirm a covenant with many for one 'seven.'" However, "in the middle of the 'seven,' . . . he will set up an abomination that causes desolation" in the temple. Jesus warned of this event in Matthew 24:15. After the Antichrist breaks the covenant with Israel, a time of "great tribulation" begins. (Matthew 24:21)

In recent days we have seen a type of this occur right before our eyes. Recently the Pope convened a Prayer Peace Summit with Israel and the Palestinian Authority. In attendance at that meeting was Syria and the Patriarch of Constantinople, Turkey. Where did that take place? The Vatican, of course! Immediately following this summit, the Pope stabbed Israel in the back! It was prophetic of the betrayal that the Antichrist will bring halfway through the tribulation. (Daniel 9:27)

The Pope recognized Palestine as a state. This announcement was a direct attempt to disenfranchise the Jewish people of their land. Meeting with Palestinian officials at the Vatican, church officials agreed, to formally recognize the "State of Palestine" as part of a deal concerning Catholic activities in the Palestinian-controlled areas. This outrageous step was a severe blow to Catholic-Jewish relations and it cannot go unanswered by Israel. Nor can it go unrequited by the

Bible believing church! Nor will it go unanswered by the LORD!

Daniel also predicts that the Antichrist will face judgment. He only rules "until the end that is decreed is poured out on him," (Daniel 9:27) God will only allow evil to go so far, and the judgment the Antichrist will face has already been planned out.

The prophecy of the 70 weeks is complex and amazingly detailed, and much has been penned about it throughout the centuries. Of course, there are various interpretations, but what I have presented is the premillennial view. One thing is certain: God has a time table, and He is keeping to His schedule. He knows the end from the beginning, (Isaiah 46:10) and we should always be looking for the triumphant return of our Lord. (Revelation 22:7) His return must be understood as imminent and not eventual.

When the number of completion came in Daniel's day, two teams were sent to Jerusalem to start the restoration project in Jerusalem. They were Zerubbabel and Ezra. Once more the Lord's symphony of love took to the world's stage. Sadly, Daniel died in Elam, in the city of the Hôzâyê1, and was buried in Shôshan the fortress. His grave site is known to this day.

This tells us that our hero, never made it out of captivity again. His feet never walked the streets of Jerusalem. He never saw the restoration of the city or heard the restored temple worship. Still, he was free. He knew a freedom greater than the sights, sounds and smells he would have experienced if he had walked the streets of his precious Jerusalem. He was free on the inside. Free to be a servant of the Lord in absolute surrender. Don't weep for him. Let's learn from his story of absolute surrender and like him, tread where many fear to tread.

Temple Worship

Ezra and Nehemiah walked hand in hand in ministry albeit in two different arenas. Ezra was concerned with the building of the temple and eventually Temple Worship. Nehemiah was concerned with the building of the city and walls of Jerusalem.

Right from the outset, we are reminded of the importance of ministries understanding the anointing that others walk in. In our day the Lord is restoring the five-fold ministry and some are struggling to find unity. Many others struggle in finding their identity within their office. Instead of turning to the Word for answers they turn to others in ministry. Some of those, don't understand that every office, must line with the qualifications laid down in the Word.

The five-fold gifts have the same goals to accomplish. The perfecting of the saints, for the work of the ministry, for the edifying of the saints. Until we all come in the unity of the faith, and of the knowledge of the Son of God, unto a perfect man, unto the measure of the stature of the fullness of Christ: (Ephesians 4:12-13)

Let's take a look at the five-fold and their anointing as they work for us. Perhaps we will garner a little better understanding of where the church today stands.

"And he gave some, apostles; and some, prophets; and some, evangelists; and some, pastors and teachers;" (Ephesians 4:11)

In the Bible the Apostle after seeing the resurrected Christ gave witness to His resurrection. (Acts 4:33) This was their only message. What did the so-called apostle tell us about at the last meeting we attended? Did they speak of gold dust, angel feathers or oil dipping from the hands? If so they have failed their office.

In the Bible the prophets were moved physically, emotional and spiritually, through time and space to see firsthand what was, coming. They spoke of God's calendar and of His timing. They explained how all lined up with what is in, the Bible. Today so-called prophets speak of new revelations that supersede the Word of God when the Canon of Scripture is closed. God is not giving any new revelations in our day. (Revelation 22:18) Our job is to vie for the faith that was once and for all time delivered to us. (Jude 3) If a self-claimed prophet does not speak only the words contained in Scripture they too have failed miserably.

The pastor he/she knows where the church stands in the present. Their job as a shepherd is to lovingly protect those in their church. Today they know that much error is flying around and that many in their churches have been snared by that error. These refuse to stand up and be counted. They refuse to confront that error head on. Why? It's difficult for a paid pastor to speak up when they know that offerings will drop as a result.

The teacher according to the Bible is to teach the whole counsel of the Word of God. Their job is not to expound anything not found in the Word. Today the church is full of hyper-grace teachers. There are also those who teach about manifestations nowhere found in the Bible. Even others teach Eschatology with a twist of the U.F.O. These say the Nephilim are returning in the end times in U.F.O.'s and the Antichrist will arrive in a spaceship. Don't laugh, hundreds of thousands of people in the church buy into this nonsense! Even more teach that healing comes by session and is not instantaneous as is the pattern in Scripture. Sozo teachings are proof positive that the temple and some teachers lies in ruins.

Evangelists their job is to go fishing. To bring in the lost. Over the past many years they have preached anything, but the cross. They have preached healing, deliverance, anything, but what they are supposed to announce. Few if any, ever tell people that surrender of all is what is needed to live a, life in freedom. They have adapted these other messages because church leaders are afraid that the truth of heaven or hell will diminish their numbers. Some self-styled Evangelists want the accolades of the pulpit more than truth.

Where does any of this bring about perfecting, edification or carry us into the unity of the faith? If the five-fold offices themselves are broken they cannot develop us in the knowledge of the Son of God. The fullness we will know cannot be the stature of the fullness of Christ. Rather, we will walk, where they walk, as they reproduce after their kind. Surrender is needed, but without the intervention of the Lord how is it possible in our time? Ah, but the Lord still has 7000 who have not bowed the knee to Baal. (Romans 11:4)

Every single surrender requires not just the priests, but those, like Nehemiah who understood the needed structures in life. This is important because in the last days, the laity will be used as never before. In these last days the Lord is restoring to the church the concept of abandonment. It's time for leadership to bring it back to the pulpits and forget the idea that their position is dependent upon how many attend their church.

The temple was the last thing to be destroyed when the nations of Israel and Judah fell into captivity. It is always the last holdout as a nation falls into apostasy. It is the last place to be rendered sterile during an individual's failure to relate to God. The temple is also the first place where God begins to set about the work of restoring that surrender. The book of Ezra, deals with restoring the temple, and gives us insight into all that is taking place in our hearts today. Notice the opening words of this book:

"In the first year of Cyrus king of Persia, that the word of the Lord by the mouth of Jeremiah might be accomplished, the Lord stirred up the spirit of Cyrus king of Persia so that he made a proclamation throughout all his kingdom and also put it in writing." (Ezra 1:1) (RSV)

Now look at 2 Chronicles 36:22:

"Now in the first year of Cyrus king of Persia, that the word of the Lord by the mouth of Jeremiah might be accomplished, the Lord stirred up the spirit of Cyrus king of Persia so that he made a proclamation throughout all his kingdom and also put it in writing:" (2 Chronicles 36:22) (RSV)

The same words exactly! The book of Ezra begins right where second Chronicles leaves off. It was the Chronicles of the Kings that Ahasuerus had read to him in the story of Esther. (*Anthem of a Throne*) Ezra became an intimate picture for us of the work of God, in the restoration of a heart that has fallen into sin. Restoration can be on an individual basis. It can be on a local church basis! It can be the work of God in a nation, bringing it back from secularism and materialism to true spiritual knowledge and the manifest presence of the King. Such transformations seem to follow a pattern of surrender laid out in the book of Ezra.

Ezra, the priest and scribe, was descended from Aaron the priest. Clearly outlined in his words is the need for the work of both the king and the priest in accomplishing restoration. The work of the king is to build or in this case, to rebuild. The work of the priest is to cleanse. The work of the Prophet is to declare truth experienced. Jesus is all three, Prophet, Priest and King. All aspects are essential in the work of assisting someone who has fallen into a sinful state to come to abandonment. Since He is the absolute Christ the abandonment must be absolute. Sadly this is missing in our day as the full counsel of the Word of God is what has been abandoned rather than lifestyles.

Restoration of a surrendered life involves rebuilding the control of the Spirit of God through obedience to the Kingship and Lordship of Jesus Christ. It involves the Lord as King ministering into our life. It means we have to recognize, God's right of ownership to our life, to direct us, to replace our plans with His, to change us, and to make both the major and minor decisions of our life. Restoration also means cleansing! The spirit and the soul are cleansed by our great High Priest who, when a human heart earnestly confesses sin, He washes away the guilt, tidies up the past, and restores us to a place of fellowship in His sight. There must be absolute oneness with the Master. (John 17:21)

There are those who today say we do not have to confess sin, that all is covered under grace. If that were the case then why are we told specifically to confess? (1 John 1:9) The church today is as broken as it was in the days of Ezra and Nehemiah.

Returning to the temple, returning from sin, is always the work of God's grace. In the first verse of Ezra, chapter one it says:

"The Lord stirred up the spirit of Cyrus king of Persia." (Ezra 1:1b)

And verse five says:

"Then, rose up the chief of the fathers of Judah and Benjamin, and the priests, and the Levites, with all them whose spirit God had raised, to go up to build the house of the LORD, which is in Jerusalem." (Ezra 1:5)

The Lord always takes the initiative. No one, after falling into a sin, can ever come back to Christ unless God brings him back. The true message of repentance has been watered down for the convenience of our generation. What we need is people who will seek the Lord with all our heart, pleading for His intervention.

Daniel set his face to seek the Lord. (Daniel 9:3) Restoration came by faith when the act or decision of man embraced the promises of God.

This is a decision that not all made! Many in Babylon, refused to return even when God opened the door. But, the Spirit of God stirred up the hearts of some and made them unsatisfied with where they lived. They had become so materialistic, so bound up by sins culture, wrapped in easy believism. They didn't understand that mere things will never satisfy the deep-seated cry of the human spirit. When some felt that deep crying need for freedom, God stirred them up to return and rebuild the things that make for spiritual strength. Is He calling us today to follow in their footsteps?

Under Zerubbabel the first return took place. This great kingly descendant led about fifty thousand people from Babylon back to Jerusalem. The account of that return is given to us in Ezra chapters one and two. When they came to Jerusalem, it was the seventh month of the year, just in time for the Feast of the Tabernacles. The

Feast of Tabernacles (*also called the Feast of in-gathering*) is the time when Israel dwell in booths to remind them of their wilderness wanderings. The feast also looks forward to the eventual re-gathering of Israel (*which started at birth of Israel in 1948*) from the vast worldwide dispersion. For Ezra it was a feast that was mingled with tears of sorrow and joy as the people saw the foundations of the temple being re-laid. It's coming again if we are willing! Remember, the household of God is "built upon the foundation of the apostles and prophets, Jesus Christ himself being the chief corner stone." (Ephesians 2:20)

The first thing they did was to lay the foundation of the temple. The work was met with mixed feelings, in chapter three, verses 11-13:

"And all the people shouted with a great shout, when they praised the Lord, because the foundation of the house of the Lord was laid. But many of the priests and Levites and heads of fathers' houses, old men who had seen the first house, wept with a loud voice when they saw the foundation of this house being laid, though many shouted aloud for joy; so that the people could not distinguish the sound of the joyful shout from the sound of the people's weeping, for the people shouted with a great shout, and the sound was heard afar." (Ezra 3:11b-13) (RSV)

Have we ever felt that way? Have we ever come back to God after a time of coldness and withdrawal? Imagine the church in the days ahead! We have been held captive by the power of sin. A great sense of joy will rise as the foundations of fellowship are rebuilt by the Spirit? There will come regret for the lost and wasted years and we will weep! That's exactly what was portrayed, by Ezra. Tears of joy mingled with tears of sorrow as the people saw the church foundation, the Apostles and Prophets, being re-laid. (Ephesians 2:20)

Next came the rebuilding the altar, on the original temple site in the midst of the ruins the sacrifices began. (Ezra 3) This is significant because the first act of a church that really desires to return from wandering in darkness, in the ways of the world, to real fellowship with God, is to build an altar. The sacrifice of Jesus must be the very first thing people need to see when they enter the church door. (Hebrews 10:12)

An altar is always the symbol of ownership. It's both an acknowledgment that God has sole right to His church and the symbol of our personal relationship to Him. Therefore, an altar almost invariably involves sacrifice, worship, and praise, the sacrifice of recognizing the truth. "You are not your own; you were bought with a price." (1 Corinthians 6:19-20) Our temple worship is then enjoying a restored relationship, when again the church is ministered to by the only one who can meet her needs.

The third factor in this return under Zerubbabel is the opposition that immediately developed. (Ezra 4-6) A force was at work in every heart, as world affairs immediately came up to oppose everything that God attempted to do. It remains the same in every age. People always rise up with hatred to oppose the work of the Spirit of God. The opposition first appeared as friendly solicitude. (Ezra 4:1-2) The enemy is sneaky! Watch out!

"Now when the adversaries of Judah and Benjamin heard that the children of the captivity builded the temple unto the LORD God of Israel;

Then, they came to Zerubbabel, and to the chief of the fathers, and said unto them, Let us build with you: for we seek your God, as ye do; and we do sacrifice unto him since the days of Esarhaddon king of Assur, which brought us up hither." (Ezra 4:1-2)

This was the birth of the Samaritans that we have read so much about in the New Testament. They had a form of godliness, but denied the real power and manifestation of God. (2Timothy 3:5)

"Let's help you? We would like to join with you in the project." They knew nothing of how God works in transformation. It must have been a hard thing to say no to them. Not all will be carriers of truth no matter how badly they desire to be used or how good they look on the outside. The only way they were able to say no, was with hearts that were willing to be obedient to the Word of God. (Ezra 4:3)

That no! May have seemed ill-mannered. It wasn't a mere arbitrary statement. God had commanded Israel not to engage with them in enterprises that concerned the faith. The Samaritans and others around them were filled with the things of the world. God rejects utterly the philosophy of the world in carrying out his work. His end time's transformation will have nothing of the world associated with His love. The Lord had also told them through Moses that when they entered the land they would have enemies to defeat. (Deuteronomy 7:1-6)

The offer of Samaritan friendship quickly turned ugly. (Ezra 4: 4-5) The builders encountered one attack after another, each growing in intensity and sophistication. The enemy can only attack through a door left open by the faults of a believer. These compromises were like a magnet for the work of the enemy. Satan uses things, earlier in our life, a seedbed, for his later program to steal, kill and destroy. The enemy works by infiltrating the church here a little and there a little, over the years. With each step he carries believers, one step at a time, further and further away from, "the whole counsel of God." Then too, some of his lies he designs for detection, so that other aspects of his plan go undetected. The more he infiltrates the church, the easier it becomes for believers to buy into another error. When discovered, it sometimes takes generations to remove the embedded wrong. Since fragments remain, they open the door for the later introduction of more error. Evils that are particularly tuned for our day to reach, and confuse people, at the point of their need.

What concessions were they that gave the enemy legal ground? Who were the cultures through whom the devil, spawned his attack? Since they were in captivity with the influence of other cultures around them they picked up many issues.

"When the LORD thy God shall bring thee into the land whither thou goest to possess it, and hath cast out many nations before thee, the Hittites, and the Girgashites and the Amorites, and the Canaanites, and the Perizzites, and the Hivites, and the Jebusites, seven nations greater and mightier than thou;

And when the LORD thy God shall deliver them before thee; thou shalt smite them, and utterly destroy them; thou shalt make no covenant with them, nor shew mercy unto them:

Neither shalt thou make marriages with them; thy daughter thou shalt not give unto his son, nor his daughter shalt thou take unto thy son.

For they will turn away thy son from following me that they may serve other gods: so will the anger of the LORD be kindled against you, and destroy thee suddenly.

But thus shall ye deal with them; ye shall destroy their altars, and break down their images, and cut down their groves, and burn their graven images with fire.

For thou art an holy people unto the LORD thy God: the LORD thy God hath chosen thee to be a special people unto himself, above all people that are upon the face of the earth." (Deuteronomy 7:1-6)

The Hittites! The Girgashites! The Amorites! The Canaanites! The Perizzites! The Hivites! The Jebusites! The Ammonites also influenced them! All these had a generational effect upon them because they disobeyed the Lord and did not eradicate them. Added to these was the influence of Egypt and everything that tracked with them. All that was and is Babylonian error licked at their heels. They were also told not to make marriages with them or give their children in marriage to them.

The Hittites were a fearful nation, they brought fear! (*Controlling church leaders and so-called prophets*) The Girgashites taught them compromise. (*Gold dust, orbs of light, angel feathers, new revelations not in the Word*) The Amorites were a people filled with pride. They were status seekers! (*See the manifestations I bring, see me*) The Canaanites were the parents of materialism. (*Prosperity preachers whose goal is to get and keep*) Along with the Perizzites came the depth of immorality. (*Same-sex marriage, ordination of practicing homosexuals and lesbians*) The Hivites were a people who were known to live a lie. They were the fathers of secular humanism. (*Secular humanism is rampant in our church today and the Church of the Way introduced spiritual humanism, where people are worshiped*) The Jebusites lived in Jerusalem who walked in the pain of condemnation and discouragement. (*Those who have never abandoned the pain and hurt at the cross, those who seek Sozo*) Then, came the influence from the Ammonites who taught them external worship. Everything for show without depth of commitment. Worship teams that are more interested in click tracks, head and foot signals, the next best thing in the music store rather than spending time in prayer. Backmasked worship to attract people. Finally, the Egyptian spirit contaminated them with the rest of the world's system. (*Worldly thinking*) If the people didn't rid the land of the first seven as instructed, a door was left open for the entrance of the other two.

Backmasking referred to is a recording technique in which a sound or message is recorded backwards onto a track that is meant to be played forward. Backmasking is a deliberate process, whereas a message found through phonetic reversal may be unintentional or intended by Satan. It is not just in secular rock songs that such things are found. They are employed in some Christian worship. What is happening to people the world over when they are soaking, listening to some music?

Many Christian worship songs today, contain subversive messages to the church. Subliminal messages in Christian worship are nothing new! Keith Green, a contemporary Christian music pianist, singer and songwriter, worshiper, and preacher, was one of the first to expose it. On July 28th, 1982, shortly after exposing these truths he died suddenly and mysteriously, in a small plane crash.

Since then, Wikipedia has carried the following article. "Backmasking was popularized by the Beatles, who used backward instrumentation on their 1966 album, "Revolver." Artists have since used Backmasking for artistic, comedic and satiric effect, on both analogue and digital recordings. The technique has also been used to censor words or phrases for "clean" releases of explicit songs.

Backmasking has been a controversial topic in the United States since the 1980s, when allegations from Christian groups of its use for satanic purposes were made against prominent rock musicians, leading to record-burning protests and proposed anti-Backmasking legislation by state and federal governments."

The very thing protested by worship leaders is now being used by them. Is it really taking place with worshipers today? Do any receive so-called worship songs through automatic or spirit writing? Where is it happening? Worship is the singularly most powerful quintessential of the church influencing the masses! Satan himself was a worshiper.

"The workmanship of your tambourines and of your flutes in you. In the day you were created, they were prepared.

You were the anointed cherub." (Ezekiel 28: 13b-14a LITV)

He knows what sort of worship, is acceptable to the Lord and how to manipulate it into becoming worship of him. He also knows how to get such songs, into the hearts of God's worship teams. He excels at reaching the masses through subliminal messaging. He is not above using spirit or automatic writing where the musician, songwriter, believes they are receiving from the Lord himself. Many wonderful worshipers, may have already been duped.

MercyMe put out a song entitled, "I Can Only Imagine," and reputable sources claim that sublimely all the way through are words. Words that I am reluctant to write, but for the purpose of knowing the truth of what is happening they need recording.

"Imagine that I'm the only God. We've made sure we'll verve with the error of Satan." (*The word, "verve," is archaic, meaning with "enthusiasm."*) It continues: "Wisdom of God the lonely one. Gnash-Damn thee, and only God. Damn the only God." (*The word, "gnash," means to grind the teeth.*) - YouTube – Stormy17

At first I completely abandoned this as total and complete, utter rubbish. Then, I felt led to listen to it both forwards and backwards. It was there! It was clearly heard on the recording I listened to!

How could this have come about? Something demonically supernatural had to have taken place in recording. Some of these groups, unknowingly have been the victims of the enemy. Some have spent hours, days, weeks or even months waiting before the Lord. They longed for something special to lead God's people, into His presence only to discover this. Still, it remains on the market as is today! One would think it would be changed especially since technology exists to remove it.

It is also heard in the Amy Grant recording of the same song. In Carmen's recording of, "Destination is there," the words, "Satan worship the mark … worship Satan," are clearly heard. The Resurrection Band's, "Between heaven and hell," is Backmasked, "Yeah Lucifer promised me more, live for a week, ooh evil I take the mark."

We have seen that Backmasking, has been intentionally created by others using technology. Hillsong in their recording of, "Evermore," intentionally use what they call, "Holy Backmasking." The very term makes me sick. In any event, it's covert manipulation, no matter what the message's contents are! There are many such Backmasked songs, in the churches today, these have been just a few. This is what they call temple worship today. It is far from the heart of godly worship. Jesus never manipulated anyone.

Can you see how the church, today, stands in the very same place as Israel? Do we stand in the need of a radical transformation? Do we need the Lord to dig about our foundations? Are we in need of the temple being rebuilt in our day? The answer is obviously a resounding, "YES!" That leaves us with only one more question in need of answer. Are we willing to have that transformation start in us? The answer requires more honesty, more transparency than we may have known in a long time. To put it simply! Are we ready to come clean? Without this step the enemies of the cross will stop the work of God before it gets a chance to complete! To be used in this last final rebuilding of the church we must become abandoned to the purposes of God. We have to be willing to accept whatever consequences may come and they will come if real worship is to be restored.

If we entangle ourselves with any of these enemies, if we permit our children to marry into a relationship dictated to by these spirits, trouble awaits. It will be a heartache second to none. Perhaps it is already too late for some who are reading this book! Only the Lord can bring deliverance! There is a way out, a way to freedom before disaster strikes. Hebrews 2:3, asks the question.

"How shall we escape, if we neglect so great salvation; which at the first began to be spoken by the Lord, and was confirmed unto us by them that heard him?"

In the days of Ezra the enemies of God were successful in stopping the work of rebuilding the temple. (Ezra 4) They deliberately attempted to frustrate the builders, by mocking them and taunting them, they discouraged Israel from doing work that God had commanded. I'm sure you can see how this same thing will come to us when we take that stand for the truth of the Word of God. Those closest to us will claim we are disrespecting church leadership. When we tell them we are standing for the truth of the Word, they will cast our name out from their numbers.

Israel's so-called friends used all legal means to undermine Israel's authority and right to build. When they do this to us, we will stand in good company. This is what goes on, every time someone wants to stand for truth in love. Get ready for their board meetings where excommunication will flow like a river. Paul told us why such things will take place.

"The desires of the flesh lust against the Spirit." (Galatians 5:17)

For Israel the work was stopped for sixteen years and the temple lay half-completed, overrun with weeds and grass. For how long will the building of our hearts lay dormant? Again, temple worship ceased. What a beautiful picture those thoughts bring. Every building that is neglected for some time gets overgrown with weeds. Jonah 2:5, says weeds were wrapped around his head. How very much like Israel that was. The contamination had choked out his ability to think clearly. It's the same contamination that keeps people in our day from thinking clearly and discovering what is happening at church. This is what happens because of the teachings of error. "The wicked spring up as the grass, and when all the workers of iniquity do flourish, they shall be destroyed forever." (Psalm 92:7) They were cast out of His sight; yet they/we will look again toward His holy temple." (Jonah 2:4)

The Lord sent two prophets, Haggai and Zechariah. These two men were God's instruments to move the people's hearts. The minute the people began to turn back to God, he also turned the hearts of the kings, Darius and Artaxerxes. They issued the decrees that started the temple work again. Finally, the work was finished. (Ezra 6) Revival is not an overnight happening. Rest assured in our day the work will be completed as we the real church become without spot or wrinkle. (Ephesians 5:27)

The first thing they did was to celebrate the Passover, marking the beginning of their life under God. Similarly, we cannot make sense out of revival not renewal, unless we are in fellowship with the living God. Without Him the church has nothing to celebrate. We have nothing to thank God for unless the church as a whole are enjoying the glory and the light of heaven when He enters our celebrations. I'm speaking about the glory cloud described in Scripture not what many today call a cloud of glitter. It is only when the church is in fellowship, with the temple builder that the Passover Lamb, Jesus, can bring us joy unspeakable and full of glory. (1 Peter 1:8)

Ezra was a most remarkable man, a priest of the line of Aaron. In chapter seven, verse six, we are told:

"This Ezra went up from Babylon; and he was a ready scribe in the Law of Moses, which the LORD God of Israel had given: and the king granted him all his requests, according to the hand of the LORD his God upon him."

He was a ready scribe, a writer! He was skilled in the word of God and as a communicator. The king, granted him all that he asked. Hudson Taylor once said: "God's work done God's way will never lack God's supply." When the tabernacle was being built, Moses went to the people and took up an offering. The response was so great he later had to tell the people to stop giving. (Exodus 36:5) Ezra was a man trusted of the Lord that even a heathen gentile king gave him everything he requested. In the last days as the church, when the people are rebuilt we too will experience this sort of thing.

There is coming a transference of wealth. Not wealth to build more big building or to grow bank accounts. The word says; the rewards of sinners are laid up for the just. (Proverbs 13:22) Unlike the treasurer, the thief Judas, the just will be good stewards of the funds. (John 12:6) Does your heart desire to walk in such depth of trust? Then, remember this prosperity is not for us. It is to be entirely dedicated to winning the lost. There is also a secret to it! The secret, was due the character of Ezra that the LORD was able to trust him.

"Ezra had prepared his heart to seek the law of the LORD, and to do it, and to teach in Israel statutes and judgments." (Ezra 7:10) (LTTV)

Not only are we to be students of the word, not hearers only, but doers of the word. (James 1:22) His heart was not for money, it was for the gold of heaven. In our day it will not be for building projects, Jesus never had a single building. Some here say, 'our job is to build a synagogue whereas Evangelists are the ones on the road without a building.' If this is true, why then is evangelism the bottom line on the church budget? 'But we need a building for those the Evangelist wins to come to.' If the Evangelist cannot go, all we will have is another empty church with empty pews. It's not structures that make a church, it's the Word of God that builds.

God sent Ezra to Jerusalem to strengthen and beautify the temple. That is the work of the word of God in His church. It strengthens and beautifies, it creates and brings forth because He is alive. (John 6:63) Ezra came to Jerusalem and found an incredible condition. The nightmare of their prior disobedience came home and bite them. In chapter nine verses one and two, Ezra writes:

"Now when these things were done, the princes came to me, saying, The people of Israel, and the priests, and the Levites, have not separated themselves from the people of the lands, doing according to their abominations, even of the Canaanites, the Hittites, the Perizzites, the Jebusites, the Ammonites, the Moabites, the Egyptians, and the Amorites.

For they have taken of their daughters for themselves, and for their sons: so that the holy seed have mingled themselves with the people of those lands: yea, the hand of the princes and rulers hath been chief in this trespass."

This was what had undermined the power of God among them. This is what has undermined the power of God in the church today. The people have been broken, the church is divided and the pews are empty. The people of God are polluted by relationships with those in the world. How is a physical structure going to change any of that?

"Wherefore come out from among them, and be ye separate, saith the Lord, and touch not the unclean thing; and I will receive you." (2 Corinthians 6:17) It's abundantly clear we still need to learn this lesson.

After seventy years in captivity, Israel had not learned a thing. After seven historic revivals, the church today has not learned a thing either. The lust of the flesh, the lust of the eyes and the pride of life has not changed. (1 John 2:16) No matter how long we have walked with the Lord, we will never get to the place where we cannot return to wallowing in the mire from where we came. (2 Peter 2:22) Are we not appalled? Listen to The Father's heartbreak in these words.

"For they have taken of their daughters for themselves, and for their sons: so that the holy seed have mingled themselves with the people of those lands.

When I heard this, I rent my garment and my mantle, and pulled hair from my head and beard, and sat appalled." (Ezra 9:2-3) (RSV)

What blatant disobedience! The actions of the parents brought an agonizing nightmare upon the children. They were trapped in relationships, knowing fear, compromise, discouragement, condemnation, materialism, pride, status seeking and devoid of all real love. Their painful solution came swiftly from the throne.

"Now therefore let us make a covenant with our God to put away all the wives, and such as are born of them, according to the counsel of my lord, and of those that tremble at the commandment of our God; and let it be done according to the law.

Arise; for this matter belongeth unto thee: we also will be with thee: be of good courage, and do it.

Then, arose Ezra, and made the chief priests, the Levites, and all Israel, to swear that they should do according to this word. And they swear!" (Ezra 10:3-5)

O, what agony we have brought upon our children? Is this another reason why our divorce courts are bursting at the seams? Lives shattered, devastated our children feel there was no other way out of prison. Our sin filled lives have condemned them to tears. Perhaps, some this day, have already made their beds in a Christ-less eternity because of the choices we have made.

Consider for a moment! When that precious little new baby came into our home. So sweet, so tender! All the baby needed was a full tummy, lots of loving and a dry diaper. He/she made the most wonderful sounds as they stretched and grew. Do we remember those very first steps? How pleased they were, life for them had taken a giant leap. Do we recall them getting on the school bus, for the very first time? We were so proud! We thought our chest would bust wide open! Then, came those horrible nights when we argued with our partners. Did our kids have to listen as punches were thrown or plates broken? Did they watch us fill our bloodstream with drugs? We said we couldn't weather the storms of life? What have we taught them?

Did they grab the first relationship just to escape from their home where they were to be safe? Did they watch as we were taken away by the police? Did they think the world had come to an end when our marriage ended up as just another number on some divorce roll? Did we teach them how to find an abortionist? Have they too, spent time in some prison cell? Will they end their lives alone and lonely with none to care? Were they tossed to and fro on a sea of tormented emotions as the enemy laughed? It is the rude awakening of the Garden of Eden, relived every day.

O, how our hearts should break over the things we have done. How we need to rend our hearts and not our garments. (Joel 2:13) Decisions must be made before life's agonies are exchanged for the torment of the fires of hell.

We too must come out from among such relationships and be separate and touch not the unclean thing. (2Corinthinans 6:17) The church must separate herself from every defilement. We must be removed from every sickness, all emptiness, every misery, from poverty and death by an act of total and complete surrender of all.

If we are separated from something, then we must be separated to something. Paul was separated unto the gospel. (Romans 1:1) He was brought into joy, gladness, happiness, health, wholeness, prosperity and everything that pertains to life and godliness. (2Peter 1:3)

Here lies the future of the church if we embrace all that Jesus has for us. Here is the beauty of the temple, living in the glory of His presence. Will we not turn around now? If not others will follow us and lie awake all night long, victims of the nightmare we have brought to them?

Right now they are running to one so-called prophet after another, seeking some word in their situation. If they could just experience a few specks of gold dust, see and orb of light or discover an angel feather they would be deceived into feeling a little better. Soon they will find a hyper-grace preacher who will tell them their sin has been covered by grace so they can go on living as they are. They are drowning in a world of darkness with no one to tell them the way of escape. (Hebrews 2:3)

Those who share with them the whole counsel of God have been rendered ineffective by the mega-churches who say they are the ones in error. They claim they themselves have superior insight into the things of God. That is Gnosticism! (*Esoteric knowledge*) It's believing that they are elevated to a higher level of comprehension which the uninitiated have no understanding. All false apostles, prophets or teachers resort to this argument. The very moment they use it, the true nature of their hearts they expose!

While all this goes on, precious souls are battered by a hurricane from hell. We claim to be the church, yet far too many are out there in the darkness are going down for the last time! It's high time we showed them a way out of the pit of sin and despair. It's time to hear the voice of our lover like a trumpet calling to us.

"Rise up, my love, my fair one, and come away." (Song of Solomon 2:10)

The Trumpet Shall Sound

The assignment given to Nehemiah was to build the walls and the gates of the temple.

Jesus often talked to people using parables as pictures of spiritual truth. The order of the gates of the temple, they also picture spiritual truth in a progressive way. Every one of the ten gates speak clearly of Jesus and the way out of the pit of sin. To understand this, we need go back again to the book of Genesis. Everything that the Lord would do or has ever done through the thousands of years is there contained.

"And God said, Let there be light: and there was light.

And God saw the light, that it was good: and God divided the light from the darkness." (Genesis 1:3-4)

The word light in Strong's Exhaustive Concordance, (*OT: 215*) renders the word, owr (*ore*); a primitive root; to be (*causative, make*) luminous (*literally and metaphorically*):

Light figuratively speaks of truth, life, salvation, freedom, prosperity, abundance, happiness joy and health. It means to make glad.

The word darkness in Strong's is: (*OT: 2822*) choshek (kho-shek'); from; (*OT: 2821*) the dark; hence (*literally*) darkness; figuratively, misery, destruction, death, ignorance, sorrow, wickedness, poverty and misery.

It represents sin, emptiness, ruin, sickness and death. Then, we come to where God divided the light, (*owr*) from the darkness. (*Choshek*) An understanding of these two words is vital to know that God has prepared a way out for those who have been taken by the enemy. There is a way out for everyone, yes, even for the church today. It is also important to know that when we are saved we are not only rescued from the jaws of hell, we are restored to what the Lord planned for us in the first place. Now let us take a look at the word salvation before we find Him in the gates of the temple.

"For whosoever shall call upon the name of the Lord shall be saved." (Romans 10:13)

Once more the Greek word in Strong's is: (*NT: 4982*) Sozo (*sode-zo*); from a primary "sos" (*contraction for obsolete saoz, "safe"*); to save, i.e. deliver or protect (*literally or figuratively*): heal, preserve, save (*self*), do well, be (*make*) whole. In Mark 5:34 the very same word is used for the word whole, Sozo.

"And he said unto her, Daughter, thy faith hath made thee whole; go in peace, and be whole of thy plague."

To save, deliver, heal and protect, preserve, do well, be (*make*) whole. This woman with an issue of blood came for a physical healing and went home with everything. She received exceeding abundantly above all she could ask or think. (Ephesians 3:20)

In the beginning Adam sold out his dominion. He surrendered it to Satan. That day we not only lost our home in the garden we lost much more. This was not the loss of a religion, we lost a kingdom. We lost all that is the light and we took upon ourselves all that is referred to in the word choshek. (*Darkness*) God's purpose right from the beginning was to restore to us all that is contained in the Hebrew word, owr. All that is included in the Greek word, Sozo.

Every passage of the Old Testament is a revelation of how and through whom that restoration would come. Remember it's not a building the Lord is out to restore. Act 7:48, tells us, He does not dwell in temples made with hands. His goal was to restore us to the seat of government, when we would again be able to rule and reign as kings in the Kingdom. (Revelation 5:10) Let's identify the Messiah from the Old Testament and then see His connection to the first gate of the temple.

Psalms 18:2, refers to the Messiah as a horn of salvation. Luke does the very same thing in chapter one, verse 69. The word salvation is the Hebrew word: yesha' yêsha', yeh-shah, yay-hah!

It means deliverance, prosperity, safety and salvation. More importantly the word is the name, Jesus! In second Samuel 22:51, He is referred to as a tower of salvation.

"He is the tower of salvation for his king: and sheweth mercy to his anointed, unto David, and to his seed for evermore."

Yet again the name of Jesus is used for the word salvation. Strong's: (*OT: 3444*) yeshuw` ah (*yesh-oo-aw*); feminine passive participle of OT: 3467; something saved, i.e. (*abstractly*) deliverance; hence, aid, victory, prosperity:

Is it any wonder the song writer penned the words, no other name, but the name of Jesus. Yeshuwah! Yeshuwah is Jesus. Come with me as we move ever closer to the temple gates. Isaiah 59:17 and Ephesians 6:17 contain similarities.

"For he put on righteousness as a breastplate, and an helmet of salvation upon his head; and he put on the garments of vengeance for clothing, and was clad with zeal as a cloke." (Isaiah 59:17)

Yet again, the word for salvation is Strong's: (*OT: 3444*) yeshuw` ah (*yesh-oo-aw*). Next we find...

"And take the helmet of salvation, and the sword of the Spirit, which is the word of God:" (Ephesians 6:17)

Right from our early days in Sunday school we learned that having on the armor of God was to be in Jesus! He is not something who is put on every day, like some article of clothing. We discovered that through Him our thinking is protected. If the Children of Israel had just run to the rock that is higher than I, their thinking would have been protected. (Psalm 61:2) They would not have got all messed up in wrong marriages. The same can be applied to the church today.

All through the Old Testament Jesus is revealed, still so many cannot see Him. 2 Samuel 22:36, calls Him by name in speaking about the shield of our salvation. David in Psalm 62:1, declares that Jesus, (*yesh-oo-aw*) salvation will come from God. Isaiah 62:1, tells us the He will not rest until righteousness goes forth as brightness and the salvation, (*yesh-oo-aw*) as a lamp that burns. Psalm 116:13, says I will take the cup of salvation. (*Yesh-oo-aw, Jesus*) The reason the Jew cannot see Him, is that there are scales upon their eyes. That is not so with us. What was it Paul said about the cup?

"Ye cannot drink the cup of the Lord, and the cup of devils: ye cannot be partakers of the Lord's Table, and of the table of devils." (1Corinthians 10:21)

The people who returned to rebuild the temple drank from the cup of evil and paid the price for it. Nehemiah set about building the walls and the gates of the temple. What he was building was far more than just a physical structure. The story he was about to tell would be the epic of the ages. In so doing he used every willing vessel, whose heart was submitted.

"Then, Eliashib the high priest rose up with his brethren the priests, and they builded the sheep gate; they sanctified it, and set up the doors of it; even unto the tower of Meah they sanctified it, unto the tower of Hananeel." (Nehemiah 3:1)

The very first thought that comes to mind at the Sheep Gate is found in these words:

"Except the LORD build the house, they labour in vain that build it: except the LORD keep the city, the watchman waketh, but in vain." (Psalm 127:1)

Eliashib, (*His name means, God will restore*) the high priest rose up with his brethren the priests built the Sheep Gate; they consecrated it and hung its doors." (Nehemiah 3:1)

The Sheep Gate is where the sheep were brought into the city of Jerusalem to be taken to the temple to be sacrificed to the Lord in compliance with the law. This is the only gate of which it is recorded that it was "sanctified" that is, dedicated to God in a special way. We read about the Sheep Gate years later in John 5:2. At that same gate was the pool of Bethesda, which means the place of the outpouring. John spoke about a man who was healed there when angels were manifest. (John 5:2-9) The heart of the supernatural will always be found at the Sheep Gate. Salvation is a work of the supernatural.

The Old Testament tells us about the sacrificial system and as we move into the New Testament, we understand why God commanded that sheep and other animals were to be sacrificed to the Lord. When John the Baptist saw Jesus one day, he said, "Behold the Lamb of God takes away the sin of the world" (John 1:29). The Sheep Gate reminds us of Jesus the Lamb of God. Every sheep that came through that gate was a prophecy of the coming of our Savior. It was a declaration of the price He would have to pay to buy us back. A cost so dear, so staggering that would reinstate us to the Government of God. The

Old Testament saints looked forward to the coming of Jesus whereas we look back to when He came. Our meeting place is Calvary that is where everything comes together.

Inside the temple just through the Sheep Gate, there were sheep pens. The animals were kept there until they were summoned. It's almost reminiscent of sheep folds today. I wonder did the sheep near the temple know peace. Do they know peace in our churches today which are our sheepfolds? Were they all together in one or broken by petty manufactured theologies? The sheep had to be without spot or blemish because Jesus would be pure. Our theologies in like manner must be pure. As individuals we too are without spot or blemish in Him, yet I wonder is that really true today? We talk a great walk, but often walk little of the talk.

The work began at the Sheep Gate. The Lord was showing to the people that provision had been made for their sin. All that needs to be done is to accept that provision in Him. So who is the Sheep Gate?

"Then, said Jesus unto them again, verily, verily, I say unto you, I am the door of the sheep.

All that ever came before me are thieves and robbers: but the sheep did not hear them.

"I am the door: by me if any man enter in, he shall be saved, and shall go in and out, and find pasture." (John 10:7-9)

He was telling them, there was a way out of the pit that has been our life. The real sheep, His chosen will not hear the other voices out there. We will follow only His Word. An end to the fear and brokenness is within the grasp of humanity. The Sheep Gate, is where the journey begins for all. It's where man begins with God. It's where the church needs to get back to and follow Him all the way through the other gates.

The sons of Hassenaah built the Fish Gate; they laid its beams and hung its doors with its bolts and bars. (Nehemiah 3:3) The Fish Gate is where the fishermen came to Jerusalem to sell their fish. Since it was on the north side of Jerusalem, perhaps the fish were primarily brought from the Sea of Galilee.

As with all other gates, the Fish Gate has a spiritual application. What does the Fish gate remind us of spiritually? Well, once we become a Christian, we have an important task. When Jesus called His disciples, He said to them, "Follow Me, and I will make you fishers of men" (Matthew 4:19, Mark 1:17). Firstly, He makes us all He wants us to be and then He makes us fishers of men. The day we got saved we were on fire. At the Sheep Gate we fell deeply in love with our Jesus. There has never been anything more powerful than our first love. Now, in the power of that love, He calls us to the requirement of the Fish Gate.

When the Comforter came into our life, the Spirit's flame burned with passion in our hearts. Our eagerness remained vibrant and strong. Do we remember? Such intimacy can never be properly appreciated. Do we recall with passionate longing the hour, the moment that wonderful second, when Jesus came into our heart? Well did such moments, cause us to resound; "More love, more power, more of you in my life."

Do we remember those sleepless nights? Nights when, we were so consumed with our Lord's words and in prayer. In those days we lived the words of the Psalmist.

"O God, thou art my God; early will I seek thee: my soul thirsteth for thee, my flesh longeth for thee in a dry and thirsty land, where no water is;" (Psalm 63:1)

In those days, nothing kept us from His Word. It's His paper sunshine, His intimate love letter to us. (1 Corinthians 13) It was designed for no other, except His cherished bride. As we read His epistle of love, our hearts jumped and we trembled under His tender touch. When we sang to Him, a wonderful fragrance filled the air. Why, we were in love, hopelessly, madly in love with our Jesus. Out we went and with passion we told the world about His love.

What warmth the memories of those quiet times bring. We cuddled in His arms and somehow we just knew that, "we are our beloveds, and His desire is toward us." (Song of Solomon 7:10 *Paraphrased*)

Who could ever forget, when He whispered to us in those tender moments? There, we learned that this whole earth and eternity was all about us. During those special, gentle times, He shared with us the secrets of His heart. In that place, we were His secret confidant. It was in His arms that we discovered our purpose was to be a gift of love to those around us. He called us to the Fish Gate, to learn how to become fishers of men. Why telling others about the lover of our soul was such a joy. As a fisher of men, have we remained faithful or has some so-called manifestation seduced us away?

Jesus said after we got saved, after He remade us that was the first thing we were to do was reach the dying. He told us, He would show us, where to find lost souls, how to fish and how to use the net to catch them. (John 21:6) From the stories of Peter we learned that the fish would surrender themselves to self-death.

In recent years evangelists have had to go line fishing instead of using the net. Not many in some churches want to get involved in winning the lost. Evangelists therefore, could not toss out the net, the church, into a sea of lost humanity. All people wanted was the presence of some so-called manifestation. Evangelism became like a sports event. A few down on the field and fifty thousand watching from the stands. Thus, fishing only with a line, they are only able to catch one or two at a time.

Some today say that mass evangelism is a thing of the past. If that were so, how then will the masses be won? Evangelism is not a church ministry. It is out on the highways and byways that the message is to go forth. The thousands saved in the New Testament were not saved in the synagogue. Obviously the current methods have not worked and it is time to get back to the biblical pattern.

Jesus said that His mission was to seek and save the lost. (Luke 19:10) It never fails to amaze me how many people say it is not their ministry to reach the dying. It was the priority of the Lord. We are to be like Him therefore evangelism needs to be our primary focus. Sadly evangelism has been relegated to a very small line on the bottom of the church financial statement.

Ezekiel reminds us: "This is what the Lord GOD says: I have gathered many people together. Now I will throw my net over you. Then, those people will pull you in." (Ezekiel 32:3) (ERV)

Jeremiah also spoke about the fishermen in the end times. His words speak of the salvation of Israel. This will be during the tribulation period when the Lord gathers the nation. It's proof that the fishing will not stop this side of glory.

"Behold, I will send for many fishers, saith the LORD, and they shall fish them; and after will I send for many hunters, and they shall hunt them from every mountain, and from every hill, and out of the holes of the rocks." (Jeremiah 16:16)

The very first symbol of the church was a fish. The Greek word for fish (Ichthys or *Ichthus*), works nicely as an acrostic form I = Jesus, C = Christ, TH = God's, U = Son, S = Savior. Everything about the Fish Gate speaks of the Lord's desire to reach the lost. It is all about bringing happiness into the hearts of those who have hurt for so long.

"And the ransomed of the LORD shall return, and come to Zion with songs and everlasting joy upon their heads: they shall obtain joy and gladness, and sorrow and sighing shall flee away." (Isaiah 35:10)

Today many claim to be in renewal leading to revival. May I say that the term renewal, appears nowhere in Scripture in this context. Revival on the other hand does. Then, again if our supposed revival meetings does not lead us to the Fish Gate? If it does not move us into the winning of souls, then it is not revival at all. It's nothing more than entertainment held in some social club. In revival whole communities are turned upside down.

The Lord knew that we would not remain faithful to His call upon our life. He knew His church would fall asleep that the walls and the gates of the temple would be broken down.

Do you remember that terrible day! It was a day that changed our life forever. Something horrible came and without notice, it defiled our oneness with our lover. That fire that once burned brightly within our heart began to grow dim. We still took little walks, to be alone with Jesus. Then, it was different somehow, it seemed to mean a little less to us. Our study of the Word that too, dwindled and slowly, ebbed away like a receding tide until we were reading just one chapter per day. Soon we never studied the Word at all, we just ritualistically read it.

Do you remember how we hungered for His Word and meditated upon its every sentence? We held His hand so tightly not wanting to stray not even an inch. Soon we began to think it inappropriate to hold His hand in public, so we tucked our Bibles under our coat or in our purse.

Before long, we didn't want Him to whisper in our ears. Why, what would people think? We needed to concentrate on what people had to say to us. Their words became more important than His. Rapidly the beauty of creation was drowned in a rush of activity, as we raced here and there. The wonderful days of those forest walks tumbled, victim to our agenda.

As we journey onward we come to the Old Gate in Nehemiah 3:6. Let our hearts be open to the trumpet of love. It is a gate that offers us more of the solution for a broken temple.

"Moreover Jehoiada (*Jehovah-known*) the son of Paseah and Meshullam the son of Besodeiah repaired the Old Gate; they laid its beams and hung its doors, with its bolts and bars." (*Paraphrased*)

Nehemiah is the only book of the Bible where this gate is referred to by that name. (Nehemiah 3:6, 12:39) Perhaps this was one of the original gates of the city of Jerusalem back in King David's reign. On two occasions the Hebrew word translated "old" is contrasted with what is "new." (Leviticus. 26:10, Song of Solomon 7:13)

"And ye shall eat old store, and bring forth the old because of the new." (Leviticus 26:10)

"The mandrakes give a smell, and at our gates are all manner of pleasant fruits, new and old, which I have laid up for thee, O my beloved." (Song of Solomon 7:13)

We have learned that the temple lay in a shambles. The people were destroyed by the nations around them. They were backsliders! The church was dead. It was the same with the church just before the seven great historic awakenings. The word old in Leviticus is: 'yaw-Shane.' A primitive root; properly to be slack or languid that is, (*by implication*) sleep (*figuratively to die*); also to grow old, stale or inveterate: - old (*store*), remain long, (*make to*) sleep. (*Strong's*) Sure sounds like the children of Israel, then again, it describes the church of our day.

In the Song of Solomon the word new is: 'châdash khaw-dash.' A primitive root; to be new; causatively to rebuild: - renew, repair. (*Strong's*) This is what was needed, then and now.

So what does the Old Gate teach us? Look at Jeremiah 6:16.

"Thus, says the LORD: 'Stand in the ways and see, and ask for the old paths, where the good way is, and walk in it; Then, you will find rest for your souls."

We are living in a generation that is always looking for something new, *(Revelations)* however, Solomon said there is nothing new under the sun. (Ecclesiastes 1:9) In the world of politics there are many who want to set aside the constitutions of the nations, and develop a new world order. Looking to the new, will not do it for the church or the nation.

There are fundamental truths and principles in the word of God that apply to every generation. We need to again look to the Ancient of Days. (Daniel 7:9. 13, 22) If we do, God says "you will find rest for your souls." If we are going to have transformation capture our heart, we must remain faithful to the old ways of the Word of God applied to our day. The message of repentance must go forth without fear or concern of reprisal. Hyper-grace must be removed from the church along with its expositors if they refuse to repent. Jesus said the only way into the Kingdom was through the gate of repentance. (Matthew 3:2) To be able to preach that message with effectiveness it requires two giant leaps forward. Firstly, we need to be motivated by love to take a long hard look at our own hearts. Secondly, we need to embrace real humility.

Jeremiah 9:1, shows us the way to move from a broken church to one rebuilt. There the prophet, recognized his heart was hardened to the condition all around him. He lifted his voice:

"Oh that my head were waters, and mine eyes a fountain of tears that I might weep day and night for the slain of the daughter of my people!"

When we the church realize where we stand, in a similar need, we will be ready to move through the Valley Gate. When we realize that for far too long, tears from a broken and a contrite heart have been absent. (Psalm 51:17) When we understand that the rebuilding of the temple takes hard work, then, we will be able to embrace the valley of humility.

"Hanun (*means move to favor by petition*) and the inhabitants of Zanoah repaired the Valley Gate. They built it, hung its doors with its bolts and bars, and repaired a thousand cubits of the wall as far as the Refuse Gate." (Nehemiah 3:13)

There are valleys especially on the west, south, and east sides of Jerusalem. The Valley Gate points us to humility. As we go through that gate it takes us into the Valley. Jeremiah was a great prophet of God! He had a reputation in his day! Yet, he humbled himself in the sight of the Lord. He said he needed to be broken over the state of his nation. That's real humility!

If we are truthful with ourselves and the church, Jesus, will work to cast out the sin of pride, and lead the church back into a life of deep humility.

"God resists the proud, but gives grace to the humble. Therefore humble yourselves under the mighty hand of God that He may exalt you in due time." (1Peter 5b-6)

One of the character qualities that the church is to put on is "humbleness of mind." (Colossians 3:12) It is a quality that needs to be seen in and around us.

There's a story about a certain Scottish preacher, a student, who was attending, class at seminary. One of the local churches invited him to preach. He was one of the top students, and he thought the church was rather privileged to have him as their preacher. He expected that he would be the next Charles Spurgeon. Even though he was prepared on paper, he was not prepared in spirit. He became frightened. He forgot everything he knew. He fumbled through the message and the message fell flat. He knew God was not in his message that day. After the service a lady, came up to him and said, "If you had gone into the pulpit as you came out of the pulpit, you would have come out of the pulpit as you went into the pulpit." He had too much pride in his heart to be used of God. - Vernon McGee, Through the Bible pp.513-514

How do we find humility? Sometimes God will take us through the Valley Gate into a time of suffering so that we may be humbled before Him, and brought to the place we need to be before Him. Jeremiah went through much suffering in his life as did all the rest of the champions whose stories we have read.

It's here at the Valley Gate that all territorial spirits find their end. It's time to get away from a small mentality of doing our thing and step into the big picture of what God is doing. The pride of the Amorites must be eradicated from the church forever. Big buildings, great swelling meetings, great oratory presentations, best worship bands must fall silent in the light of His glory and grace. The church needs to become empty of self, and full of the Holy Spirit, and we will have humility.

No matter how much the Lord pleads with humanity, some will not be able to go beyond the next step, which is the Refuse Gate.

"Malchijah (*means appointed by the king*) the son of Rechab, leader of the district of Beth Haccerem, repaired the Refuse Gate; he built it and hung its doors with its bolts and bars." (Nehemiah 3:15a)

It is also called the Dung Gate. (Nehemiah 3:14) It was on the south side of Jerusalem leading to the Valley of Hinnom. That was where, the garbage of Jerusalem was carried to be burned. Years later Jesus compared hell to Gehennah, which was another term for the Valley of Hinnom. Garbage was constantly burning in that valley. Jesus said that place is, where their worm does not die, and the fire is not quenched. (Mark 9:44) It is a portrait of the gates of hell itself. A gate beyond, which lies agonies unimaginable!

What warning does the Refuse Gate offer us? There is a lot of garbage in our life and we need to get rid of it. There is much garbage that has contaminated the church in our time. If we refuse to permit the Lord to deal with it then one day, at an appointed hour, we too shall be cast into that lake of fire. For a second let's recap who they are! Only the dung, the refuse will go there. How un-politically correct is that truth. Dumped there will be the polluters of truth: (*The Girgashites*) those who teach people to compromise the Word, for something less and far from the pattern of Scripture. (*The Hittites*) with their controlling church leaders and so-called prophets. Those who teach that new revelations today supersedes the Word of God. (*The Amorites*) Filled with pride. All status seekers who are filled with pride. These shout come see the manifestations I bring, see me, me, and me. (*The Canaanites*) The parents of materialism. Preachers whose only goal is to get and keep for themselves. (*The Perizzites*) Those who keep the door open to deep immorality. Expositors of same-sex marriage. Those who ordain practicing homosexuals and lesbians and think they do God a service. (*The Hivites*) Teachers of humanism and those who have introduced spiritual humanism. Those who encourage people to worship man. (*The Jebusites*) Those who have never abandoned the pain and hurt at the cross, those who seek Sozo Ministry rather than abandonment. All those who teach people that freedom can only be found in one session after another will scream in agony if they refuse to repent. (*The Ammonites)* Teachers of external worship. Worship teams who are only interested in attracting people to their sound. All perpetrators of so-called Holy Backmasking to manipulate listeners will never know peace again. All these have added to or taken away from the sure word of prophecy. To them the Lord promises this:

"And if any man shall take away from the words of the book of this prophecy, God shall take away his part out of the book of life, and out of the holy city, and from the things which are written in this book." (Revelation 22:19)

In that day, all will cry out for a drop of water to cool their tongues. (Luke 16:24) None will be offered. It is not easy to write these words. I know in some quarters a price will have to be paid for writing them. Will I be delivered from those vicious tongues? I know not. This one thing I do know.

"If it be so, my God whom I serve is able to deliver me from them. Then, He will deliver me out of their hand. Still if He chooses in His wisdom not to, be it known I will not serve their gods, nor worship their gold dust, orbs of light, angel feathers, Backmasked worship, hyper-grace, Sozo error or a thousand other things that they have introduced to the church."

So let us come to the Refuse Gate and get the garbage of our life. Let's take it all to the cross so that it may be tossed into the valley of garbage and left there. In 2 Corinthians 7:1, we read,

"Therefore, having these promises, beloved, let us cleanse ourselves from all filthiness of the flesh and spirit, (*human spirit*) perfecting holiness in the fear of God."

Notice that we need to cleanse ourselves not only of the filthiness of the flesh, but also of the human spirit. We need to get rid of jealousy, hatred, lust, unforgiveness, and bitterness. This can only happen at that place of total surrender. Be warned the time is short. The clock of grace is running down as we race towards the end. Don't gamble any longer with our eternal destiny. It is not worth it! Consider what awaits.

The refuse shall be driven away. Away, away from all they hold dear. Away! Tumbling down, down, down into the caverns of a Christ-less eternity. Falling deeper, ever deeper, in agony and despair. Their screams will be heard echoing, bouncing from the walls of the caverns of hell. This is the message of the Dung Gate!

"Shallun the son of Col-Hozeh, leader of the district of Mizpah, repaired the Fountain Gate; he built it, covered it, hung its doors with its bolts and bars, and repaired the wall of the Pool of Shelah by the King's Garden, as far as the stairs that go down from the City of David." (Nehemiah 3:15)

This gate was at a very strategic location near the Pool of Siloam, the old City of David and the water tunnel built by King Hezekiah (2 Kings 20:20). The Gihon Spring that fed the water system was an important source of water in the city. Now we have come to the east side of Jerusalem.

Regardless of the fact that some listened to the message of the Dung Gate, others refused. These had created their own systems of belief. They spent days, weeks, months and even years coming up with dogma totally contrary to truth. Still some made their way back to the Fountain of Living Waters.

"For my people have committed two evils; they have forsaken me the fountain of living waters, and hewed them out cisterns, broken cisterns that can hold no water." (Jeremiah 2:3)

In John 9:7, we find Jesus speaking about this area. He had made some mud from his spit and told a blind man to go wash in the pool of Siloam. I bet if that happened in our day there would have been a church board meeting. Our politically correct world in many places has eliminated the Lord working like this. Today many churches would not even allow Jesus in the door.

He is too radical, too challenging and too confrontational. Men like Smith Wigglesworth were termed as being too blunt and were refused opportunity to preach. They called him a brutal Yorkshire plumber with the Master's plumb line. His messages made the people very uncomfortable. The same today is hailed as an Apostle of the faith.

The Fountain Gate also reminds us of the woman at the well with whom Jesus spoke. The Samaritans were mongrel Jews. They were the despised of His day. Here, Jesus demonstrated preaching that brings forth fruit that remains. He spoke just seven times. He didn't get into some long drawn out discourse. Even when the woman wanted to get him tied up in some theological debate He brought her back to truth. (John 4:22-24) This was the Fountain of Living Waters at work. (John 4:10, 13-14) He moved in the supernatural by a word of knowledge. (John 4:16-18) In the end He gave her revelation as to who He is. (John 4:25)

He could say in a few words what preachers today, take forty five minutes to say. Power is not in a multitude of words; rather it is in a single word delivered from the Throne Room. A minister of the Gospel is sent to turn people from darkness to light and from the power of Satan to God! (Acts 26:18) In the modern church there is something wrong. Preaching seems to be devoid of all real power. Ministers of the gospel have lost all ability to move God for man and man for God. To put it bluntly, preaching today seems to accomplish nothing. People turn more to the river dance than to the Spirit to be ignited.

With preaching aflame, hearers, whole congregations should be slain in the Spirit. This is what happens when the Fountain of Living Waters speaks through His servants. Others should cry out for mercy. Weeping and wailing should fill the house. Even others should know the laughter of healing. In real revival meetings where love is manifest, noise should come to such heights that the speakers are compelled to stop speaking. As the Lord drowns pride in love, He will preach His own messages, in a supernatural manner. On the other hand, when the Lord, grants man to come to the Fountain Gate then stand in His pulpit, the hearer will never thirst again.

Jesus is the one that can satisfy every thirsting soul. He can satisfy the deepest needs of our life. If we look at John 7:38, we see another reference of how God brings this to pass. Jesus said, "He who believes in me, as the Scripture has said, out of his belly will flow, rivers of living water." In the next verse John says that Jesus was referring to the Holy Spirit, who would become in us like a fountain or rivers of living water. He is a fountain of water that never runs dry!

Just think we His church, could see once more, His fountain of words poured out from the pulpits bringing wonderful, glorious things in our day. He also told us how to find the place of transformation. He said:

"For I will pour water upon him that is thirsty, and floods upon the dry ground: I will pour my spirit upon thy seed, and my blessing upon thine offspring:

And they shall spring up as among the grass, as willows by the water courses." (Isaiah 44:3-4)

As a church do we thirst? O, well should we sing: "As the deer pants for the water, so my soul longs after thee." In one mini revival the participants gathered every night for six months. The participants prayed and waited upon the Lord. Night after night they declared that He will pour water upon him that is thirsty. Nothing happened! They soon came to an end in their search. Suddenly a young man stood up in prayer and asked the Father, "is my hands clean, is my heart pure"? The very next morning revival was poured out. The people of that island sprang up from among the grass.

Do you remember how we learned that apostasy rendered the church abandoned and broken down? The grass and weeds grew all over. If the children of Israel, if we would get to the Fountain of Living Waters, we too will spring up from among the grass. Transformation always comes in response to heart purity when the timing lines up with heaven's calendar.

Then, one day soon, when the last trumpet sounds and we are gathered by the Lord. At that great wedding feast, at the consummation of the ages, He will speak, in no sweeter words that has ever be spoken.

"It is done. I am Alpha and Omega, the beginning and the end. I will give unto him that is athirst of the fountain of the water of life freely." (Revelation 21:6)

As we journey onward towards the Water Gate let the excitement of our heart continue to mount, reaching towards the ultimate climax. There is much more waiting for us with each new step along that way. As we go deeper and deeper until we come to that place where deep calls unto deep, press on into Him.

"Moreover the Nethinims (*Temple Servants*) who dwelt in Ophel made repairs as far as the place in front of the Water Gate toward the east, and on the projecting tower." (Nehemiah 4:36)

This was a gate that was near an important source of water for the city of Jerusalem. In fact, the Water Gate led from the old City of David to the Gihon Spring, located adjacent to the Kidron Valley. A point to note here, it does not say this gate was repaired. Perhaps it survived the Babylonian destruction. Since water is a symbol of the word of God we are reminded that the word of our God stands forever. (Isaiah 40:8) In fact, it says that the grass withers, the flower fades, but the word of God stands forever. In the New Testament it says, the word of the Lord endures forever. (1 Peter 1:25)

When Ezra assembled the people to read the word of God, he did so at the Water Gate. (Nehemiah 8:1)

All through the Bible we are told that the water, the word, cleanses. (Psalm 119:9, John 15:3) Sanctification comes through the word. (John 17:17) His word is a lamp unto our feel and a light unto our path. (Psalm 119:105) The word hidden in our heart keeps us from sin. (Psalm 119:16)

The psalmist in conversation with the Lord said. "My soul thirsts for the living God!" (Psalm 42:2) Job said he placed the word of God before his eating. (Job 23:12)

The psalmist also remembers the days when the people were happy. "My heart breaks as I remember the pleasant times in the past, when I walked with the crowds as I led them up to God's Temple. I remember the happy songs of praise as they celebrated the festival." (Psalm 42:4) I wonder does anyone today think back to the days when real Holy Ghost laughter and joy filled heaven and the churches as souls came home. (Luke

15:7) Look around us next Sunday at the empty seats and long for a return to those wonderful times.

Have we been waiting for the Lord to do something in our day? Are we tired of the same old services week after week? When we abandon, replace the precious word of the Lord with a watered down gospel, we miss out on so very much.

Are we thirsty today for a fresh drink of the word of God? Is our life like a parched field in a drought? Has there been a famine because there has been no real word preached? In these last days the final battle will be for the return of the full counsel of the Word of God to our churches. In the end the Word will win out over all these so-called new revelations in our day. His word stands forever. Remember those words we read a moment ago. I will pour water upon him that is thirsty and floods upon a dry ground. He promises to pour out His spirit upon us one more time. (Isaiah 44:3)

The psalmist also tells us, we will again be able to praise Him. He reports that in the spirit he is able to hear the roar of waters coming from deep within the earth. (Psalm 42:5-6) (ERV) That's you! That's the whole counsel of the Word pouring out of us one more time. We are the earth! We are treasures hidden in earthen vessels! (2 Corinthians 4:7, Luke 12:2) God, says through the psalmist in 42:7, "Your waves come one after another, crashing all around me." Glorious days could be just ahead as we come into personal revival! Let's not just stand there watching the waves. Jump in! Onward now, we must go, onward on our road to glory. Carrying the lessons of the Water Gate with us, we must race quickly to the Horse Gate.

"From above the horse gate repaired the priests, every one over against his house." (Nehemiah 3:28)

The Horse Gate was near the temple. That's why, the priests were involved. This gate is mentioned two other times in Scripture. (2 Chronicles 23:15, Jeremiah 31:40) Since it was also close to the King's Palace, this is where the King's horses came in and out of Jerusalem.

Everything about the Horse Gate is prophetic of the two comings of the Messiah. Horses were used in war. Here, the all-conquering hero will enter the city. The Jews were looking for the Messiah to come and liberate them from the hand of Rome. They sought for the deliverer however, they could not see that He first had to come as the faithful suffering servant. (Gospel of Mark) When Jesus entered the city on His way to Calvary, He entered riding on a donkey. (Matthew 21:2) The donkey is a symbol of peace. He came in peace. However, the horse was used in war. When Jesus comes again, the Bible says he will ride up on a white horse.

As the church moves towards the end, we need to embrace the peace symbolized in the donkey. At the same time, we must endure all that will come as the days or sorrows begins. We are told in 2 Timothy 2:3, "You therefore must endure hardship as a good soldier of Jesus Christ." If we are to walk triumphantly in these last days we have to take hold of all that belongs to us.

"And from the days of John the Baptist until now the kingdom of heaven suffereth violence, and the violent take it by force." (Matthew 11:12)

This means spiritual warfare. However, remember for kings in the Kingdom, spiritual warfare is different for us. We are to stand still and see the salvation of our God. (2 Chronicles 20:17) There is no need to fight as we imagine fighting. We have an army for that purpose, they are the angels. Every kingdom has an army. Your nation has an army. Who does the fighting for you in a time of war? It's certainly not the citizens unless they enlist. The word, "force," referred to in this verse is not force as you might have been taught. A better translation for the statement, "the violent take it by force," might be: "Men with minds made up take back the kingdom using their authority."

All around us we see people shouting at the enemy. They scream at him as though he were deaf. The kind of spiritual warfare we are to engage in is supernatural, filled with authority. It's an adventure in peace. When we engage the enemy it's not something to get excited about.

A king, always displays a certain deportment and manner of speech. A king, any king never has to raise their voice. The power of a king's voice is not in its volume, it is in the authority of the position. They simply know the authority of that position. They speak and things happen. In the last days as we come to understand the authority given to us as sons of God, wondrous things will take place. Let's move on through the Horse Gate!

When Jesus comes again, He will ride a white horse. Other horses will also ride that day. They will include a pale horse. The pale horse is the only one where the name of the rider is revealed. "Death and hell follows him." (Revelation 6:8)

This is the end! Then, the clock of grace will have stopped. There will be no more time to make a decision for Christ. Eternal damnation is permanent. It will then, be time to turn away from the lost and focus upon an eternity spent with our Bridegroom. It will then be our time! To this end we now journey to the East Gate.

There we read, "After them Zadok, (*Means righteous or just*) the son of Immer made repairs in front of his own house. After him Shemaiah, (*Means Yahweh has heard*) the son of Shechaniah, the keeper of the East Gate, made repairs." (Nehemiah 3:29)

The East Gate was near the Temple facing the Mount of Olives. It was the first gate opened each morning. Tradition says that Jesus entered the temple on Palm Sunday through this gate.

This is the next to the last gate. It also points us to the return of Jesus. If you were to go to Jerusalem today and look at the east side you will see the modern day East Gate. What is unusual about that gate, is that it is sealed up. That's, because they believe that the Messiah is going to come through the East Gate and no one else may use it. That is partly based on Zechariah 14:4, "And in that day His feet will stand on the Mount of Olives, Which faces Jerusalem on the east."

They believe that He will then enter into Jerusalem through the East Gate. Orthodox Jews are still looking for His first coming, but we know that He comes from the east at His second coming. Jesus said in Matthew 24:27; "For as the lightning comes from the east and flashes to the west, so also will the coming of the Son of Man be." Jesus is coming from the east according to that Scripture. When that happens something powerful will take place.

"At that time he will stand on the Mount of Olives, the hill east of Jerusalem. The Mount of Olives will split in half. Part of the mountain will move to the north, and part to the south. A deep valley will open up, from the east to the west." (Zachariah 14:4)

The mountain will split right in two. The Jerusalem News Wire in 2004 reported an earthquake struck Jerusalem cracking the Knesset, the Parliament. Active fault lines run throughout the State due to the active tectonic structure of the Dead Sea Rift that runs the full-length of Israel. Jerusalem is only 15 miles to the west of the rift. A crack could happen at any moment. Israeli seismologists suggest that this area is due for an earthquake at any time.

Unfortunately, the churches over the years have replaced the imminent return of Christ with the idea of His eventual return. This has left us without the benefit of understanding that He could come as a thief in the night.

Are we looking and longing for the return of Jesus Christ? Does our heart cry out to finally be one with our Bridegroom? Is that our heart's desire? The apostle John said, "Even so, come Lord Jesus." If we are not longing for Jesus to come there is something wrong. Have we truly come to Jesus, the Lamb of God? If so, let us move onward to the last and final gate. The Inspection Gate!

"After him Malchijah, one of the goldsmiths, made repairs as far as the house of the Nethinim and of the merchants, in front of the Miphkad Gate, and as far as the upper room at the corner." (Nehemiah 3:31)

Miphkad is actually a transliteration of the Hebrew word found only here. However, the same word is found in a different form in Ezekiel 43:21:

"Then, you shall also take the bull of the sin offering, and burn it in the appointed place (*miphqad*) of the temple, outside the sanctuary."

This gate and the Sheep Gate where the two closest gates to the Temple.

Some believe Miphkad means "review" or "registry." (*Others translate it as Yahweh id King*) When a stranger came to Jerusalem, he had to stop at this gate and be registered. Their names were written on a scroll or in a book. The Hebrew word has a military connotation and refers to the mustering of the troops for numbering and inspection. Tradition says that David met his returning troops at this gate and inspected them. The north side of Jerusalem was the most vulnerable to attack, so this was a logical place to locate the army.

Thus, after the last battle of life, when Jesus comes again, we must appear before the throne in judgment. On inspection day. 2 Corinthians 5:10 says:

"For we must all appear before the judgment seat of Christ; that every one may receive the things done in his body, according to that he hath done, whether it be good or bad."

Someday our life will come under review by the Lord Jesus. Are we ready for the greatest inspection of all? In that day I can imagine our accusers rising up one last time. They may point at us and say what about this or that. But then, our advocate, Jesus Christ will rise to His feet. "Yes Father," He will say, "but look my blood is upon that heart." Immediately we will pass from death to life.

In verse 32 of Nehemiah three it says:

"And between the upper room at the corner, as far as the Sheep Gate, the goldsmiths and the merchants made repairs."

We started at the Sheep Gate and now we end at the Sheep Gate. Doesn't that speak volumes? It seems to me the Sheep Gate was the most important gate of all. Even so, Jesus Christ, the Lamb of God, is the most important person of all. His importance is clearly specified in John 14:6:

"I am the way, the truth, and the life. No one comes to the Father except through me."

Jesus is the "Alpha and Omega, the beginning and the ending." (Revelation 1:8)

We are now coming to the end of our earthly sojourn. We are racing to the end of the story of our life. When the books in heaven are opened what will be read aloud? Everything not surrendered will be exposed to all. How will the church stand in that day?

The future of the church lies in our hands. Will we answer the call to rebuild the temple? Will we be involved in the restoration of the walls and the gates? The doctrines of Scripture are the very bricks and mortar, Jesus is He who holds it all together. Will we heed His' symphony of love that is calling forth the builders in our day? The Master is coming soon to build His eternal temple! Surely the trumpet shall sound, perhaps, even before the words of this book makes its way into the home of your loved ones. As we turn the last page of our life story before we go to heaven with Jesus, consider this one last thought.

"Look unto me, and be ye saved, all the ends of the earth: for I am God, and there is none else." (Isaiah 45:22)

Freedom, joy, happiness, all that is salvation, all that love is and how to find Him, is summed up in these few words. Look unto me! All we have to do is look. We don't have to have a college education to look. We need nothing of the world to look. We came into this world with two eyes. Whether sighted or blind in the natural we can still look.

Once I considered taking an 84 year old, blind lady, into the jungles of Guyana and into the heart of Africa on mission's trips. I questioned the Lord if I should and asked Him to confirm it for me. Instantly a still small voice called to me. "Yeh though she is blind she sees more than you."

Look, look away right now! Look quickly! The trumpet is about to sound! Anyone can look! We can look, our children, our husband or wife can look. It costs nothing to look unto Him. If we do we will be saved, says the prophet Isaiah.

Saved! There is that word again that precious name that is above every other name, yaw-shah. (Philippians 2:9) We can have everything that is contained in His name. Isaiah offered his invitation to all the ends of the earth. We are the earth he was speaking about. It is for all humanity, black, white, yellow brown, olive, race or gender makes no difference. It's an invitation that is full and free. An invitation that can only be accepted by grace through faith. We cannot work for it! It's ours just for the asking! (Ephesians 2:8-9)

"For I am God and there is none else." Acts 4:12, tells us the same thing. Salvation is found in no other than Jesus. Here is a revelation that stirs the very soul. He, Jesus is the King, He is Lord, and He is the only wise God. To Him, be glory and majesty, dominion and power, both now and ever. Amen. (Jude 1:25)

Oh glory! He is coming! The time is far spent. His hallelujah chorus is beginning to fill the air. Come let's go, the hour of our departure has come. Let's run to Him quickly. The bright resonance of the trumpet is calling us home.

Hallelujah Chorus

We are on our way! Our wedding day has come! The long wait is over! Jesus as promised came for His bride! The fanfares of glory have sounded. (1 Corinthians 15:52) Their echoes reverberated throughout eternity, space, time and into the hearts of men. The Mount of Olives split in two as He said it would. (Zachariah 14:4) Scientists had told us for years there had been in crack in the mountain, still many did not listen. The end has come and we are on our way to our wedding!

When we left earth we felt as light as a feather. Contrary to the laws of nature we drifted upwards. Every ascending eye was fixed upon our Bridegroom. The rafters of buildings couldn't hold us down. The concrete and steel of great soaring structures were powerless to prevent our departure. John the apostle also saw what we have just experienced.

"After this I looked, and, behold, a door was opened in heaven: and the first voice which I heard was as it were of a trumpet talking with me; which said, Come up hither, and I will shew thee things, which must be hereafter." (Revelation 4:1)

He only had a glimpse of glory, although, he did hear the command to come. Just like John we were empowered by the Spirit to take the journey. It was within our power to obey or disobey. God never asked us to do anything He had not empowered us to accomplish. In our last days on earth our bridal preparations intensified. With every passing day we took on more and more of His glory. Then, one day in response to the command to come, we simply stepped into eternity. Who will ever forget those wonderful words filled with unattainable beauty. "Rise up, my love, my fair one, and come away." (Song of Solomon 2:10)

Who is like unto Him? (Micah 7:18) He spoke to the darkness and called forth light. (Genesis 1:3) He commanded the mountains and the very peaks penetrated the heavens. He created rivers and commanded them to cut their way through the earth ordering them by His Word. (Genesis 1:7) Nothing was lacking to the glory of the living word of God back there on earth. He was in the beginning with God, (John 1:1) and called those things that were not as though they were. (Acts 4:17) Now He has called us home!

He is exalted in the earth. He is exalted on high. (Psalm 46:10) He was that beam in the Tabernacle, made of incorruptible wood, upon which all things hung. (Exodus 25:10) The keys of death, and hell, are fastened to His belt. (Revelation 1:18) The government that too, is upon His shoulders. His name is called Wonderful, the mighty God, and the Prince of Peace for you. (Isaiah 9:6) For the second time marvelous words of Him were spoken as we ascended to glory.

"Lift up your heads, O ye gates; and be ye lift up, ye everlasting doors; and the King of glory shall come in.

Who is this King of glory? The LORD strong and mighty, the LORD mighty in battle." (Psalm 24:7-8)

He is Jesus, our all-conquering King. The enemies of the cross, our enemies have been destroyed. What shivers went through us when we heard our Bridegroom announce. "The King of Glory is coming." Coming with His bride, coming not as a crucified King, but as the King of Glory. Jesus, His name, is like no other name. It is a name far above every name. (Philippians 2:9) It's the only name, to which everything and everyone now bows, in heaven, and earth, and under the earth. (Romans 14:11) He is Lord over all. He was, He is and is to come and to Him all must ascribe glory, honor and praise. (1Timothy 1:17) He is worthy of nothing less than our absolute praise.

Our Bridegroom is absolute! He rules in His unlimited Kingdom. He paid sins price. He bought us back and His place as our Bridegroom was assured. The Prince of Glory, laid aside all His Kingly robes and being moved with compassion, humbled Himself and entered into a union with the very nature of man. It's again as Savior, the Father seeks to honor Him as His Son. That great wedding feast is not just to honor His person. It is to honor His personality in a new and wonderful relationship with His family. To this wedding we have now come!

To all loyal subjects in any realm, a marriage in a royal family usually commands the attention of nations. In the United Kingdom, when Prince William and Kate Middleton were joined together, London's streets were lined with cheering subjects. Such an expression of celebration is commonplace in the land of my birth. To the cheering crowds of the redeemed Jesus now marches us through the Gates of Glory.

In the celebration described by Matthew, this wedding called for joy and jubilation from all His subjects. (Matthew 22) Here, is the revival of the ages! His union is with whom? Is it with angels? Far from it! It is with His Kingdom citizens, those who were created to rule with Him. It's a marriage with the very seed of Abraham.

What a day of rejoicing it was when Christ, became incarnate. Just think of how He stooped down to redeem humanity from the ruin of the fall. The angels still rejoice, yet they can never share in the joy of the coupling of the ages. Only with their eyes can they watch as the ceremony unfolds. It is the pinnacle of joy to the heart of everyone who has long awaited this day. "Such knowledge is too wonderful for me; it is high, I cannot attain unto it." (Psalm 139:6)

As we stand at the entrance of glory we recall with passion the hour, the moment that wonderful second, when Jesus came into our hearts? The gifts of the Spirit a symbol of our betrothal, were ours. Well did such moments, cause us to sing; "O the glory of His presence." How much more now that we are unbroken fellowship with Him forever?

Do we fondly remember nights alone with Him? Nights, so taken up with our Bridegroom's words and in prayer. In those days we breathed the words of the Psalmist.

"O God, thou art my God; early will I seek thee: my soul thirsteth for thee, my flesh longeth for thee in a dry and thirsty land, where no water is; "(Psalm 63:1)

Back on earth, nothing kept us from His Word. Now we are totally one with the Word. He is the Logos, the Living Word. (John 1:14) There is no more seeking, we are one with Him. It's an oneness that the mortal mind of man cannot express. The Bible was His intimate love letter to us. (1 Corinthians 13) It was designed for none other than His cherished bride. As we read His epistle of love our hearts jumped and we trembled under His tender touch. When we sang to Him, a wonderful fragrance filled the air. Why we are in love, so hopelessly head over heels in love with our Jesus.

What warmth the memories of those quiet times bring. We cuddled in His arms and somehow we just knew that we were our beloveds, and His desire was toward us. (Song of Solomon 7:10 *Paraphrased*) Soon, we, will have no more memory of our days on earth. They will be exchanged for the oneness of glory. Let's enjoy them one last time before we experience the pinnacle of love.

Who could ever forget, when He whispered to us in those warm moments? There, we learned that everything He ever did was done with us in mind. During those special gentle times, He shared with us the secrets of His heart. In that place, we were His secret confidant. It was there in His arms that we discovered our purpose, to be a gift of love to those around us. O, how He lives for us. Now we know what He meant when He said we are the apple of His eye? (Zechariah 2: 8) You and your time was all He longed for and now, He is with us forever! Everything He created was given to us as a gift of love.

On fire, when the storms of life blew without mercy, we rested safe and secure. He was there and nothing else mattered. He was our anchor in every tempest. We were firmly grounded upon the Rock of love! No circumstance was able to overwhelm us! We took hold of the sides of the boat and in His peace; together we rode out the squall. The cares of the world grew strangely dim in the light of His glory and grace. (Psalm 84:11) We were so in love with Jesus and nothing could ever quench our love for Him. Now all the storms are past, the days of trouble gone forever!

In glory we again take little walks together! O, how different those walks are! Still the lover of our souls, carries our hearts in His hand. It's the same grasp that holds the stars in the heavens. The same creative hand that fashioned every snowflake. Everything is wonderful and alive in our world of love as we admire His wonderful creations in heaven. What joys we now know watching the wolf lie down with the lamb? (Isaiah 11:6a)

By glorious streams we amble along. At times, He brings the little animals to the edge of the steam and we are amazed by the glory of their splendor. A fatted calf, a lion, a young goat! To sing His grace, it is a spectacle beyond compare.

He did the same for Adam when each creature was given their names. In heaven we now know more, not less than what we knew on earth. The perfumes of the halls of glory and the essence of the ramparts mingle as a congregation of fragrances from the Holy Ghost fills the air. With each step we take with Him, it seems as though, Jesus is giving us one bouquet after another.

"And the city had no need of the sun, neither of the moon, to shine in it: for the glory of God did lighten it, and the Lamb is the light thereof." (Revelation 21:23)

A strange quiet descends all across our heavenly view as we stand in awe in the brilliant light, exploding all around. The blues of the sky gave way to the purples and gold's of the shining Son. Wonderful shadows frolic from the walls of jasper. The foundations of New Jerusalem radiate the light of all manner of precious stones. The sapphire, the chalcedony, the beautiful emeralds all add their beauty to the dance of His glory. The sardonyx, sardius, cheysolite, beryl, topaz, chrsoprasus, jacinth and the amethyst radiate a blinding light. The gates of pearl and the streets of gold they too offer their radiance to a symphony of grandeur. (Revelation 21:17-21) It's alright, Jesus is right by our side, showing us the beauty of our great wedding hall. His grip of grace holds firmly, ever confident.

His devotion for us is unwavering. We rest in His promises! Inside, we know the delight in His heart as together, we explore the wonders of glory. Soon we will be summoned and the bridal song will sound. Why words, are not necessary. His love for us knows no limit, no bounds and no end. Captivated by our Lover's smile we want to walk on with Him forever.

Do any memories remain of the days when we viewed ourselves as insignificant? Now at long last a new confidence rises. No longer do we need to be reassured of His love. Soon He will take us to His throne and remind us that we are kings. On earth when we felt that things were hopeless, He met us in the darkness with the light of His love. Now there is no more darkness, earth's vain shadows have flown away. We will never again know, even a second of darkness, just the light of His glorious love.

On earth when we were sick, He restored our health. When we were weak, He strengthened us. When we were weary, He held us, close and we rested. When we felt burdened down, He gave us that wonderful garment of praise for the spirit of heaviness. (Isaiah 61:3) When we felt useless, the God of the whole universe, our lover, our Master, our Father, our King, lifted us by His grace and poured His power through us. Why, now, there is no more sickness or death. Every tear has been wiped away from our eyes. No more sorrow. No more crying. No more pain, all these former things have passed away. (Revelation 21:4)

Like an expectant Daddy, our Father God, waits with longing in His heart for us to enter the great banquet hall. Everything for that great wedding feast is ready. We will dine on the Bread of heaven and drink the Water of

Life freely. We will even get drunk on the new wine of the Holy Ghost. (Acts 2:13)

That great banquet table has been set before us in the very presence of our powerless enemies. It's a table filled with all the riches of heaven. (Psalm 23:5) Soon we will be ushered to our seat at that great table and seated in the promises of God. The table will be arrayed with the choicest of fruits. They are the fruits of the Spirit. Love, joy, peace, long suffering, gentleness, goodness, faith, meekness and temperance. (Galatians 5:22-23) What a wedding feast it is!

All is free! It is ours without money and without price (Isaiah.55: 1). All these wonderful things came at a price. So expensive was its cost that the very heart of Christ was drained to pay a debt He did not owe. A debt we could not pay and yet it's free and at long last we have come home.

The credentials of invitation have been fulfilled. Nothing we have ever done warranted such communion. All the works of man could not bring forth so much as one of the fruits that grace His table.

Again we are reminded of the very last words the Lord spoke to us. He said; He was going away to prepare a place for us. He said that if this was not so He would have told us. He also told us that He is going to come again and take us to that place He prepared for us. (John 14: 2-3)

The usual practice in a Jewish wedding was for the young man to return to his father's house and build a honeymoon room there. This is what is symbolized by the chuppah or canopy, which is characteristic of Jewish weddings. It is like a tent or tabernacle. He was not allowed to skimp on the work and had to get his father's approval before he could consider it ready for his bride. If asked the date of his wedding he would have to reply, "Only my father knows."

He did it! He kept His word! He came again and we are now entering that great hall. We are all dressed for the occasion! Wearing His robes of righteousness we move towards the door. (Job 29:14)

An invitation to a royal wedding is a rare honor to those who attend. Only the elite of society are asked to attend such functions. Going to that Celestial Wedding is the greatest day of our life, second only to the day we were redeemed.

Despite all of the love, all the preparations it is a heart breaking day. Not all said yes, to the invitation. Tears begin to flow from the hearts of those who chose a Christ-less eternity. The preparations for love's banquet were in place, still not all churches chose to be rebuilt during our final days of earth. Those days of personal revival were a great celebration on earth's side of eternity. Babylon the great, the mother of harlots, the parent of earth's abominations, the apostate church turned their backs. (Revelation.17:5) They had their chance and we now turn away looking towards the angels who are about to sound the fanfare of the bride.

Nothing we can ever do can ever rival the blood of Jesus Christ. We came! Came, in all our guilt! Came just as we were and experienced the mercy that Jesus freely offered. His mercy is the element of His love that eliminated us from having to face the consequences of our sin.

The fatted calf was slain. (Luke 15:30) The tables set with extravagant love. Invitations went out through the mouths of the Lord's fishermen. Those wonderful

Evangelists who remained faithful to their calling. Perhaps we are looking around for that precious soul who introduced you to Jesus.

Think of the honor His Majesty bestowed upon us. He did not leave the table preparations for the wedding to some servant. Lovingly and tenderly He himself set each place. (John 14:3) The plates, the napkins, the table decorations were precisely positioned. It is a table that seems to stretch into infinity. At each place there is a name card. On each card there is inscribed a different name. These are the names of the invited kings. I want to melt as I think of how much love the Lord put into getting my place ready. To top it all off, the Father had to give His approval. If you look along that long line of place settings, you will discover a place with your name on it. No one else can sit in that chair.

Soon we will be ushered into that Chuppah, the bridal canopy. Can you imagine the size of it? As we make our way to the entry, the angels begin to rejoice. There is such a hustle and bustle of heavenly business going on. Some angels carry a Shofar as they make their way to their places on the ramparts of glory. The candles on the tables are being lit and the sounds of the angelic choir begin to stir the air. "They're coming!" An angel shouts! "The bride is coming?"

Suddenly everyone looks toward the entrance. As the angels fuss together one indicates that Jesus can be seen over by the gates. Another points out Peter and yet another Paul standing with us near the Chuppah. Soon all of the original eleven disciples arrive with much grandeur. Every giant of the faith assembles with the rest of the bride! There is none greater than the other. We are one in the Spirit, we are one in the Lord. The angels start singing their welcome. Jesus has longed for this moment, when He presents His bride before the Throne. Before long the procession of eternity begins, as we make our way towards the throne. Every nation and tribe and tongue have come home. (Revelation 7:9)

In a chorus of unity we begin to sing. What are we singing! 'Coming home, coming home. Never more to roam! Open wide, thy arms of love. Lord I'm coming home.' I think not.

As we come closer and closer, the arms of Jesus spreads wide to embrace His bride. The closer we get to Him our voices stir in a strange unity of words, powerful words; fantastic words that fills the air with song. It is a song no one has ever heard before. Why, it's our new anthem! It is the song of the redeemed! (Revelation.5:9)

"Thou art worthy to take the book, and to open the seals thereof: for thou wast slain, and hast redeemed us to God by thy blood out of every kindred, and tongue, and people, and nation; and hast made us unto our God kings and priests: and we shall reign on the earth." (Revelation 5:9-10)

Entering the room we mingle for a short while. Again, we look around for old friends and acquaintances. As we make our way forward, joy rises from our inner most being. Our laughter, the joy of our hearts grows in intensity. Once more our eyes are drawn to the door. Other guests are still coming. They look a little different! They are dressed all in white. They make their way directly to the throne. As they near the angels standing around the throne the angels fall upon their faces. They cry out; "Blessing, and glory, and wisdom, and thanksgiving, and honour, and power, and might, be unto our God for ever and ever. Amen." (Revelation 7:11-12)

One of the angels begins to speak with John the Apostle! "What are these which are arrayed in white robes and where do they come from?" John replies, "I don't know, but you do!" The angel brings understanding! "These are they that came out of great tribulation, and have washed their robes, and made them white in the blood of the Lamb. Therefore, are they before the throne of God, and serve him day and night in His temple: and He that sitteth on the throne shall dwell among them." (Revelation 7:14-15)

Soon, New Jerusalem will descend to the new earth. All memory of the former earth in which we lived is now gone! (Isaiah 65:17) As preparations continue for God to be revealed in all of His goodness we glance again at the city.

A river clear as crystal flows through New Jerusalem. The apostle John declared: "And he showed me a pure river of water of life, clear as crystal, proceeding from the throne of God and of the Lamb." (Rev. 22:1)

Just as in Eden there was a river to water the garden, so also in the New Jerusalem there is the river of life. It begins at the throne of God, the very uppermost part of the city, and it courses downward through the entire area. No one on earth ever knew such a wedding planner! In New Jerusalem, the river of crystal water flows on forever, reminding us for all eternity that God continually provides for our every spiritual need.

Remember, life in eternity is not some vague existence in some nameless place. No! Here, we lead rich and full lives in glorified bodies. We will soon dwell on a renewed earth in a real city of gold with our life filled with significance and meaning as we give praise to our Bridegroom, our King and lovingly follow His desires.

This crystal river flowing past us sparkles in beauty and has a clarity beyond the purest water man has ever seen. Think of it! Together with Him we stroll the banks of this glorious crystal river. What a joy is ours!

Some Bible teachers feel that the river flows through the middle of a broad street, and alongside the river on each bank will be the trees. Others believe that a grove of trees is centered between the avenue of gold on one side and the river on the other. Now all that uncertainly is gone. You may have thought that here we do nothing, but sit on golden stairs playing harps. We were grossly mistaken. Life in heaven is filled with beauty and variety.

Everything is radiant with the light of God's glory shining through the jasper walls, its jeweled foundation, and its gates of pearl. This city, New Jerusalem, is our eternal abode. In our perfect society we realize our full spiritual potential as individuals. Nothing can compare with the communion, fellowship, and love unending that we enjoy.

The explosion of color before our eyes peeks our curiosity. Naturally we want to know more! The primary colors that appear seem to represent the core attributes or the character of God. The secondary colors represent the roles of God as He reconciled one character to another within us. Just as He used numbers prophetically and symbolically, God uses colors symbolically in His sanctuary and its services.

Looking at the colors and combinations and their symbols a pattern emerges. Examining the roles assigned to the members of the Trinity and the use of color in the Bible, we begin to speculate about the meanings of the secondary colors and how the combination of primary colors interact to demonstrate a truth.

"The heavens declare the glory of God; and the firmament sheweth his handywork.

Day unto day uttereth speech, and night unto night sheweth knowledge. "And according to the Psalms." (Psalm 19: 1-2)

The reds speaks to us of life, blood and atonement. (Leviticus 17: 11) Red is the sacrifice. It means life. When life is taken, red can appear to mean death. It is the blood of Christ which cleansed us and covered us from the penalty of sin. The Tabernacle had a covering of red so does the Chuppah. This symbolizes the protection the blood of Christ offered us. This covering is the mercy seat over us. Upon the Mercy Seat in glory, the blood of Jesus was applied. (Hebrews 9:12)

As the yellows appear we are reminded we had to buy from Him gold tried in the fire so that we would become rich. (Revelation 3:18) These yellows and gold are twofold. It signifies the divinity of our King. It also signifies our character. Our character is the gold tried in fire. It was achieved through receiving the Holy Spirit as He wrote the Law in our hearts. What a wonderful testimony to His character worked out in our life.

The orange gleaming from the rainbow of His faithfulness speaks of the flames of the Holy Ghost. Orange combines red and yellow. As Witness and Comforter on earth, the Holy Spirit had the task of making us perfect. Because of the sacrifice of Jesus, He changed our character and reconciled us to God. He sustained us and comforted the saints as we waited for our deliverance.

While we were on earth, He provided our daily link to heaven. He searched our hearts, cutting away the evil, repairing the damage of sin, placing us in the fiery furnace until we emerged perfect. Everything in heaven and earth is all about our Bridegroom, it is also all about His bride.

Ah, the beauty of the blue sapphire now bursts onto the scene. Moses recorded the first time he experienced this sight. "And they saw the God of Israel: and there was under his feet as it were a paved work of a sapphire stone, and as it were the body of heaven in his clearness." (Exodus 24:10)

Ezekiel experienced a similar wonderful sight that we now enjoy. "Above the firmament that was over their heads was the likeness of a throne, as the appearance of a sapphire stone: and upon the likeness of the throne was the likeness as the appearance of a man above upon it" (Ezekiel 1:26)

The Blue Throne! What a magnificent sight it is, as it begins to appear. In silence we stand there for a time amazed by its beauty.

"Speak unto the children of Israel, and bid them that they make them fringes in the borders of their garments throughout their generations, and that they put upon the fringe of the borders a ribband of blue:

And it shall be unto you for a fringe, that ye may look upon it, and remember all the commandments of the LORD, and do them; and that ye seek not after your own heart and your own eyes, after which ye use to go a whoring:

That ye may remember, and do all my commandments, and be holy unto your God." (Numbers 15:38-40)

Blue is the Law, which is a part of the throne of God. It is also a reminder that Jesus fulfilled the Law. The Israelites wore a blue tassel to remind them of that Law. (Numbers 15: 38-41) The same blue tassels they now wear in glory. The priest's garment have gold, red, blue and purple. The, "Mother or Harlots," of revelation was adorned in everything except blue - she violated the Law, yet she wanted riches, priesthood and sacrifice. She is no more!

Yet more colors burst into sight. They shall take away the ashes from the altar, and spread a purple cloth thereon. (Numbers 4: 13)

Purple has always been the symbol of royalty, but it clearly is a symbol that is related to the priesthood and sacrifice when God used it. This color was in the priest's garments and the coverings of the tabernacle and the doorways. Significantly, the altar of sacrifice was covered in purple when the Tabernacle was moved. Once more we understand why Jesus was dressed in purple at the trial. These purples also testify that even at the crucifixion when they pleated a crown of thorns for Him, they also put a purple robe on Him. (John 19: 2; Mark 15: 17) His sacrifice, the price paid to enable us to stand here will ever be before us.

A purple covering holds amazing revelation. Purple is a combination of red and blue. Our High Priest fulfilled the demands of the Law by becoming the sacrifice. He atoned for the broken Law (*blue*) with His red blood. Therefore, when the law and sacrifice combined it formed purple. No wonder the place of sacrifice was covered in purple. Thus, we are kings and priests unto our God forever.

The emerald green, now offers its beauty. Green is the symbol of royalty and His presence in life. It is a combination of blue and yellow. The King has laws and He does His duties in love. The blue combines with the gold to produce one harmonious society. We are now at the very center of oneness. The answer to the prayer of the Lord in John 17, is at long last manifest.

"That they all may be one; as thou, Father, art in me, and I in thee, that they also may be one in us."

I in them, and thou in me, that they may be made perfect in one;

Father, I will that they also, whom thou hast given me, be with me where I am; that they may behold my glory, which thou hast given me: for thou lovedst me before the foundation of the world." (John 17:21a - 24)

We see the green color in at least four places in the Bible, three having to do with happy times spent with the King. Happiness abounds all around us now. Gone are the days of wondering what tomorrow holds. We are now with our Bridegroom, the one who holds tomorrow!

"And He who was sitting was like a jasper stone and a sardius in appearance; and there was a rainbow around the throne, like an emerald in appearance." (Revelation 4: 3)

Jasper can be red, yellow or green. Sardius is a blood red color! The yellow also represents leprosy as a plague of sin. (Leviticus 13:30, 32) The red of course is the blood that covered our sin. Yellow also represents glory, life and light. The green, however, has wonderful symbolism to understand. It speaks to us of eternal life, of love and even of the Feasts of the Lord.

It's the King who made the covenant to combine the Law with love, in our hearts. The covenant says that He will be our God and King and we will be His people. (Psalms 95:7) To do that He wrote the Law in our hearts. (Hebrews 8:10) Here, He combined the blue and the yellow. Blue and yellow makes green!

When Jesus entered Jerusalem on that last Sunday before his crucifixion, he was greeted as the king with green palm branches. (John 12:13)

The Feast of Tabernacles celebrated a future living with God in His presence!

"And ye shall take you on the first day the boughs of goodly trees, branches of palm trees, and the boughs of thick trees, and willows of the brook; and ye shall rejoice before the LORD your God seven days." (Leviticus 23: 40)

The Feast of Tabernacles is adorned with green branches. Green is clearly the symbol of royalty and being in the presence of the King and therefore life. We now live in the Feast of Tabernacles eternally. Everything around us emanates His love, devotion and glory. Everything around us is the story of Jesus love within us. Everywhere are joys unspeakable and full of glory.

All over the place we are embraced by Him. The goodness of God completely surrounds us. He undergirds us and above us is His banner of love. Why our heart wants to bust wide open because of His unending love. Everything we see, touch and experience is unrestricted love. The very best of heaven is for us, every part of us. Only love was able to set us free from the bondage of earth. He loves us as He sees us, the way He created us, whole and perfect, uniquely spiritual and complete.

Tenderly He whispers to us! Though the mountains be shaken and the hills removed, yet my unfailing love for you will not be shaken. (Isaiah 54:10)

Who can describe the love that bursts out before us? The words of man fail miserable in their task. Still, we try with every combination known to the literary world. Alas they fail...

Could we with ink the ocean fill?
Were every blade of grass a quill?
Were the world of parchment made?
And every man a scribe by trade,
To write the love of God above
Would drain the ocean dry?
Nor would the scroll contain the whole,
Though stretched from sky to sky.
- By Unknown Author

Can you hear Him whisper to you right now? Of all the things I have created, the universe, the stars, and the sky with great big fluffy clouds. Of all the things I have every spoken into existence! Of all the miracles I have ever preformed! Above all the glories of heaven, you are by far the greatest and most precious to Me. "Eye has not seen nor ear heard, neither has it entered into the heart of man all the things I have prepared for you." (1Corinthians 2:9 *Paraphrased*)

I love you with an everlasting love and right at this very moment, I am drawing you. (Jeremiah 31:3)

Jewish marriages were generally arranged by the fathers of the bride and groom, typically at the initiation of the father of the groom.

In all periods of Jewish history, almost all marriages were arranged by the young couple's respective fathers, who were obligated, to see their children married. Thus,

Jeremiah, charged the exiles in Babylon, "Take wives for your sons and give your daughters to men." (Jeremiah 29:6)

"During the biblical era, sons and daughters alike were completely under the authority of their parents. The match would be made between the heads of families, the fathers, and the father of the son taking the primary initiative."

The parents could employ a trusted agent to find the bride. Thank God for the trusted Evangelists who searched us out! Only now in glory do they realize the honor that the Father bestowed upon them.

"And Abraham said to his servant, the oldest of this household, who had charge of all that he owned, "Please place your hand under my thigh, and I will make you swear by the Lord, the God of heaven and the God of earth, that you shall not take a wife for my son from the daughters of the Canaanites, among whom I live, but you shall go to my country and to my relatives and take a wife for my son Isaac."(Genesis 24:2-4)

As in all betrothals without the consent of the bride there is no marriage. Without our express consent we could not stand here today!

Then, they called Rebekah and said to her, "Will you go with this man?" And she said, "I will go." (Genesis 24:58)

Romance could be (*but was not necessarily*) a factor in the match.

"So Jacob served seven years for Rachel and they seemed to him, but a few days because of his love for her." (Genesis 29:20)

When it comes to our Bridegroom, He romanced us and we fell deeply in love with Him. His upright character through all of His dealings with us, we knew His loving-kindness and compassion.

"And I will betroth you to me forever; Yes, I will betroth you to me in righteousness and in justice, in loving-kindness and in compassion, And I will betroth you to me in faithfulness. Then, you will know the LORD." (Hosea 2:19)

As we stand near the Chuppah we begin to realize many things. Fasting is no more! On earth we fasted and prayed. We lived a fasted life, but now:

"And Jesus said to them. While the bridegroom is with them, the attendants of the bride do not fast, do they? So long as they have the bridegroom with them, they cannot fast. But the days will come when the bridegroom is taken away from them, and then they will fast in that day." (Mark 2:19-20)

Jewish marriages were legally formalized by a written marriage contract, called a ketubah, (*pl. ketubot*) that stated the bride price, the promises of the groom, and the rights of the bride. The word `ketubah' literally means a written instrument, and hence the reason for its application to the marriage deed. As the bride of Christ we have the spoken Word, the written Word, the price paid at Calvary and the promise of eternal life. This is our ketubah, sealed by the blood of our Bridegroom!

We are about to be presented before the Throne of His Glory! Excitement fills the air! What will He look like? Show us the Father someone cries out! On earth no one could look on the face of God and live. Speaking to Moses He said:

"Thou canst not see my face: for there shall no man see me, and live." (Exodus 33:20) That was then, we are no longer man. We are spirit, standing in our glorified bodies. "Blessed are the pure in heart, for they shall see God." (Matthew 5:8) We are now pure in heart therefore we shall see Him. Revelation 22:4, refers to those in the New Jerusalem who "will see (*God's*) face." What will He look like the question is repeated over and over again? Ezekiel tried to describe Him through human eyes!

"And above the firmament that was over their heads was the likeness of a throne, as the appearance of a sapphire stone: and upon the likeness of the throne was the likeness as the appearance of a man above upon it.

And I saw as the colour of amber, as the appearance of fire round about within it, from the appearance of his loins even upward, and from the appearance of his loins even downward, I saw as it were the appearance of fire, and it had brightness round about. (Ezekiel 1:26-27)

"The light shining around him was like a rainbow in a cloud. It was the Glory of the LORD. As soon as I saw that, I fell to the ground. I bowed with my face to the ground, and then I heard a voice speaking to me." (Ezekiel 1:28) (ERV)

Yet his description falls terribly short and incomplete! John also tried!

"His head and hair were white like wool, as white as snow, and his eyes were like blazing fire. His feet were like bronze glowing in a furnace, and his voice was like the sound of rushing waters. In his right hand he held seven stars, and out of his mouth came a sharp double-edged sword. His face was like the sun shining in all its brilliance." (Revelation 1:14-16) (NIV)

From a distance, from the ramparts of glory the sound of trumpets command our attention. Trumpets and cornets gather in crescendo. The air is electric. (Psalm

98:6, Numbers 10:2) Instinctively we know what is about to happen, we are going to meet Him face-to-face.

Wow! Are you nervous we're about to meet Him face-to-face? Moving ever closer. The Light is blinding. Noticing our clothing we stand amazed in the presence of His Majesty. We're wearing robes of pure white linen. (Revelation 19:8) The walls of glory begin to resound. The voices of every angel, the beasts and the elders numbering one million rises in a thunderous chorus. Even other voices join in the splendiferous sound. Every creature which in heaven add their voices singing. "Worthy is the Lamb that was slain to receive power and riches, and wisdom, and strength, and honour, and glory, and blessing. Blessing, and honour, glory and power, be unto Him that sitteth upon the throne, and unto the Lamb for ever and ever." (Revelation 5:11-13)

More powerful energy has never been known, gathers in percussion. Suddenly there is something very familiar in the brightness. A face begins very slowly to emerge in to view. The sound of distant thunder echoes across eternity! The noise of tumbling avalanches! The booming heartbeat of the universe explodes! The drums of glory roll! (2Samuel 6:5) The harps deliver reassuring comfort as the symphony comes together. The lyres add their perfection to a wonderful aria of grace. The low-pitched, warm tones of cymbals blends into the surrounding music. Suddenly the high symbols clash and we stand transfixed on the figure emerging from the throne. (Psalm 150:5) It's so pure, so crisp, so crystal clear that the very walls of glory radiate with the sound.

The closer we get the more powerful we seem to become. People press in to get as close as they can. The voices change drifting into a chorus of love. The voices of multitudes arises in His anthem. "Hallelujah! For the Lord God omnipotent reigneth. The kingdoms of this world is become the kingdoms of our Lord, and of His Christ: and He shall reign for ever and ever. King of Kings, and Lord of Lords." Glory, Hallelujah! (Revelation 11:15, 19:6, 19:16)

Then, we see Him! Astonished cheers and shouts of joy erupts. A voice of thunder rumbles from the blazing glory. (Revelation 14:2)

"Have I been so long time with you, and yet hast thou not known me, He that hath seen me hath seen the Father; and how sayest thou then, Shew us the Father?" (John 14:9 *Paraphrased*)

In that instant we realize that until that moment we have seen through a glass darkly. (1 Corinthians 13:12) Now we see Him face-to-face in the purity of His holiness. Hallelujah, Hallelujah! He is our Jesus!

The End

An Invitation

Dear reader;

Jesus right now is singing a song of love over you. Suddenly in the twinkling of an eye, we will soon be gone to the greatest wedding feast known to humanity. To show you how precious you are to Him. To show you how loved you are to Him. He came and gave His life to buy you back from the pit of sin. YOU, yes, you.... Really you! The gift He offers us is exactly that, a gift. We don't have to work for it. It's ours just for the asking. He gives it to us by grace through faith in Him. All we have to do is ask Him to come into our heart and life and we will enjoy all the splendors of heaven you just read about.

If we have been confused by the things we have been taught in church. If error has abounded Sunday after Sunday. We need to know that He was there with us through it all. Just like His precious Israel, we too are the apple of His eye. All we have to do, is come back home to Him.

If the Lord has spoken to you through the words of this His, "Symphony of Love," know that it was written especially for you. If you truly want a better life and assurance that when Jesus comes you will spend eternity with Him in heaven, then why not pray this simple prayer with me.

'Father, in Jesus name I come to you. I ask you to forgive me for all of my sin. Wash me in the blood of Jesus. Lord Jesus I completely surrender to you my life, my plans, my goals, my future and accept your plans and purposes for my life. Lord Jesus come into my heart and life and be my Savior and Lord. In Jesus Name.'

If you prayed that prayer and meant business with God, I want you to know that your sins are forgiven and your name is written in the book of life.

If you prayed that prayer I would like to hear from you and pray for you. Jesus is still in the miracle working business and I give you His word. No matter what the need Jesus will meet you at the point of that need.

Please contact me at the phone number, email address or the website below. I would love to hear what Jesus has done in your life.

As a reminder of your decision and this your special day fill in the portion below.

On this date: _____

I (Enter your Name) _____

Accepted Jesus as my Lord and Savior.

Signature: _____

Any time you question your decision open this book again as a reminder that Jesus will never leave you or forsake you.

About the Author

George Jenkins, is an ordinary guy who has spent a lifetime seeking out the deeper truths of the Word of God! He lives in Kitchener, Ontario, Canada from where he reaches out to fulfill his purpose in life.

George founded Kingdom Ministries Canada, a mission's group that reaches out around the world. He attends The Bridegroom's House Church, where he hosts an interdenominational Thursday-night Joshua Mission group for people in his city. Because of his burden for unity in the body of Christ, for a return to truth, George counts serving ministries of all denominations at home and abroad as one of his greatest privileges in life.

© George Jenkins 2015 ©

Other Books in Print

Final Warning
Master of Mystery
In Search of Love's Revival

You can reach George at:
7-16 Bonfield Place,
Kitchener, Ontario. Canada. N2E 1H5
Telephone: 519-804-2973
Email: ciskitchener@gmail.com

www.ingramcontent.com/pod-product-compliance
Lightning Source LLC
Chambersburg PA
CBHW061634040426
42446CB00010B/1408